Essex Workhouses

John Drury

Farthings Publications

First published in Great Britain 2006

By the same author:
A History of Upminster and Cranham
Domesday Havering
Treasures of Havering
Felsted Parish Council 1894 - 1944
A History of Felsted

Published by:
Farthings Publications
Pudneys
Causeway End Road
Felsted
Essex CM6 3LU

ISBN 0 9536154 1 3
ISBN 978 0 9536154 1 4

Printed by St Edmundsbury Press
Bury St Edmunds Suffolk
IP33 3TZ

Contents

Acknowledgements

The author wishes to thank the Essex Record Office and the
Museum Service of Braintree District Council for granting
permission for the reproduction of the following illustrations in
this book:

Reproduced by courtesy of Essex Record Office

Page 182   Workhouse receipt for coal purchased 1812
            ref. D/B 3/8/9
Page 200   Maintenance a/c for Stanford Rivers parish 1833
            ref. D/P 140/12/8
Page 241   Part of 25" 1873 Ordnance Survey showing Rochford
            Union Workhouse
Page 332   Receipt for work at Hatfield Peverel workhouse 1717
            ref. D/P 42/12/6
Page 336   Election of Guardians for Witham Union 1842
            ref. D/P 42/19/2

Braintree District Museum Trust

Page 44   Bocking Church Street around 1890 negative no. 251
Page 44   Bocking Church Street around 1900 negative no. 258
Page 58   Braintree Union Workhouse around 1905
            negative no. 208

I would also like to thank my wife Kitty for her invaluable help at
the editing stage of this book and for her expertise in the
technicalities of the computer.

Preface

I have tried to produce a work that will give some interest to every reader and have not tried to produce the definitive A - Z work on Essex workhouses. I am sure that there have been a number of parish workhouses in the county that I have not mentioned and the reason for this is that I have not traced sufficient information about them to justify inclusion. If the reader feels that a particular parish had a workhouse at some time that I have not mentioned then it might prompt the reader to conduct their own research into this fascinating subject. I appreciate that readers will be more interested in their own area if they hail from Essex but if they venture into other parts of the county in this publication I am sure they will find snippets of interest. Occasionally bits of information get repeated in subsequent chapters and for this I apologise.

I hope that readers from wherever they live will get the flavour of workhouse life both in the period of parish workhouses which lasted until the 1830s and thereafter in the seventeen Union workhouses in the county which were in being until 1930. For some years prior to 1930 the title 'workhouse' was a misnomer as various Acts in the early part of the twentieth century meant that there was no need to enter this institution by virtue of being poor. In the twenty years prior to 1930 the predominant occupants were the aged and infirm.

John Drury
2006

The typical Union Workhouse exercise yard of the late 1830s

Chapter 1

HISTORY OF THE WORKHOUSE

There have been two types of workhouse, the parish workhouse which was run by the church wardens and the overseers of the parish and the Union workhouse which was established in the 1830s by amalgamating a group of parishes and run by a Board of Guardians elected by the parishes. Thereafter parish workhouses closed. There have been up to 150 parish workhouses in Essex which were built from the early 1700s up till their demise by 1840. There were over 400 parishes in Essex including those now in the London Boroughs and nearly 40% had a parish workhouse at some time or another. Although the majority stayed open for the whole of their life some opened then closed and opened again when there was a need.

There is no strict description of a workhouse or poorhouse but generally a workhouse would have had resident inmates that were overseen by a workhouse master or governor whose basic job it was to cloth and feed the paupers. The cost would either have been at the expense of the parish or within the master's annual salary. The inmates would be put to work on jobs that could be carried out within the workhouse. The poorhouse would probably not have had a master or governor but just a property, usually a cottage that the parish owned that was used to give rent free accommodation and also financial assistance to the poor of the parish. Some poorhouses were just used to give employment to parish residents that were out of work but had their own accommodation. They would come to the poorhouse on a daily basis and were probably overseen by the overseer for the poor. The majority of Essex's parish workhouses get a mention in the text but there were some that were only open for a short time for which there was no information. A few workhouses were open for longer periods that would have justified an entry but records have not survived to make this possible. The principal source of reference for the information on the parish workhouses has been the Essex Record Office and whereas for some parishes there is a wealth of information for others there is almost nothing. Consequently the quantity of text for the various parish workhouses fluctuates according to what information has been available at the Record Office. I do refer though to every one of the Union Workhouses that were set up in the 1830s but even with these I have picked out the more interesting bits and pieces of their life and interesting snippets over their next 100 years. Parish poorhouses and workhouses came to an end when Union Workhouses were established and consequently those parish buildings still in existence are now mainly private houses. Parishes invariably sold off their workhouse in the late 1830s when they were usually converted into a number of cottages. Since then these cottages have often been amalgamated into a lesser number of dwellings and it is often difficult to imagine what the original workhouse looked like.

I felt it right when tackling the subject of workhouses to mention almshouses which are an entirely different type of institution. Almshouses pre-date workhouses by a number of centuries and were founded originally in the Middle Ages by the monastic bodies who gave pilgrims and travellers hospitality and overnight accommodation. Often those that stayed more than one night were sick and monasteries soon built infirmaries in their grounds. From the word hospitality came the word hospital. Monastic hospitals were dissolved in the reign of Henry VIII and their successors were almshouses where benefactors could build a row of cottages for the relief of the poor and infirm of a parish. Almshouses, therefore, were usually built and endowed by private benefactors whereas the parish poorhouse or workhouse was usually built by the parish.

The reign of Henry VIII was followed by Edward VI in 1547 and in 1552 an act was introduced which was the first of the Poor Laws which was concerned with the collection of funds from the wealthy for the relief of the deserving poor. It seems that the system was not effective and all that happened to non-payers was that they were reported to the local parson by the churchwardens whose job it was to collect the money due. The parson would admonish the offender who might then be reported to the bishop but the church did not have any powers to enforce the poor rate. Over the next forty years or so there were various Poor Relief Acts and Poor Law Acts but it was not until the reign of Elizabeth I that the Poor Law Acts of 1597/98 passed the responsibility for the relief of the poor from the church to the local parish vestry who were now allowed to levy a Poor Rate. The parish 'vestry' was not the 'Parish Council' as we know it today, as this body did not come into existence until 1894, but a group of principal residents who assumed the responsibility for the running of the parish. A typical vestry might consist of the lord of the manor, the clergy and his churchwardens, the doctor and a small number of principal local residents. In addition the parish appointed one or more overseers who were in charge of administering relief to the poor. The parish was now able to levy a Poor Rate which had the backing of the courts for those non-payers. Consequently by the early 1700s we see parishes possibly having surplus funds from the poor rate to be able to build firstly a poor house and following an act of 1723 parishes had the power to set up a workhouse with a workhouse master. This important act also gave the parish the authority to stop any out-relief being given to an individual if he or she did not enter the workhouse. Parishes if they wished could establish a joint workhouse and we see examples of this in the chapter dealing with the parishes in the Orsett area.

The Knatchbull's General Workhouse Act of 1723 was the vehicle for allowing villages to decide whether they wished to continue to just provide financial relief for the poor in their own homes or build a workhouse to accommodate paupers which would make savings on the poor rate. If there was a need then extra rates would be raised to build cottages for poor families on waste ground or common land which would just be houses for the poor rather than a proper workhouse with a workhouse master. It was also incumbent on the parish to put teenage paupers into apprenticeships. The workhouse would have a master appointed to look after the inmates and put them to work. The name 'poorhouse' and 'workhouse' are both used to describe a building used for the relief of the poor and if one wished to be more specific a poorhouse could be just that, a place that accommodated poor people where work might be brought to them, whereas the workhouse would

A typical parish workhouse (Upminster) which was converted into cottages after the 1834 Act

probably have had a workhouse master where the able inmates would be obliged to undertake work in return for their board and lodging. Soon after the Act of 1723 a survey was conducted which showed that there were 20 'workhouses' in Essex and presumably these were proper workhouses with a workhouse master and not just a parish poorhouse where the poor of the parish were lodged. Although there were no planning laws as we know them today, in the seventeenth and eighteenth centuries it was against the law to build a cottage without there being four acres attached to it for this was considered to be the minimum amount of land required to sustain a family. The average village family in the eighteenth century had little use for money as they were virtually self sufficient with their four acres or more and any rent they had to pay would be minimal. This new law ensured that all new properties had sufficient land to be mainly self supporting which helped to keep the numbers reliant on poor relief down to a minimum.

The various Poor Law Acts covered many issues relating to the poor one of which was on the subject of bastards as this was always a problem in the nineteenth century with its increasing levels of illegitimacy. Basically the father, if identifiable, was to bear the financial responsibility for the child and all the Poor Law acts supported this edict. The mother and child invariably relied upon the parish for financial support whether on out-relief or actually in the workhouse. The parish for their part were keen to identify the father and apprehend him as he invariably disappeared from the parish where the lady lived. The parish would, through the court, get a warrant for his arrest and if successful he would be brought before the court and an arrangement made for the support of the child. Research has been done on the cost of supporting a mother and bastard child compared with the money recouped from the father. For Essex the average amount recouped was 35% in the 1830s. For Great Waltham, at this time, £82 was recovered out of £266 expended on illegitimate children. Essex seemed to be less efficient than other counties whereas Yorkshire, for example, recovered over 60% of illegitimate expenses. The blame for the poor return was mainly attributable to the inefficiency of the parish vestry and its overseer of the poor who was not chasing up defaulters. One can understand though that if someone did not want to pay, even after appearing before the court, then it was easy to disappear and very difficult to find the person again.

One of the new Poor Law Acts also made the parish responsible for their poor even if they wished to move from their village to another village. People tended to live and die in their own parish and travelled little but it is feasible that those on poor relief might wish to move elsewhere possibly to get a new start in life. A parish would still have a financial responsibility to their own poor and would have to provide the individual or family with a certificate stating where they had come from and that the parish would send money for their keep. Conversely a parish would only accept the poor of another village provided they brought a certificate with them.

Whilst most cases were accommodated in the parish workhouse some were housed in village houses where the occupier received 'outdoor relief' or 'out-relief'. Parishes were allowed to 'name and shame' residents by putting up posters listing those on out-relief and inviting anyone to advise the parish if they thought someone was an impostor. Whether those on out-relief living outside the workhouse worked or not, we do not know but those capable of work within the master's control were given jobs to do like making beer or, more importantly in many parishes in Essex, the spinning of yarn that was supplied by the overseer. Spinning was a considerable cottage and workhouse industry in the seventeenth and eighteenth centuries although in decline by the second half of the eighteenth centuries although in decline by the second half of the eighteenth century. Yarn was made and sent to the baize weavers in the north Essex towns of Gt Dunmow, Braintree, Bocking, Halstead, Hedingham and Colchester.

To keep the numbers down in the workhouse, children were invariably put out to work even if their parent(s) were still inmates. The overseer would draw up a formal agreement with the prospective employer whereby an allowance was made to clothe and feed the child who would normally be put to work on a farm if the pauper was a boy or sent into service if a girl. The parish payment to the employer decreased as the child became more useful ending up with the child being no longer a drain on the parish and receiving wages to complete his or her independence. You might ask why the parents were not working and this is invariably because they were either too old or too sick to take on employment. Here are some extracts of Agreements of 1781 and 1782 by the parish of Felsted at vestry meetings:

April 5 1781 Mrs Agness agreed to take Widow Jegons' daughter for one year from the date hereof and to find her clothes, at the expiration of which the Parish to allow Mrs Agnes two pounds two shillings.
3 May 1781 William Lazell hath agreed to take Thomas Aylett for one year at one shilling per week
June 6 1782 Mr John Skill agreed to keep Thomas Aylett for one year at nine pence per week.

Either Thomas Aylett did not prove to be a good worker for he changed employer after one year and the new employer was paid less, or alternatively, the vestry felt that being a year older he was contributing more to the farm and it was felt that he was earning his keep more and they could justify giving the farmer a lower allowance. The children would only be aged seven or eight when put out to work. The administration of poor relief was in the hands of the vestry up who were an un-elected body, who usually met in the church vestry, and from this venue the body took its name. Prior to the Poor Laws, as was said earlier, the church looked after the poor of the parish and presumably at that time the clergy conducted their business relating to the poor from the church vestry. When the Act of 1597 was passed, the parish body that took over the administration of poor relief also made use of the vestry to conduct their business.

One of the essential elements in the provision of assistance to the poor whether by out-relief or admittance to the workhouse was the question of to what parish did the person belong. The Act of Settlement in 1662 laid down the rules for this decision and once this had been established a person had the right to ask for assistance when required. In general ones parish was that of his or her father's place of birth. Circumstances change and on marriage the settlement rights for the woman assumed the same settlement rights as her husband. If a man or woman completed a year's hiring in another parish or served an apprenticeship elsewhere then the right of settlement changed to that parish. A person could only have one parish as their right of settlement. In practice it was not always that simple and cases crop up in the Union Workhouse Guardians' minutes in the post 1834 period where investigations are made to establish the correct settlement parish as no parish vestry or Union workhouse wished to incur the expense of someone or a family who was not their responsibility.

A typical settlement certificate would read something like this:

We .... and .... Churchwarden and Overseer of the Poor of the parish of ...., do hereby own and acknowledge Joe Bloggs, his wife and family, to be inhabitants legally settled in the parish of ....aforesaid.

The certificate would probably be attested by four of the parishioners.

Now that we have set the scene and know how parish poorhouses and workhouses came into being and operated, let us look at where the workhouses were located in Essex. It is difficult to say definitely how many there were and in which village there was a workhouse as the situation often changed from decade to decade. A parish may start up a workhouse in a property, which it rented, only for that workhouse to close some years later as things were not working out or the parish poor rate could not support the running of a workhouse. For some years subsequently that parish would be without a workhouse. Later when the parish was more in funds it may build its own workhouse and was therefore back on the list again. A good indication of where the workhouses were and how many available places there were is seen in a Parliamentary survey of 1776/7 which looked into poor relief expenditure in England and Wales. The survey listed 140 parishes in Essex which had workhouses in 1777. In Essex one third of parishes had a workhouse but in Oxfordshire, for example, the proportion was only one in nine. The spelling of some of the parishes was different in 1777 and I have used the modern parish names to identify the parish. Some of the names may not be recognisable as parishes today, as parish mergers have taken place subsequently. The following list is a little suspect as there were a number of parish workhouses that were definitely open in 1777 which do not feature in the list. Also the number of available places for inmates is possibly wrong in a few cases.

Essex Parish Workhouses in 1777 and available places

Abberton	16	Aldham	20	Ardleigh	40
Ashdon	30	Aveley	40	Gt Baddow	20
Bardfield Saling	12	Barking	70	Gt Braxted	16
Beaumont/ Moze	14	Belchamp Otton	9	Belchamp St Paul	15
Lt Bentley	26	Gt & Lt Birch	24	Bocking	140
Boxted	30	Bradfield	12	Bradwell	13
Braintree	60	Brentwood	14	Gt Bromley	30
Broomfield	20	Bures	9	Burnham	24
Gt Burstead	40	Buttsbury	10	Chelmsford	100
Chigwell	33	Gt Clacton	30	Gt Coggeshall	50
Lt Coggeshall	15	Colchester All Saints	28	Colchester St Boltophs	35
Colchester St Giles	30	Colchester St James	24	Colchester Lexden	34
Colchester St Martin	12	Colchester St Mary	30	Colchester St Nicholas	14
Colchester St Peter	20	Earls Colne	42	Colne Engaine	30
Copford	30	Corringham	20	Dagenham	30
Danbury	18	Dedham	48	Fordham	22
Gt Dunmow	50	High Easter	33	Epping	20
Faulkbourne	25	Felsted	20	Finchingfield	25
Foulness/Shoe	30	Fryerning	20	Goldhanger	18
Gosfield	20	Gt Hallingbury	24	Halstead	80
West Ham	155	S Hanningfield	9	Harlow	20
Harwich D/Cour	8	Harwich St Nich	60	HatfieldB/Oak	60
Hatfield Peverel	30	Hedingham Cas	65	SibleHedingham	30
Hockley	20	Gt Horkesley	26	Kelvedon	30
Langham	25	Lambourne	40	Lawford	22
Layer de la Haye	15	Gt Leighs	15	Leyton	30
Maldon, St Mary	40	Manningtree	20	(Layer)Marney	25
West Mersea	18	Messing	100	Navestock	25
Black Notley	16	Gt Oakley	20	Pebmarsh	12
Pitsea	12	Purleigh	20	Ramsey	14
Rayleigh	20	Ridgewell	24	Rivenhl	25

Rochford	24	Roxwell	20	St Osyth	30
Shenfield	30	Southminster	30	South Weald	17
Springfield, Chel	35	Stanford(Rivers?)	30	Stanford le Hope	20
Stansted	40	Stanway	18	Stebbing	30
Steeple	6	Steeple Bump	25	Stifford	20
Stock	10	Stow Maries	10	Tendring	20
Terling	20	Great Tey	28	Thaxted	50
Theydon Garnon	30	Grays Thurrock	10	Thorpe(leSoken)	50
Tillingham	6	Tollesbury	30	Tolleshuntd'Arcy	10
Tolshunt Major	10	Toppesfield	30	Gt Totham	20
Lt Totham	16	Upminster	20	Gt Waltham	100
Lt Waltham	20	Waltham H/Cr	100	Walthamstow	50
Wethersfield	25	Weeley	16	GtWigborough	20
Willingale Spain	12	Witham	60	Wivenhoe	30
Wix	25	Woodham Ferrers	30	Writtle	100
Gt Yeldham	20				

There are a few anomalies in the above figures. In general the number of available places per parish workhouse relates to the size of the village or town but it seems unlikely that Bocking, a small parish of only a few hundred souls in 1777, would have had a workhouse capable of housing 140 persons. Similarly, Messing, Gt Waltham, Writtle and possibly Waltham, Holy Cross was unlikely to have had workhouses that could accommodate 100 persons. Chelmsford with 100 places on the face of it might appear correct but statistics of Chelmsford's inmates in 1818, over 40 years after the 1777 survey, state that there were only 61 inmates. Of course Chelmsford's workhouse could possibly accommodate 100 inmates but in 1818 there may have been a low point with only 61 inmates. Possibly the figure for West Ham is correct at 155 as this parish was very large taking in East Ham, Wanstead and Leyton. Colchester is also probably correct at 227 when one adds up all the wards of the town.

The above statistics could therefore contain some inaccuracies and so I have looked more closely at the situation of Bocking where the workhouse in 1777 is recorded as being able to accommodate 140 inmates. By just relating the size of the community to its workhouse capacity the figure for Bocking looks wrong. The other factor to take into consideration though is the situation regarding employment in the area. The Essex cloth trade was in decline by the late 1700s and as Bocking was one of the centres of this industry this may be the reason why the Bocking parish workhouse was so large. The cloth industry, although controlled by the "clothiers" who were at the top end of the production chain, was reliant on the cottage industries to provide the cloth. The residents of Colchester, Braintree, Bocking, Halstead and Coggeshall, invariably in their homes, undertook the combing, the spinning and the weaving with the fulling mill extracting the grease from the cloth. Literally thousands were employed in the north east Essex area in these trades and with the decline of the cloth trade it must have increased the population of parish workhouses. The reasons why this happened are not easy to identify. Essex cloth was exported to Europe with Spain and Portugal buying the majority. Wars in Europe at this time would obviously have curtailed the export trade and it is possible that diversification of interests by the 'clothiers' saw them cutting down on their wool interests. The manufacture of silk partly replaced the wool trade but the majority of firms did not last long. Whatever the reasons for the decline of the wool trade one can now see possibly why the Bocking workhouse could accommodate 140 persons, the one at Halstead 80, Braintree 60 and the two at Coggeshall totalling 65 inmates. These four wool areas all had much larger workhouses than in most of the other Essex locations apart from those near to London and the principal towns of Chelmsford and Colchester. We have seen previously that workhouses or poorhouses in Essex, as in other parts of the country, were administered by the parish vestry. The Poor Rate was always rising and eventually there were many critics of the old Poor Laws. Parishes had made economies by building their own workhouse to save on paying outdoor relief to residents to look after the poor and infirm but nevertheless many ratepayers were finding themselves in financial difficulty by having to pay a fast increasing Poor Rate. One way that a parish sought to relieve the distress of the poor was to introduce the Speenhamland scheme which was implemented by many of the rural parishes in Essex as well as in other counties in southern England. This system gave poorly paid labourers a supplement to their wages the funds coming from the parish poor rate. The scheme was started in 1795 in the village of Speenhamland in Berkshire when it was decided to link the financial relief of the poor to the cost of a loaf of bread. The loaf selected was the 'gallon' loaf weighing nearly nine pounds and costing one shilling. Based on the cost of this loaf, Speenhamland parish paid out three shillings to the head of the household and one shilling and six pence for every other member of the family. When the price of bread changed the weekly allowance changed accordingly.

There were two reasons why the number of poor was on the increase in the eighteenth century. One was the various Enclosure Acts that allowed landowners to enclosure millions of acres of common land throughout the country depriving the less well off from growing crops and grazing cattle on their village commons. The second reason was the decline in the spinning industry in Essex which effected this cottage industry as well as those employed in large firms. In view of the foregoing situations and also the depression following the Napoleonic wars it became clear to the government in the early 1830s that for every parish to cater for its own poor was inefficient and that there was a need for the old poor laws to be brought up to date. Consequently in 1833 the Prime Minister, Earl Grey, set up a Poor Law Commission to examine the system for looking after the country's poor and to make recommendations. One of the systems that the Commissioners looked at was that at Southwell, Nottinghamshire where the Rev. J T Becher had established a workhouse in 1824 to cater for all the parishes surrounding Southwell. This purpose built three storey building catered for over 150 paupers who were segregated according to sex and age and who all had their separate exercise yards. A similar system was started at Stanford Rivers in 1829 (see Ongar chapter) and it is clear that the Southwell and Stanford Rivers workhouses helped to form the basis of Union workhouses of the future.

The recommendations, incorporating the two examples above, were far reaching and the report to parliament was the forerunner of the Poor Law Amendment Act of 1834. The new act decreed that 'external relief' for the poor was to be stopped within two years which meant that parishes would then no longer be responsible for their poor and it also meant that if a parish maintained a workhouse then it would no longer be used to house the poor and could be sold. Those previously living in the parish workhouse would have to leave and would either starve or be admitted to a new Union Workhouse. It looks from the report that many undeserving cases were getting handouts from the parish poor rate which every parish had to collect from its residents. The new Poor Law said that if a person was able bodied and chose not to work then the only way that that person could receive help was to enter a Union Workhouse and as you will see that would be a bad choice as against going out and getting a job. One of the main recommendations of the Commission was to root out the 'undeserving poor'. One of the advantages of the new Union system was that where previously the poor of the parish had been looked after by the parish officials, where the overseer might have been the only paid person, the new Union system created a new salaried class of official to run the Union workhouse from the master down to the porter where their prime responsibility was the well being of the poor in their care.

Nevertheless one writer of the time said, when referring to the new Union Workhouses, 'the workhouse should be a place of hardship, of coarse degradation and humility; it should be ministered with strictness and severity; it should be as repulsive as is consistent with humanity'. The Poor Law Amendment Act stated that adjacent parishes would be grouped together into Unions and the Union would build a large workhouse to accommodate all the poor from those parishes. The report even stated that the workhouse was to be a large grim building built to look like a prison. The underlying principle of the new workhouse was that conditions would be less comfortable than conditions in society outside. Consequently only those in desperate need would seek admittance to a Union workhouse. A Local Board of Guardians would be elected by the ratepayers to run the workhouse supervised by the Poor Law Commission.

As you can imagine from the above comments conditions in a Union workhouse were very harsh and the rules and regulations drawn up by the Poor Law Commissioners were strictly adhered to by those in charge of each Union Workhouse. It soon became clear to the populace that to enter a Union Workhouse would bring shame on the inmate although this feeling might be lessened in the knowledge that the person would be getting fed and watered which would be better than starving in the outside world. The next deterrent to entering a workhouse was one of slavery. Although slavery is a harsh word inmates worked very hard for long hours for little or no money. The third deterrent was confinement. As we have said before life in a workhouse was similar to prison life which also included harsh punishments for quite trivial misdemeanours. The farming community noticed a wind of change after the establishment of Union Workhouses. Farm labourers had obviously heard of the conditions endured by being taken into the workhouse and farmers suddenly saw that farm workers were working harder and keen to keep their jobs rather than being sacked and ending up in the workhouse. Admittance to a Union workhouse was not compulsory and it was left to the parish resident to agree to be admitted although there was invariably no alternative if he or she and their family had nowhere to live and no income.

When a new pauper entered the workhouse he or she was first placed in a probationary ward. Whilst in this ward they would be seen by the medical officer, thoroughly cleansed, and their clothes taken away for cleaning and held in store for return if they subsequently left the workhouse. There were roll calls and times for breaks and meals with the whole regime being based on the lines of a prison. Boys and girls would have three hours a day of teaching to include reading, writing and religious instruction. The days for everyone began at 6am and went through until 6 to 7pm for supper which was followed by bed at 8pm.

We are all aware of Charles Dickens' *Oliver Twist* although the film *Oliver* probably had a wider audience. The original book was completed in 1839 which was only five years after the 1834 Poor Law

Act was passed. Oliver was born in the workhouse and spent all his early years there. Charles Dickens relates Oliver's trials and tribulations in the workhouse and we all know of him 'asking for more'. Workhouse food was deliberately very poor and only sufficient to keep the inmates alive. Dickens refers to Mr Bumble the Beadle and although this may have been a minor workhouse official in London there is no reference to a member of the staff of an Essex Union workhouse having this title. Although the book was written after the establishment of Union workhouses Dickens is probably taking his workhouse experiences from the period prior to 1834 as he makes reference to Oliver being looked after by the parish rather than the Union. Consequently the Beadle was probably an official of a London parish prior to 1834. There is reference to West Ham Parish Workhouse having a Beadle on its payroll up to about 1819. The Beadle's role was similar to that of Overseer of the Poor. Charles Dickens also refers to the workhouse master ladling out the meals assisted by responsible inmates in the 'asking for more' incident. There were a number of dining rooms in the Union workhouse and the Master may have assisted on a rotation basis just to check that portions were adequate but not too large. At the age of nine Oliver would not have been grouped with the younger children but would still not have been placed with the adult males. The other piece of artistic license by Charles Dickens was his mention of an advertisement outside the workhouse offering for someone to take Oliver off their hands for £5. The workhouse Guardians in the post 1834 period were always very keen for young males to be taken into an apprenticeship and likewise young females to be taken into domestic service. It was not unusual for the Guardians to make a payment of about £5 to whoever was taking the child to offset the initial expenses but it is unlikely that named inmates would have been advertised for apprenticeship or domestic service.

Men and women were separated, even if married, as were the children if over seven years old although children under the age of seven were grouped together. Workhouses all had uniforms for men and women which, in the case of women, were shapeless dresses down to their ankles which invariably had pale blue vertical stripes on an off-white background. The men had shirts similarly patterned together with badly fitting trousers. The children also were garbed in ill fitting clothes similar to the adults. Some workhouse would have the letter 'P' sown on to the clothes to show that they were paupers and this letter invariably was followed by another letter signifying the parish from whence they came. During the day the men would be employed breaking stones, probably for roads, or cutting wood or grinding corn. Women would be employed washing scrubbing and cleaning.

It is clear that the Union workhouse regime from 1834 was harsher for paupers than the life of a parish workhouse previously and there are many cases where individuals or families having experienced a short time in the workhouse soon left if they were able to put their life together again. No one went into a workhouse for an easy life and this kept numbers down to a minimum and similarly reduced the cost of looking after the poor of the community. From the government's point of view they were also pleased that by doing away with parish workhouses and combining the resources into one Union workhouse there were financial benefits. Despite the gradual rise in population in the country the cost of financing the country's poor reduced from £6.3 million in 1834, when parish workhouses came to an end, to £4.9 million ten years later.

The new Union Workhouses up and down the country were all subject to the same rules and regulations and all were built to look like, and to be run like, prisons. Essex was divided up into 17 areas by grouping together about 20 parishes to form a local Poor Law Union. The seventeen groups were as follows:

Billericay	Halstead	Romford
Braintree	Lexden & Winstree	Saffron Walden
Chelmsford	Maldon	Tendring
Colchester	Ongar	West Ham
Dunmow	Orsett	Witham
Epping	Rochford	

Before moving to the individual workhouses I will just mention fleetingly the mentally ill and also the changes that took place in the twentieth century that gradually saw the end of the workhouse for the poor. There was no formal provision in Essex for sufferers of mental illness prior to the setting up of the Union Workhouses and the mentally ill would have been looked after at home if they were of no danger to the public. There are examples of parishes sending those of unsound mind to an asylum, usually in London, but of course the parish would have to pay for their keep which would have been more than looking after them locally. Following the establishment of the Union Workhouses in the 1830s the Essex County Lunatic Asylum was opened at Warley, Brentwood in 1853. It changed its name on several occasions over the next 150 years before closing in 2001. A small unit has now been built alongside. Severalls Hospital, Colchester opened in 1913 as Essex's second asylum with Runwell Mental Hospital opening in 1934.

The following chapters record snippets of information of many of Essex's parish workhouses prior to 1834 and the setting up of the seventeen Unions. Not every single parish workhouse is featured as for some parishes there have not been available records. There are also extracts from the Union Workhouse minutes which show what workhouse life was like between the period of their establishment in the 1830s to 1930. It has not been my intention to record all the information and facts about every parish workhouse and Union workhouse in Essex as this would be rather boring. I do not think that readers are interested in knowing the names of every medical officer, for example, for every workhouse over the years of their existence. What I have tried to do is give the reader the flavour of how workhouses were run and the sort of things that cropped up in the day to day life of inmates. There were 140 parish workhouses in Essex at the time of the survey of 1777 and the majority are featured in the following chapters. In the case of the Billericay and Braintree Union workhouses I have mentioned more about how the Union was set up in the 1830s and its early years whereas for Epping I have dealt more with the layout of the building. For the other workhouses I have taken periods over the next one hundred years to show the sort of situations that were cropping and how they were dealt with by the Guardians. In the case of Lexden and Winstree I have expanded on the census data to show the make up by age, sex and circumstance of a typical workhouse.

The stories from the seventeen Essex Union Workhouses run through to the twentieth century demonstrating the hard life that inmates had if they were unfortunately admitted to a workhouse. The first major change came in 1908 with the Children's Act which gave local authorities new powers over children, who would otherwise have entered a workhouse, from not being admitted to this type of institution. Arrangements were made for children to be housed in special villages, cottage homes or individual homes in the community. This meant that children were no longer admitted to a workhouse from 1908 and this Act was followed within the year by the start of Old Age Pensions which meant that there was no need for another category to have to go into the workhouse. The effect of these two new laws was immediate and it is recorded that by 1913 the only admissions to Essex's workhouses were the old who were sick. Consequently one sees the name 'workhouse' being dropped by these institutions to be replaced by 'infirmary' and the workhouse building became more a hospital than a workhouse. The Local Government Board was replaced by the Ministry of Health in 1919 and this fourth name for the body that originally looked after the poor of Essex was now wholly concerned with the population's health. The establishment of the Workhouse Guardians as a body still continued until Essex County Council took over the administration in 1930 which saw the end of the workhouse although this change had gradually taken place over the previous twenty years.

I have grouped the Essex parishes into their groupings that became the Essex Union Workhouses in 1834 following the passing of the Poor Law Amendment Act. Not all Essex parishes though were combined into an Essex Union and a surprising high number of parishes were allocated to a Union in an adjacent county where the parish was near to a county boundary. Cambridgeshire, Suffolk and Hertfordshire took a number of Essex parishes into one of their own Unions. For example, Stansted Mountfichet parish was taken into the Bishops Stortford Union in Hertfordshire. However, there are no examples of parishes in other counties being incorporated into an Essex Union. The list of Essex parishes in Unions in other counties can be seen in Appendix 1.

George R Sims was a journalist and wrote many articles in the mid 1800s campaigning for better conditions for the poor. In 1877 he wrote a poem *In the Workhouse: Christmas Day,* which is much longer than produced here, which tells the story of life in the workhouse through an inmate called John.

It is Christmas Day in the workhouse,
And the cold bare walls are bright
With garlands of green and holly,
And the place is a pleasant sight:
For with clean washed hands and faces,
In a long and hungry line
The paupers sit at the tables,
For this is the hour they dine.

And the Guardians and their ladies
Although the wind is east,
Have come in their furs and wrappers,
To watch their charges feast;
To smile and be condescending,
Put pudding on pauper plates,
To be hosts at the workhouse banquet
They've paid for - with the rates.

Oh the paupers are meek and lowly
With their 'thank'ee kindly, mum's
So long as they fill their stomachs,
What matters it whence it comes?
But one of the old men mutters
And pushes his plate aside;
"Great God!" he cries
"But it chokes me!
For this is the day *she* died"

The Guardians gazed in horror,
The master's face went white;
"Did a pauper refuse their pudding?"
"Could their ears believe aright?"
Then the ladies cluthched their husbands.
Thinking the man would die,
Struck by a bolt or something,
By the outraged One on high.

There, get ye gone to your dinners;
Don't mind me in the least;
Think of the happy paupers
Eating your Christmas feast;
And when you recount their blessings
In your smug parochial way,
Say what you did for *me*,
Too, only last Christmas Day.

I do not think that the Guardians came with their wives to the workhouse on Christmas Day although I have seen that Guardians' meeting were often held on Boxing Day. It was usual though to lay on extra food on Christmas Day although as readers will see in the story of the Rochford Union the Guardians were not always keen for every inmate to receive a Christmas dinner.

Chapter 2

BILLERICAY AND ITS ENVIRONS

PARISH WORKHOUSES

The following 26 parishes in the above area were grouped together in 1834 following the Poor Law Amendment Act to form the Billericay Union. Before 1834 each parish may have had its own poorhouse or workhouse.

Basildon, North Benfleet, South Benfleet, Bowers Gifford, Brentwood, Great Burstead, Little Burstead, Childerditch, Downham, Dunton, East Horndon, West Horndon, Hutton, Ingrave, Laindon, Mountnessing, Nevendon, Pitsea, Ramsden Bellhouse, Ramsden Crays, Shenfield, Thundersley, Vange, Little Warley, South Weald, Wickford.

Billericay does not get a mention as it was historically part of Great Burstead parish.

The government undertook a survey of parish workhouses in 1777 and the following parishes in this area had a workhouse open in that year.

Gt Burstead, Brentwood, Shenfield, Pitsea, South Weald

Great Burstead

Before the 1930s and the formation of Billericay Urban District Council the town of Billericay fell within the parish of Great Burstead. Consequently references to Great Burstead parish workhouse are referring to the workhouse that was built in what we now know as Billericay. The parish house was built probably in 1719 as the parish records mention a bond for £50 borrowed in connection with the erection of a house for the poor. The year 1719 was very early for a parish workhouse to be built as the Act to formalise the building of a parish workhouse was not passed until 1723. It is possible that this 1719 building was just a house owned by the parish in which the poor were accommodated rent free and not a formal workhouse with a workhouse master. The government survey of workhouses in 1777 recorded that Great Burstead's workhouse, and by this time the parish had a proper workhouse, could accommodate up to 40 inmates. This workhouse may not have been in the same location as the 1717 building mentioned above. This later property stood in the Laindon Road opposite School Road. The building became an iron foundry after the new Union workhouse was built in 1840 and then the site for the local gas works. Even today the site in the Laindon Road is still owned by a gas company and one can see the area that the workhouse and its surrounding garden covered.

At a general meeting of the parishioners in 1815 chaired by the Rev. John Newman Clark it was decided that all matters relating to the poor of the parish would be placed under the direction of a committee of 20 parishioners together with the overseers of the poor. If three or more committee members were absent from the meetings then the business would be adjourned. It meant therefore that at least 18 members of the committee had to attend every meeting to get any business transacted. This seems a much too large a committee and one wonders if anything got done. It was not surprising that one month later the rules were amended to have four sub committees of five members each to work on a four week rotation basis with either a churchwarden or overseer to be in attendance. This was a much more workable number.

The parish vestry minute book for the early 1800s lists the names of all the workhouse inmates with their ages and a sample of the numbers during 1819-1821 are as follows:

	1819	Jan 1820	March 1820	Dec 1820	June 1821	Sept 1821
Men	8	8	4	5	9	4
Women	3	1	1	1	1	1
Boys	5	7	5	5	4	4
Girls	1	4	2	2	2	2
Family				5		
Total	17	20	12	18	16	11

The family of five were admitted on the 4 December 1820 and stayed until after Christmas. The one woman during the period was the same 60 year old widow and the two unrelated girls aged 8 and 10 were also in the workhouse for the whole period 1820-1821. The parish record, which lists all the arrivals and departures of the inmates in the 1830s, shows that on the 5th July 1830, for example, there were 16 inmates but within two years only three remained although five died in this period. Those that left or died were replaced by others and so the numbers always remained about the same.

The parish accounts list at almost every meeting those paupers on out-relief and on average about 35/40 individuals or families were in receipt of cash every week in 1819. When all the wives and children are taken into account then the total number is well over 100 persons a week. In this year the parish authorised the overseers to "provide proper brewing utensils for the use of the workhouse immediately". Weak beer was a standard drink in many institutions and presumably the workhouse master had requested an upgrade of his equipment.

In September 1829 Great Burstead parish appointed Robert Crick and his wife to run the parish workhouse. The terms of the Agreement were that Mr and Mrs Crick were appointed 'for the care and management and concerns of the poor'. The rate of payment to the couple was three shillings per person in the workhouse paid weekly. The Agreement went on to say that the Cricks were at liberty to employ the inmates in spinning and carding (preparation of wool for spinning with a card). They could also be employed in any other occupation as the Cricks think fit. The Cricks, said the Agreement, 'shall not suffer any degree of idleness'. The workhouse master was to provide good and sufficient meat and drink and he and his wife were to wash and mend all the inmates' wearing apparel and linen. The Cricks could use the workhouse as their own accommodation. The workhouse was to be furnished with sufficient beds, bedding and linen and other useful and necessary furniture including spinning wheels. This clause in the Agreement was an obligation on the part of the parish to provide all the furniture etc. This long Agreement went on to recite that if a woman inmate was 'brought to bed' (became pregnant) then the master was allowed a further thirty shillings for the extra attendance (midwife) and nourishment. The master and his wife were obliged to teach and instruct all the children in the workhouse in reading by books supplied by the parish. All the children shall also be instructed in church catechisms and upon the Lords day and Christmas shall attend the parish church. The parish on their part will provide a surgeon and apothecary and midwife, if necessary, to attend any of the poor when required.

Robert Crick signed the Agreement with his mark being an 'X' and one wonders that if he could not write his name then how was he going to teach the children to read and write. The Agreement finished with an inventory of all the rooms in the Great Burstead workhouse as follows:

Workhouse Master's room	1 oak table, 8 windsor chairs, 1 writing desk, 30 hour clock, a cupboard, a range, curtains, box for papers, fire tools, 2 bells, 1 quart mug and 1 window shutter.
Cellar	Kitchen implements and garden tools
Middle Room	Paupers keeping room (day room)
Upstairs Sick Room	1 flock and feather bed
Great Bedroom	Paupers bedroom – beds
Governor's Chamber	
Nursery	Children's bedroom – beds
Girls Room	Female bedroom – beds
First attic	2 beds
Second attic	1 bed
Kitchen	Cooking equipment

In 1832 we see the appointment of William Carter as 'Surgeon, Apothecary and Man-midwife to attend the poor of the said parish of Great Burstead ....in all cases of midwifery, surgery, vaccinations and in all fractures and casualties whatsoever ....at a yearly salary of forty pounds'.

The new Billericay Union incorporating all the parishes mentioned above was established in 1835 although the new Union Workhouse was not built until 1840. The Great Burstead parish vestry had been directed by the new Union Workhouse Guardians to dispose of parish property used by the poor. This directive, initially by the Poor Law Commissioners, instructed all parishes who owned property either as a workhouse or a poorhouse without a master, to dispose of that property and forward the proceeds to their new Union to offset the cost of the building of the new Union Workhouse. Parishes would no longer have a need for property to house the poor. Consequently the vestry minutes of 1836 refer to the disposal of the parish workhouse in the town, which was very premature as the property was not actually sold until after the inmates were transferred to the new Union workhouse. The minutes also covered the cottages belonging to the parish on Burstead Common. These cottages would have been other property belonging to the parish which were occupied by the poor without the supervision of a workhouse master. The parish workhouse is described in the vestry minutes as the equivalent of six freehold tenements. A row of six cottages in the 1830s would not have been very large and they would probably have been two up and two down cottages with attics. Some partition walls would probably have been taken down, if the building was originally built as cottages, to give large day rooms as described in the inventory of 1929 above.

It was not until 1841 that the parish workhouse was eventually sold by which time the inmates had been transferred to the new Union workhouse a year earlier.

Brentwood

Brentwood workhouse was mentioned in the national survey of 1777 and consequently was established some time before this date. That survey recorded that the workhouse could accommodate a maximum of 14 inmates although it does seem that the workhouse was capable of taking more inmates over the next ten years. The location of the workhouse was in Back Street, now Hart Street, just to the south of the High Street. An agreement with the workhouse master records in 1786 that he should receive a standard daily allowance per head of inmate but if the number dropped to below 16 then a lower sum would be payable. Although the workhouse could accommodate up to 14 inmates in 1777 by nine years later in 1786 the overseers could accommodate at least 16 inmates. The rules and regulations for the workhouse ran into three pages in the parish minute book and contained one or two interesting regulations:

The labour of the poor to be proportionate to their strength and abilities and not to exceed ten hours per day. New Years day and two days after each of the feast of Easter, Whitsuntide and Christmas to be allowed to them as days of recreation and relief from labour. The profits of their labour to be the property of the master of the house.

The officers of the Hamlet (of Brentwood) to have full power to remove any poor person affected with the smallpox or any contagious or epidemic disorder to such place as they shall think proper. The master to provide a nurse and the persons so removed to be maintained at the expense of the Hamlet.

It looks as if by 1808 the parish vestry had changed the rules again as to how many inmates could be accommodated in the workhouse as an agreement with Thomas Guyver said that he was to be paid at the rate of four shillings and four pence per week for each inmate up to 12 inmates but no more if further paupers were accommodated. Out of this sum Mr Guyer was to provide meat, drink and firing (wood) and also washing and mending. The running of the workhouse went smoothly until the 1830s when the inhabitants of the 'Hamlet of Brentwood', as the area was described in the parish records, were obviously unhappy at the way the parish workhouse was being run and also the method of assessing the financial reimbursement to those on out-relief. These concerns were raised at a parish meeting and a group of parishioners asked for new proposals for the running of the workhouse and for those on out-relief . The chairman at that meeting decreed that if changes were to be made then the 'plan', as it was being referred to, would have to be presented at a properly constituted vestry meeting. This meeting was held on the 13 June 1833 when sixteen proposals were put forward incorporating, in addition to proposals for the running of the workhouse and for the control of out-relief, a request for a general rate revaluation of all properties in the hamlet. It rather looks as if the poor rate being charged to households was getting out of control and the residents wanted their properties reassessed and also they wanted a say in how the workhouse was to be managed if they were going to be asked to finance it. The most interesting of the sixteen proposals were:

That the workhouse be provided with every comfort and convenience possible consistent with the welfare of the inmates.

That the new paupers being admitted into the (work) house should be examined under oath before a magistrate to confirm the genuineness of their legal settlement (that they are Brentwood residents).

That those applying for out-relief be examined more closely before the granting of the same to ensure that they have used every means in their power to support themselves and their family.

That relief shall not be given in the form of money except in 'necessitous cases' but shall be provided by way of food and clothing in the workhouse.

That any goods owned by paupers who are admitted to the workhouse go with them to the workhouse and can be taken away again should their circumstances change and they wish to leave the workhouse.

That the workhouse master shall keep a diary in which all details referring to the inmates shall be placed in respect of the age of paupers, when admitted, where last resided and occupation. The comments were also to include 'the state of the (work) house'. This weekly entry was to be signed by the doctor, the overseer and the master.

That the overseer shall keep an account of any earnings of the paupers which is to be transferred to his rate account.

That the master shall keep a record of all grants of clothing to the paupers and that clothing shall be marked with the hamlet's mark to prevent the paupers selling the item.

The sixteen resolutions were passed unanimously. One can read into the individual resolutions that things had got out of hand with paupers being admitted that were not Brentwood residents, that money was being paid to out-relief paupers that was not justified, that paupers were selling their clothes and that proper records were not being kept by the various officials concerned with the workhouse. The above improvements in 1833 had really come too late as by 1835 the new Union Workhouse Guardians had been appointed and the control of the

Brentwood parish workhouse passed to the new Guardians. Hopefully though they found the Brentwood workhouse in good working order. In March 1836 we see the Guardians of the new Union arranging for the paupers in the Brentwood workhouse to be transferred to either the Billericay (Gt Burstead) or Thundersley parish workhouses pending the building of the new Union workhouse at Billericay. In June of that year the parish vestry passed a resolution that the workhouse should be sold by public auction. The proceeds would not be retained by the parish but passed on to the new Union to offset the cost of the new Union workhouse. When the vestry was agreeing to the sale of the workhouse its location was described as being 'a brick built messuage situated in the Back Street in the said Hamlet with a garden and outbuildings'.

East Horndon

At the vestry meeting on the 29 March 1785 an agreement was made between Jeffery Crick of Billericay and the parish vestry for him to look after the poor of the parish for one year at the rate of two shillings and six pence and to 'find them good and sufficient meat and drink, lodgings, washing, firing (wood) and candles'. The vestry also allowed Mr Crick to spend up to 'sixteen shillings towards wheels (spinning wheels)'. The Crick family gets a mention as master of the Great Burstead (Billericay) workhouse in 1829 and possibly this was a family occupation. The poor get a mention in 1802 when Mr Adams, presumably the village doctor, gets paid £3 for inoculating the poor. There is reference that the workhouse was used for the poor residents of the parishes of East Horndon, Ingrave and Dunton. The East Horndon workhouse functioned right up to the time that the new Billericay Union Guardians took over in 1835 and was still mentioned in the Guardian's minutes of 1836 when £20 was budgeted for expenditure for the forthcoming period. The inmates would have been transferred to one of the larger parish workhouses shortly afterwards. The workhouse building was still owned by the parish in 1841 as the name is in the list of ratepayers although of course any inmates would have been transferred once more and this time to the new Union workhouse in Billericay in1840.

Pitsea

Pitsea workhouse was mentioned in the government survey of workhouses in 1777 when it was recorded as being able to accommodate up to 12 inmates. There is no mention of a workhouse at Pitsea when the

Billericay Guardians took over the parish workhouses in 1835 and consequently it must have closed at some time before this date. There is mention of a 'Workhouse Field' in a lease of 1805 in connection with the Pitsea Hall estate and it is quite likely that the workhouse itself was built on land owned by this large estate.

Shenfield

The government survey of 1777 stated that the Shenfield workhouse was capable of housing up to 30 inmates. The parish vestry minutes of 1759 record that a previous house used for accommodating the poor of the parish was pulled down and a new property built on the same site. A Mr John Bradley was paid ten shillings and six pence to remove all the possessions of the poor to a farm house in Billericay belonging to a Mr Howard pending rebuilding. The new workhouse was a brick building 100 feet long and 16 feet deep (roughly 30 metres by 5 metres) which was the building that could house up to 30 inmates.

A publication dated 1906 described the workhouse as being 'at the top end of the High Road'. When the Billericay Guardians took over in 1835 there is no mention in the minutes of a workhouse at Shenfield and presumably the workhouse had closed some time previously. When the property was sold in 1837 it was converted into six small cottages probably of the two up two down variety. The workhouse was sold by auction at the Green Dragon public house and realised £380.

Thundersley

Unlike Brentwood above, Thunderley parish was much more organised in respect of the records it kept for its workhouse. In the parish vestry minute book are some copies of entries that the governor (master) of the workhouse had entered into his journal. It seems that this journal did not commence until 1832 which was only a year before recommendations were made to the Brentwood vestry for something similar. Thundersley though recorded the state of health of the inmates which was not specifically mentioned for Brentwood although the Brentwood doctor was asked to sign the journal.

The Thundersley workhouse was not included in the national survey of 1777 which indicates it was not open at this time. The inventory of the workhouse showed that it had the following rooms:

Kitchen, bakehouse, keeping room (day room), pantry, bedrooms (probably 2)

The inventory and the list of inmates indicate that the workhouse was jointly run by Thundersley and South Benfleet parishes. The journal gives a comprehensive record of the comings and goings of individual inmates but there is only one entry that actually indicates how many were in the workhouse at any one time. This was in March 1835 when there were five inmates, two from South Ben fleet and three from Thundersley. Four were aged over 64 with the fifth being Lucy Maylen aged seven. Lucy entered the workhouse when she was five years old with her mother who was described as a widow aged 45. Lucy Maylen senior also brought into the workhouse a son, Jonathan, aged nine months. The entry records that both children were bastards, Lucy by a Mr Reevs and Jonathon by James Johnson. The mother and Jonathan are not recorded as inmates later in the year and one can only presume that she either died or left the workhouse with Jonathon and left Lucy there. Many of those taken into the workhouse only stayed a short time presumably until someone could look after them or they got their financial affairs in order or they could find alternative accommodation. A typical example was that of John Dodd, aged 50, his wife and three children aged 13. 9 and 2 who came into the workhouse on the 20 January 1832 but they all left on the 24th of that month. The governor and the parish would have assured themselves that the family had accommodation to go to and there would be future family income. The Thundersley parish workhouse closed in November 1836 with the inmates being transferred to the parish workhouse in Billericay.

South Weald

The workhouse at South Weald had opened fairly early compared with others in Essex as there is a reference to the workhouse in 1748 when Mrs Francis Maxwell had died in the workhouse and her daughter Mary Chadsey agreed that the workhouse could dispose of her mother's possessions. In 1760 the parish records contain an inventory of all the contents. The rooms are named as the kitchen, the brew house, the parlour and the buttery. Upstairs were three bedrooms containing ten beds. Outside was a stable which contained a spinning wheel and a kneading trough. The government survey of 1777 listed the South Weald parish workhouse as being capable of accommodating up to 17 inmates. The location of the workhouse is recorded in a tenancy agreement of 1803 between the parish vestry and John Brown a farmer of Langtons Farm, South Weald. The tenement was referred to as 'Goodwins or the Workhouse now in the occupation of the Churchwardens and Overseers'.

Langtons Farm is in Sandpit Lane, South Weald and almost certainly the workhouse was in this area.

In the parish records for 1827 there is a letter on Chelmsford Goal headed note paper, from presumably the Governor, recommending one of his staff to the position of workhouse master at South Weald. The letter says that Richard Clark was 29 years old, married, and had been employed at the Goal for five years. Originally he was employed as Night Watchman and then as Assistant Turnkey during which service he had 'prevented many desperate attempts to escape'. The recommendation went on to say that Richard Clark could 'write a good hand and keep accounts'.

In March 1836 the inmates of the South Weald workhouse were transferred to either the Great Burstead (Billericay) or Thundersley workhouses and the workhouse was sold soon afterwards.

THE BILLERICAY UNION WORKHOUSE

Each parish in the list at the start of this chapter submitted one name to be on the Board of Guardians for the new Union but three parishes had two representatives each, namely Brentwood, Great Burstead, in which the town of Billericay was situated, and South Weald. None of the 26 parishes had a very large population in the 1830s, with the exception of Brentwood and Great Burstead (Billericay), and it is unclear why South Weald was offered an extra place on the Board although South Weald parish was probably much larger in area than it is today. This gave a total of 29 Guardians. The parish of Basildon, Lee Chapel was added to the Union in 1858.

The minute book records that their first meeting was on the 13 October 1835. Little business was conducted at this first meeting apart from the election of officers but a sub committee was formed to look into the state of the existing parish poorhouses and workhouses which of course were still functioning and would continue to so do until the new Union Workhouse was built. Although subsequent Guardians' minutes do not contain the report on the state of the parish poorhouses it is noted that no further expense was to be allowed on the existing workhouse or poorhouse buildings within the 26 parishes.

Billericay Union Workhouse now converted into apartments

The porter's lodge of the Billericay Union Workhouse

When the new Board of Guardians for the Billericay Union took over the parish workhouses in 1835 there is reference to one at Thundersley in addition to that at Great Burstead, Brentwood and South Weald. There is no mention by the Guardians of a parish workhouse at Shenfield or Pitsea and so these two must have closed prior to 1835 or as soon as the Guardians took them over.

In January 1836 the Guardians in their minutes mention for the first time a workhouse at East Horndon when budgeting for the forthcoming period. Thundersley did not get a mention in the budget although it did not close until November 1836. Maybe in the knowledge that it was to shortly close the Guardians did not consider it necessary to provide any further funds. The budgeted amounts indicate that the East

Horndon workhouse was quite small compared with the other three. East Horndon workhouse does not get any more mentions in the minutes after 1836 and one wonders whether it closed shortly afterwards.

Budgeted amounts for expenditure on parish workhouses - 1836

South Weald	£60	Brentwood	£65
Great Burstead	£50	East Horndon	£20

Whilst the parishes still owned the land and buildings of their workhouses and poorhouses the administration and funding was now in the hands of the newly formed Billericay Union Workhouse Guardians. One sees in the minutes that various bakers and flour merchants were being contacted to supply samples of bread and flour for the Guardians to decide who was to provide these items to the existing workhouses and those on poor relief and also in the future when the new workhouse was built. The poor rate (tax) that the parishes collected from their residents was now to be sent to the Board of Guardians for them to pay the bills for running the parish workhouses and also to make payments to those poor residents who were on out-relief. The Guardians appointed relieving officers for this purpose that would organise the victual ling of any parish workhouse in their area and also arrange for a convenient location to pay out weekly those residents who needed financial assistance.

As soon as the Guardians had met for the first time in 1835 they started keeping separate ledgers for each parish which showed the expense on food and clothing in order that the parish could be charged out the total expenditure which they in turn would collect from the residents by way of Poor Rate. Here are the quarterly entries for clothing for the Great Burstead parish workhouse and those on poor relief:

Elizabeth Bonner	1 shift being 3 yards of calico
Sarah Bayford	1 pair of high shoes (not high heeled but high ankled)
James Bickett	7 yards of calico
Elizabeth Bonner	1 apron being 1 yard of check
Sarah Bayford	2 shifts and 2 aprons being calico and check
John Nash	4 yards of flannel
Robert Elvin	1 waistcoat, 1 pair trousers, 1 shirt
	1 pair shoes, 1 pair stockings, 1 cap
John Wright	2 yards flannel and 1 pair high shoes
Sarah Bayford	1 yard of muslin for 2 caps
Total expenditure	£3

The above is a typical quarterly account for the various parishes that now made up the Union. Most of the items listed for all of the parishes were similar to the above but for one Brentwood pauper the parish supplied a 'drab jacket' and the parish purchased 'smocking'. A Thundersley pauper was supplied with 'ticking' for pillow making at a cost of just over ten shillings When the Thundersley parish workhouse closed in November 1836 the Billericay (Gt Burstead) workhouse took over all their goods and chattels and the inmates, if there were any at this time, would also have been transferred to the Billericay parish workhouse. The extensive list of furniture, bedding, pot and pans etc. contained the following more interesting items:

> 4 day caps and 2 night caps
> 16 chamber utensils
> 1 tin gruel ladle
> 12 large and 12 small breakfast tins
> 18 half pint tin mugs
> 12 writing books, 6 slates and 20 pens
> 6 bibles and 6 prayer books

The new Union workhouse did not open until 1840 but it looks as if the Guardians had already decided what the inmates would be wearing as an entry for the Great Burstead (Billericay) parish workhouse in 1836 refers to expenditure on a 'Union suit and braces' for a number of the paupers which was to be grey. As well as looking after the financial side of the various parish expenses, in this interim period before the new workhouse was built, the Guardians also dealt with the advertising for new parish workhouse masters. In the Guardian's minutes in 1835 they placed an advertisement relating to the Great Burstead parish workhouse. The advertisement was looking for a workhouse master and wife to 'take charge of 30/40 able bodied paupers'. A workhouse master's Agreement for Great Burstead of 1829 can be seen in the Parish Workhouse section above.

Extracts from the Guardians' minutes

January 1836
Keeper of the stores
Although the new workhouse was not completed until four years later the Guardians were already ordering stores and equipment to be housed at various sites within the district. Expenditure on these stores started in September 1836. They appointed a Keeper of the Stores who was charged with obtaining brands marked 'Braintree Union' to mark all the

stores and clothing. I suppose that this was to stop pilfering as it would be some years before the items would be needed.

February 1836
Dismissal of doctor
The minutes for February 1836 record the case of the appointed doctor for the Basildon area. Whereas previously the medical officer was a parish appointment, the Billericay Union was now responsible for looking after the sick in their parishes whether the person was in a parish workhouse or just a local resident on relief. A resolution was passed which sacked the Basildon doctor for being guilty of 'gross negligence and inattention to the poor of Basildon'. The case referred to a Mrs Lowe and a Mrs Marshall and the Board ordered the overseer of Basildon to discharge the doctor from further attendance. No reason was given in the minutes for the incompetence but presumably the two ladies may have died without receiving adequate medical attention.

March 1836
Two Billericay workhouses
We see in this month the appointment at one meeting of two sets of workhouse masters and matrons for the 'Great Burstead Workhouse' and the 'Great Burstead Workhouse late Barracks'. It seems that two locations were being used in 1836 one of which, the Barracks, eventually became the site of the new Union workhouse in Norsey Road in 1840. From the middle of 1836 the Guardians started referring to one workhouse as the Great Burstead workhouse and the other as the Billericay workhouse although as mentioned before both were located in what we now know as the town of Billericay.

April 1836
The first thoughts on the new Union workhouse
Although eventually a completely new workhouse was built on the Norsey Road site the original thoughts were to make alterations and additions to the existing parish workhouse buildings to accommodate up to 250 inmates and advertisements were placed for architects to come up with plans.

June 1836
Changing round the inmates
The Guardians decided to reallocate the inmates along the lines recommended by the Poor Law Commissioners. The Great Burstead (Billericay) workhouse was to house the women and the Thundersley

workhouse was to house the children. Although not mentioned in the minutes it follows that the men would be housed in the other Billericay workhouse.

October 1838
Husband transported to Australia
The clerk was asked to write to the Poor Law Commissioners concerning the case of Elizabeth Nash whose husband had been transported to Australia for 14 years. Elizabeth was originally in the Great Burstead parish workhouse with her four children but she now wished to leave as a family as she had been offered accommodation by another man. There is no record that Elizabeth was divorced from her husband or of the outcome of the request but the Guardians would probably not object as the workhouse would have five mouths less to feed and clothe. Inmates would not be allowed to leave until the Guardians had made their enquiries and were satisfied that those leaving would have accommodation and be well provided for.

March 1839
Purchase of hearse
It was proposed that the Guardians purchase a one horse hearse to transport paupers who died in the parish workhouses, and subsequently the Union workhouse, back to their own parish for burial.

April 1839
Building committee
A committee had been formed to inspect likely plots of land for the new workhouse. Six sites were reported on and although one site was selected another site in Norsey Road was eventually bought from Mr Butler for £350 guineas.

May 1839
No tea for aged paupers
The Guardians passed two unusual resolutions in May which said firstly that no tea was to be allowed to paupers in any of the parish workhouses except males over 60 and females over 50. The second resolution was that single women with child are not allowed to have any communication with their friends during their residence at a workhouse.

July 1839

Advertisement for tenders for new Union Workhouse

Architects George Scott and William Moffat had won the contract to design the new workhouse which was to be sited between Stock Road and Norsey Road, Billericay. The architects also designed Dunmow, Tendring and Witham Unions. Basically the structure was a large 'H' shaped building with the two long sides of the 'H' facing the Stock and Norsey Roads. An infirmary was built later to the north of the block with other additions subsequently. When one sees that the workhouse was built in 1840 for up to 300 inmates out of a total population of the parishes of around 13,000 this indicates that over 2% of the population were potentially classed as in need of relief in the workhouse as well as those that would have been on outdoor relief in their own parish. In fact there were only 126 inmates in the workhouse in 1841 although there would have been probably twice this number in receipt of 'out-relief' who was not actually resident in the workhouse.

October 1839

Problem with water supply

The Guardians contended that the contract to build the workhouse also included the sinking of a well and the supply of water. The builder disputed this but the matter seems to have been resolved without any further reference in the minutes. The new Union workhouses would not have had mains water initially and it seems generally that the new workhouses were always having problems with the supply of water from their well and in various cases an extra well was dug. The provision of an adequate water supply was a common problem in many of the Essex Union workhouses as possibly a standard single supply of water would not be sufficient for up to 2/300 inmates.

November 1839

Completion dates

The builder reported that the main building would be finished by the 25 December 1839 and the entire work by the 24 January 1840. Before Christmas though the builder reported that he was not going to meet the dates previously given. The new Billericay Union Workhouse eventually opened in the spring of 1840 although all the work was not completed until the September. It seems that the inmates took up residence later in the year.

April 1840

Inmates with the 'itch'

There is reference in the minutes in April of 1840 that several children in the old Great Burstead parish workhouse 'had the itch' indicating that it was still open at this time and it appears that as they had their meals in the new workhouse the Guardians put them in a separate room. The Guardians were not referring to the new Union workhouse. Different writers in the Guardians's minute book often referred to the two Billericay workhouse locations as the 'old' workhouse and the 'new' workhouse as well as referring to them as described in the jotting for March 1836 above. During the months of 1840 there are many references to the Guardians chasing the architects to get the new Union workhouse finished. Eventually the Guardians took over their new board room on the 1st September 1840 and the inmates were transferred by the end of that month.

The number of inmates

In the first chapter the government survey of 1777 recorded that Great Burstead workhouse could accommodate up to 40 inmates. In a few paragraphs above reference is made to an advertisement in 1835 for a new parish workhouse master to take charge of 30/40 paupers. In August 1838 reference is made in the Guardians minutes to there being 89 paupers in the parish workhouse and also that the monthly bill for bread was £15 and just over £8 was the bill for bread for the 'old house'. Although it is not clear from the Guardians' minutes which location they are referring to when mentioning the 'new' parish workhouse and the 'old' parish workhouse it is felt that the 'old' workhouse was the one in the Laindon Road opposite School Road and the 'new' workhouse was the one on the Barracks site which eventually became the location for the new Union workhouse. If the £15 fed 89 paupers then £8 represented about 50 paupers. This seems to confirm that there were two workhouses in Billericay/Gt Burstead in the late 1830s totalling about 139 inmates which is borne out by the 1841 census figures for the new Union workhouse three years later where the total was 126 inmates and 3 staff. The total number in the Billericay workhouses has been swelled by the closure over the years 1836/38 of the other parish workhouses so that there were just the two parish workhouses in Billericay pending the building of the new Union workhouse.

The new Union workhouse

The new Union workhouse was built on land known as the Billericay Barracks. The location of the new workhouse was in Norsey Road where the main gates and the porter's lodge were sited although there was another entrance in the Stock Road where tramps and vagrants were admitted into a Casual Ward. This Casual Ward was a timber built ward on the site of the present modern houses opposite Cromwell Avenue in Stock Road. The porter's lodge and the main workhouse buildings are all still standing and have been converted into apartments. The plaque over the main workhouse entrance is still there and says:

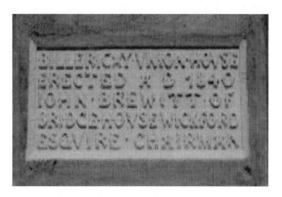

Billericay Union House Erected A.D. 1840 John Brewitt of Bridge House, Wickford Esquire, Chairman

Classification of inmates

When paupers were admitted to the workhouse one of the administrative duties was to classify them into one of seven categories. There were three categories for males, three for females and one for children:

1) Men infirm through age or any other cause
2) Able-bodied males over fifteen
3) Boys between seven and fifteen
4) Women infirm through age or any other cause
5) Able-bodied females over fifteen
6) Girls between seven and fifteen
7) Children under seven

The separation policy laid down by the Commissioners for all workhouses was to be strictly adhered to and all categories of inmates must live, sleep and take their meals in separate parts of the building. The categories also had separate exercise yards. The only concession was that infants under school age could be with their mothers but not all institutions obeyed by this rule. There were no rules for troublesome inmates, those mentally ill or sick inmates with infectious diseases. In practice the troublesome would probably be put into a separate room and the mentally ill would be transferred to an asylum outside Essex as the asylum at Brentwood had not opened at this time. As will be seen from the various snippets from the minutes of the other Essex Union workhouses those with infectious diseases were placed with the other sick inmates in the infirmary ward although eventually this class of sick were separated into a special ward for those with smallpox or other infectious diseases.

The census of 1841

The first national census after the workhouse opened in 1840 was in 1841 and the census data shows that there was now only one workhouse being the new Union Workhouse.

The number of staff and inmates was as follows:

Males	79	The total includes 3 staff and 54 children under14
Females	50	The percentage of children to the total number of inmates was 43%
Total	129	

1880s

Mr Lewis, clerk to the Guardians

The following story occurs forty years after the Union workhouse opened and is concerned with an outbreak of smallpox. Contagious diseases were common in all workhouses, as they were in the community at large, during the ninety year period of Union workhouses and the Guardians always took these problems very seriously.

Charles C Lewis was a solicitor whose office was in Brentwood and like many business people of the time kept note books of the letters he had written, by hand of course, there being no copying facilities in those days. Mr Lewis as well as being a solicitor with his own private and business clients was also a coroner for South Essex, a clerk to the magistrates at Billericay Court and also the clerk to the Guardians of the Billericay Union. This notebook is now lodged at the Essex Record Office and among the many jottings of letters he had written was one in reply to the Guardians at the workhouse who had written to him and he responded wearing his clerk to the Guardian's hat. The Guardians had asked him to enquire into the circumstances surrounding the three cases of smallpox which had appeared at the workhouse in the early months of one of the years between 1885 and 1889. Unfortunately the year of the jotting is not recorded. If the rules concerning the isolation of cases with infectious diseases had been carried out the three unaffected men should not have come into contact with those isolated with the disease and the Guardians wished to know how the three had contracted the illness.

The letter by Mr Lewis says that the research was conducted in conjunction with the Board's medical officer. Case number one was a John Gentry who was an inmate of one of the infirm wards who had been admitted a few months previously. Case number two was a Mr J W Hasler who was on the Young Men's Ward who was admitted shortly after Mr Gentry. The third case was a Mr W Saunders from the Old Men's Ward who was also admitted about the same time as the other two. None of the three could give any reasons why they had caught the disease. There was obviously by the 1880s an Infectious Diseases Ward at the workhouse and the report says that Mr Gentry, being very infirm, had had no contact with that ward prior to his illness. Mr Hasler has been at work in a field near to the Infectious Diseases Ward but also had had no contact with the inmates of that ward. Mr Saunders also said he had had no personal contact with anyone from that ward other than with the coalman who had delivered coal to the Infectious Diseases Ward. Mr Lewis, our solicitor, went on to state to the Guardians that every inmate had had the opportunity to be re-vaccinated and all the wards had been disinfected. As a piece of background for the Guardians Mr Lewis advised the body that the advance of the new railway lines in and around the Billericay area had seen a large influx of navvies and that there were many cases of smallpox within their number some of which had been brought to the workhouse if they eventually became to be out of work. Mr Lewis seemed to be blaming the navvies for bringing the disease into the Billericay workhouse as it looks as if the three inmates did not have contact with anyone in the Infectious Diseases Ward but contracted the disease from other new inmates.

We will now jump forward another twenty years to the census of 1901 to see how the numbers have changed compared with the first census after the Union workhouse opened.

The census of 1901

Males	127	The total includes 12 staff and 20 children under 14. The percentage of children to total number of inmates was 11%.
Females	62	
Total	189	

The first census in 1841 gave a total of 126 inmates compared with 177 inmates in 1901. The majority of the seventeen Essex Union workhouses had more inmates in 1901 compared with 1841. The number of inmates at most workhouses peaked in the period 1871/81 with numbers falling slightly by 1901. Although the total number increased it was the mix of inmates that changed. In 1841 that there was a very high percentage (43%) of children under 14 in the workhouse which dropped to only 11% by 1901. Conversely the number of aged and infirm increased considerably reflecting the gradual change in the policy of admission to the workhouse where the institution was moving more towards that of a hospital rather a home for paupers.

The end of the Union Workhouse

During the 1914-1918 War part of the workhouse was used to house German prisoners of war with the function of the workhouse Guardians ending in 1930. From that date the workhouse became the Billericay Public Assistance Institution which was initially controlled by Essex County Council and then latterly the building became St Andrews Hospital when the National Health Service came into being. Statistics were compiled by the workhouse on a weekly basis and these show the number of people either resident in the workhouse, at other institutions or on out-relief. When the Union Workhouse ceased to be under the control of the Guardians there were 256 inmates in the workhouse, 13 persons in other institutions and 233 cases of out-relief involving 523 men, women and children.

Bocking Parish Workhouse in about 1890

Bocking Parish Workhouse from the bridge over the river about 1900

Chapter 3

BRAINTREE AND ITS ENVIRONS

PARISH WORKHOUSES

The following 14 parishes in the above area were grouped together in 1834 following the Poor Law Amendment Act to form the Braintree Union. Before 1834 each parish may have had its own poorhouse or workhouse.

Black Notley, Bocking, Bradwell, Braintree, Cressing, Finchingfield, Great Saling, Pattiswick, Panfield, Rayne, Shalford, Stisted, White Notley and Wethersfield.

The government undertook a survey of parish workhouses in 1777 and the following parishes in this area had a workhouse open in that year.

Braintree	Bocking	Bradwell	Black Notley
Finchingfield	Wethersfield		

Braintree

There was a parish poorhouse or workhouse in Braintree from 1636 and its location was the Hyde which is now Market Street with the exact location being where Tescos is today. Most of Essex's poorhouses or workhouse came into existence in the early eighteenth century and consequently Braintree's poorhouse was very early for this type of institution. The site was originally donated as land for almshouses in 1596 and subsequent deeds refer to the site as having been used as a 'hospital house'. The Essex Record Office in Chelmsford has been my source for the original records but occasionally there has been deposited at the Record Office note books and hand written notes of past village historians who do not always quote their references. A note book covering the seventeenth century mentions the case of Harvey the tinker in 1636 who was asking (the vestry) for work. He was offered work at the hospital, now referred to as the workhouse, in spinning and carding which he declined. He was told that if he did enter the workhouse he would have to earn his keep by completing an allocation of work and if there was a shortfall then he would have make good the deficiency.

Like any building money needed to be spent on it to keep it in good order but of course any expenditure would have to be paid for out of the poor rate. In 1716 the vestry agreed to spend £28 on repairs but in 1722 a further £107 was spent making a total of £135. The vestry provided for this expenditure by charging £85 to the parish poor rate with the balance of £50 coming from Mr J Olmins, the lord of the manor. There were a total of 28 paupers in the workhouse in 1720 and the parish vestry decided what work should be undertaken by the inmates to provide for their board and lodging. Five of the adults were required to undertake spinning and carding up to a certain value of work and nine others only had to undertake carding to a certain value. Of the remaining fourteen, five were allocated light work like errands, cutting wood, pumping water and general housework. The residue of nine were probably the sick and the children who did not have any duties.

Braintree Parish Vestry Minutes
January 1723
Overseer for the poor
The parish vestry agreed to pay John Westwood two shillings whilst not at work and caring for his wife during her pregnancy. The Westwoods were not in the workhouse but they had obviously applied for relief for a period of the pregnancy. This was rather unusual and presumably there must have been some problem with the pregnancy for the parish to make this allowance. The midwife received three shillings and sixpence for the week she delivered the baby and three shillings the following week.

June 1724
Desertion by father
The minutes record that Mrs J.....? was awarded two pence a week as an interim measure until the next vestry meeting. Apparently her husband Martin was 'going for (to be) a soldier' and had left his wife and their three children, John 4, Mary 2 and James 6 months, destitute. It does not look as if the family ended up in the parish workhouse as their names do not appear in a subsequent workhouse list of what work the inmates should accomplish on a daily basis.

August 1724
Robert Saward
Robert's wife was sick and he had been ordered into the workhouse. The minutes did not say if she was to be admitted as well or why he should

be sent to the workhouse. He had not obeyed this order but brought to the vestry an order from Mr Sumers (presumably the overseer for the poor) for out relief. The vestry had not agreed with the overseer's recommendation but ordered that he be brought to the workhouse with his family. It transpired that the landlord has seized his possessions in lieu of rent arrears. The vestry then agreed to pay the arrears of rent in return for the goods and chattels which were to be sold for the benefit of the parish.

When the vestry next reviewed the work to be done in the workhouse the notes included the newly arrived Saward family. Like most families at this time some spinning or weaving was conducted at home as a source of income. The vestry minutes indicate that Robert Saward could carry on with his own bays winding but that part of the day was to be for benefit of the workhouse. When his possessions were bought back from the landlord he obviously got back his spinning and weaving equipment. His wife was obliged to carry out two pence worth of work per week and their daughter Katurah was obliged to complete three pence worth of winding.

October 1725

The Watson family

The vestry minutes record that the John Watson was having his goods and chattels seized for non payment of rent. Subsequently the family was evicted from their cottage and they were admitted into the workhouse. At the next vestry meeting the case was considered again and it was decided that Mr Watson was to be employed in the workhouse spinning and carding to the value of seven pence a day. The family of five, Mr and Mrs, two girls and a boy now had to be clothed as well as fed in the workhouse. Between October 1725 and February 1726 the following expenditure appears in the vestry minutes in respect of expenditure on the Watson family:

October 1725	Two Watson children to be allowed a pair of shoes each
November	Watson boy - a coat and breeches
	Two Watson girls a new shift each
	Mrs Watson a new pair of shoes and the biggest girl an apron

In November the vestry were negotiating with the landlord of the Watson cottage to buy back 'the best loom and winding wheel'. This entry infers that the family had more than one of each and probably extra income was earned by the daughters working for the family unit.

December 1725	The biggest Watson girl a pair of shoes
January 1726	Eliza Watson an apron

The minutes for the 21 February record a complaint against John Watson that he was neglecting his work in the workhouse and that a warrant (for his arrest) be procured. It looks as if he had absconded from the workhouse leaving his family behind. A month later the vestry minutes record a 'deficiency' by the Watson family and it appears that the whole family had now disappeared.

March 1818
Appointment of new workhouse master
John Fish Junior was engaged to look after the poor in the workhouse and allowed five shillings per inmate for the period of one year. He was also allowed to keep any earnings by the poor and he was also allowed forty shillings for a lying-in woman (midwife) for a month. Out of his income he was to find his own materials for 'making and mending' (clothes). The poor were to be provided with three good hot dinners per week on Sundays, Wednesdays and Fridays. Mr Fish and his wife were ordered to attend church with the inmates every Sunday morning and afternoon.

Census 1821
At the 1821 census there were seven males and nine female inmates with the master named as being John Irish aged 41 assisted by his wife. In 1821 the silk industry was firmly established in Braintree and the town's prosperity may well reflect why there were so few inmates in the parish workhouse.

September 1826
Parish poor houses
Most parishes owned property, which were usually small cottages in a terrace that they used to accommodate the poor of the parish probably on a rent free basis. These properties would not be workhouses with a workhouse master but just a subsidised parish owned property. Depending on the circumstances of the occupants, work may have been brought to them to offset their rent free occupancy. The Braintree parish vestry considered the situation concerning one of the poorhouses they owned in two tenements in Coggeshall Lane, Braintree which had until recently vacated been occupied by James Collins and Widow Hockley . After inspecting the property the vestry decided to sell the cottage by public auction and invest the proceeds in repairing four other tenements nearby which were also in a very bad state of repair. A year later in 1827

the vestry were talking about selling all the remaining properties in Coggeshall Lane and investing the money in improvements to the parish workhouse.

April 1828
Rules for vagrants
The vestry drew up a set of rules for vagrants being admitted to the workhouse. At the same time the vestry order a building to be constructed in the workhouse yard which would probably have been of a wooden construction and resembled a large shed. It would have two wards, one for men and one for women. The rules included the following:

> The vestry clerk shall keep a register of all vagrants
> No money shall be given to vagrants
> No vagrant shall be omitted without a ticket signed by a parish officer
> Set menus to be provided which will comprise bread and beer for all meals
> All persons shall be discharged every morning in summer at 6am and in winter at 8am
> Vagrants found begging in Braintree shall be apprehended
> Vagrants shall be searched on entry with any money or personal possessions passed to parish officers
> Children under six years of age are allowed to sleep with their mothers

November 1838
Sale of the workhouse
By the time the workhouse was sold in 1838 there were eighteen inmates twelve being men and eight women. The sale of the Braintree parish workhouse took place on the 22 November 1838 by public auction. From the auction particulars it looks as if the property, where Tescos is now in the market, was a self contained block which could be divided up into a number of tenements. The block was 120 feet deep and 80 feet wide. The description was as follows:

On the west side was a watch house, committee room, women's room, dining room, kitchen and pantry with bedrooms above.
On the south side was a general room, pantry, cellars and men's workshop. There were bedrooms above.
On the east side there was a wood house and coal house, a mill house and wash house with also a cart shed. All these buildings would have probably have been of wood construction and in a yard.
On the north side were the entrance gates, travellers room, grinding house and tool house.
There was also a brick cage (small prison buildings) built into this north side.

The buildings were sold for £370 and probably converted into tenements. Later the block was pulled down and the Crown and Anchor public house built on the site before this was pulled down and finally the Tescos supermarket was built in the 1970s.

Bocking

Bocking parish workhouse was located in Church Lane just adjacent to the bridge over the river and opposite the old entrance to the Courtaulds Bocking factory. The building still stands and carries the date 1500 and there is evidence that this building has been used as the parish workhouse since at least from the 1720s. In the first chapter on the History of the Workhouse there is a reference to a government survey of parish workhouses which records that Bocking parish was capable of housing up to 140 inmates in 1777. Although this was not a record of the actual number in the workhouse at that time the figure of 140 was very high compared to other Essex workhouses apart from those in large towns. The explanation for such a large workhouse could have been, as was said in the first chapter, that the declining spinning and weaving industry in this part of Essex meant that many were out of work and ended up in the workhouse which resulted in a building capable of housing over 100 inmates. Although this figure of 140 possible inmates was a little suspect for 1777 there has fortunately survived an accurate survey of the parish of Bocking for 1793.

The survey names Joseph Walker as governor (master) and the total number living in the property as 63 which would have included his family if he had one. This number is less than half the 140 possible for 1777. One can only assume that the parish made the property large enough to accommodate this high number at the peak of the time of high unemployment but subsequently those out of work had moved from the spinning and weaving industry to other employment by 1793 and consequently the occupancy of the workhouse was much lower sixteen years later. By 1807 the number of inmates had fallen even further with only 44 residents including the governor and his family.

The Essex Record Office has a document relating to lists of donors in respect of the supply of coal for the poor of the parish and also for celebrations for Queen Victoria's coronation in 1838. Whilst not specifically relating to the poor in the workhouse it appears that the two lists for coal in January 1838 and the Queen's coronation in the summer were published and placed on the parish notice board for all to see who donated what for these two occasions. The allowance of a bushel of coal for needy families was delivered by volunteers to all those on out-relief three times 'during the severest part of the winter'. The summer donations allowed one pound of meat to each adult and half a pound to each child. In addition each family received flour, plums and one pint of beer to every person. As the list of donors was published there must have been some prestige in being the largest donor and it is noted that the top donation of £5 was contributed by six residents that included Sir Herbert Oakley, the Very Rev. Dean and Rector and Mr Charles Tabor a well known name locally. The workhouse was used up to 1838 when the Union workhouse opened in Braintree.

Bocking Parish Workhouse as it is today

Bradwell next Coggeshall

In the national survey of parish workhouses in 1777 the Bradwell workhouse could accommodate up to 13 inmates. Many of the parish records relating to the workhouse have been lost and it is not known when it was built but by the size of the property when it was sold it was fairly small compared with other Essex workhouses and could accommodate up to about 15 inmates. The workhouse was put for auction in May 1838 with the sale taking place at the Bull public house. The property was described as being 'a substantial property' which had been converted back into its original four cottages. The property was duly sold and a deed dated 9th July 1838 showed that old workhouse had been sold for £94. The location is described was 'Hardings' in the parish of Bradwell next Coggeshall although I have not been able to identify the property today.

Finchingfield

There was an agreement by the parish vestry to build a workhouse in 1763 although the actual date of building is unknown. There is also an undated plan for a Finchingfield workhouse in the Essex Record office which shows the workhouse to be a building 76 feet long and 15 feet deep. There were to be two storeys with the lower storey having eight windows and a central front door and nine windows upstairs. The layout had seven rooms on the ground floor and was planned as follows starting from the far left:

women's sitting room - women's work room - governor's room - store room - men's work room - men's sitting room. The seventh room was a wash house and bakehouse at the rear.

Upstairs there were to be eight rooms which were probably seven bedrooms with a further room over the wash/bake-house at the back. One wonders whether this workhouse was actually built as the description of the property does not agree with that described by Eliza Vaughan in her book which was a workhouse that was in use in the 1830s. There is an inventory in the parish records for the late eighteenth century which does not seem to agree with the rooms proposed in the plan mentioned above.

Finchingfield Parish Workhouse as it is today

The inventory mentions the following rooms:

buttery - dining room - governor's room - dwelling room - ward - brew house -
coalhouse - first chamber -hall chamber - governor's chamber - first garret - second
garret

The Eliza Vaughan workhouse definitely had, and still has, garret windows which means that the descriptions of the two storey building is referring to a different workhouse to that described by Eliza Vaughan which had three storeys. It is possible that a purpose built workhouse was built in the 1760s but it was not in use later in the century as a workhouse. It rather looks as this project did not go ahead and the parish ended up using an older building. In 1777 the workhouse, and presumably we are referring to the three storey building, could accommodate up to 25 inmates and this ties in with figures in the vestry minute books which number the inmates during the period 1813 to 1824 as having 27 inmates in 1813 falling gradually to about 20 in 1824. The numbers did peak though in 1821 when there were 33 people in the house which did include the family of Simon Turner, the governor. During this period just over 100 families in the parish were on out-relief receiving amounts ranging from two shillings a week to seven shillings a week for a family with three children or more.

Finchingfield's workhouse was described by Eliza Vaughan in her book *The Stream of Time* as being by the river's side and being a picturesque gabled building with fine 16th century chimney stacks. In 1926, when the book was written, the old workhouse was a butcher's shop with a slaughterhouse to the rear. This gabled property, which still has two rooms in the gables, is by the pond at Finchingfield and now known as Bridge House. There are memories in the book of the paupers going to work in the Hop Grounds in about the 1830s which was a field that still retained that name in the 1920s although by then the cultivation of hops in the village had long ceased. The master of the workhouse was described as being a resident of Finchingfield. He was very stern and much feared and wore a kind of smock with grey breeches and stockings. It was common for paupers to abscond from workhouses and the Finchingfield master was said to go in search of fugitives with a whip. This recollection of the workhouse would have been for the period up the 1830s.

As readers will note from previous pages smallpox and other infectious diseases were always a problem up to the twentieth century and Finchingfield tackled this problem in 1803 by the parish vestry agreeing to inoculate all the poor of the parish against smallpox or cowpox. The vestry appointed Mr G Willsher to inoculate at the rate of one shilling and six pence per person.

In 1807 the parish vestry agreed to build four cottages for the use of the poor of the parish. These would probably have been rent free accommodation for poor families of the village who may have been turned out of their own cottage through non payment of the rent or having to leave a tied cottage on a farm if the agricultural worker had lost his job.

Wethersfield

The vestry minutes record that in April 1727 that the parish workhouse should be inspected and the overseer was authorised to purchase what was wanted to put it in good order. The workhouse was probably set up a few years earlier. In 1729 there were eleven inmates in the workhouse, three from the Nash family, four from the Carter family, two from the Boule family together with Mary Spleen and Thomas Joarock. A few weeks later Thomas, who is described as the son of Widow Joarock, was allowed to have twenty shillings for clothing. Presumably Mrs Joarock could not afford to keep him at home as she was probably on out-relief.

In 1730 a new governor of the workhouse was appointed. Robert Carter was allowed seven shillings and six pence to keep seven paupers in the workhouse in 'meat, drink, washing and lodging'. Out of the list of seven only Mary Spleen was still in the workhouse from those listed a year previously.

A new agreement with a new governor, John Meadows, appeared in the vestry minutes in 1764 and this time, in addition to the basic requirement seen in 1730, the vestry required twelve other stipulations. Among these were rules regarding pregnant women being admitted and the amount that would be paid to the woman during pregnancy and the amount to be paid to a subsequent child. Mr Meadows was also required to bury at his own expense any inmate that should die whilst in his care. The agreement also made obligations on the part of the parish which included the adequate supply of bedding and furniture for the inmates. Mr Meadows had to agree that all the contents of the workhouse were in the ownership of the parish, apart from that which he brought in, and that he had no right to sell any parish owned property. It seems that any previous arrangement with a workhouse governor/master must have been very loose and this new long agreement brought all the previous contentious issues together.

Two years later in 1766 the parish vestry conducted a survey of all the clothing of the inmates in the workhouse. There were 19 inmates at the time and the report details all the clothing owned by each inmates and the condition of each item. The comments ranged from 'very good' to 'pretty good' down to 'indifferent, old or very bad'. Credit must be given to the parish vestry for attending to their responsibilities to the poor of their parish. The number of inmates at this time was up to 25 as this was the number given in the return to the government which the workhouse could accommodate.

It is clear from the foregoing that Wethersfield vestry took the care of their paupers very seriously and it seems that they were not satisfied in 1785 with their present workhouse master and his wife. The vestry minutes record that Samuel Turner and his wife were given three months notice to quit their positions. Unfortunately the minutes do not record the reasons for their dismissal. The minute book shows that some of the meetings were held at the church vestry and some were held at the Lion public house.

The vestry in 1792 took an inventory of the workhouse which detailed every item in every room down the last copper pot. The workhouse was spread over three floors with two garret rooms in the gables (similar to Finchingfield). The wool industry was in decline in Essex at this time but the workhouse still had one spinning wheel in the 'Great Bed Room' and there was one in the 'Wool Room'. This latter room may well have had more wheels earlier in the eighteenth century. From the inventory of the number of spoons, pans and pots it looks as if there were enough eating utensils for up to 20 inmates. New inmates could occasionally bring their own bits and pieces into the workhouse and at the end of the inventory the vestry records that Thomas Gunn was in ownership of a bed, bedstead, linen and blankets. Also he brought in a chair, a box and a cupboard. The workhouse survived right the way up to the time that the Braintree Union was formed but was not one that the new Union took over in 1835 pending the building of the new workhouse. The workhouse closed and the contents were sold off in October 1836.

THE BRAINTREE UNION WORKHOUSE

The first meeting of the Board of Guardians was held on the 18 December 1835 at the White Hart Inn, Bocking. Locals would today refer to this public house as being in Braintree but presumably it was referred to as being in Bocking in the 1840s. The Braintree Board of Guardians was made up of representatives of the 14 parishes in the list at the start of this chapter with Braintree and Bocking getting four places each on the Board and Finchingfield and Wethersfield getting two each.

This totalled 22 representatives and I note from the minutes that all 22 were in attendance at the first meeting.

I commented in the chapter on the Billericay Union regarding the make up of their Board in that the extra representative from South Weald did not seem to reflect that parish's population. In Braintree's case though Braintree and Bocking had the highest population and justified their four places each and of all the small remaining parishes Finchingfield and Wethersfield come third and fourth in the population league table to justify their two places each.

When the new Board of Guardians took over the parish workhouses in 1835 they inherited the workhouses at Braintree, Bocking, Finchingfield and Bradwell-next-Coggeshall. The parish workhouses at Black Notley and Wethersfied closed soon after the Board of Guardians took over the control of parish workhouses. The inmates at these two parish workhouses would have been transferred to probably either the Braintree or Bocking workhouses.

Extracts from the Guardians' Minutes
December 1835
The weekly Guardians meeting
It was decided early on at the first meeting that the Union would have weekly meetings at the White Hart at 10am on Mondays. I note that two months later the Guardians formalised the renting of the room at the White Hart by agreeing a rent of five shillings (25p) a week with the landlord for the use of the room to include a fire and the supply of candles for light. It is easy to forget that there was no central heating and electric light in those days.

January 1836
Advertisements for supply of food and goods
One of the first jobs that the Guardians had to do after all the appointment of officers had taken place was, like Billericay, to place advertisements in the local paper for the supply of food and goods to the existing parish workhouses as the administration of these was now in the hands of the new Braintree Union Guardians. One of the early meetings agreed an advertisement for 'the supply of good seconds flour and bread of the same quality'. There was no equality in those days. Those in the workhouses were regarded as second class citizens and so got second rate produce.

Changes at existing parish workhouses

Now that the new Guardians had assumed responsibility for the four remaining workhouses in the fourteen parishes (Braintree, Bocking, Finchingfield and Bradwell) they, as well as ordering the food and other supplies, undertook surveys of the parish workhouses and made various changes. The rules for operating the new Union workhouse, when it was eventually built, provided for men and women to be separated and it seems that the Guardians took this on board in respect of the existing parish workhouses at Braintree and Bocking. It was suggested that Braintree workhouse be divided into two parts for men and women and Bocking workhouse be divided into three parts. The records do not say what the third part at Bocking was to be used for but this was probably for mothers and young children. The Guardians appointed a sub-committee to look into various aspects of the running and costings of the existing workhouses. The old parish workhouses at Bradwell and Finchingfield were small and did not feature in the Guardians' plans regarding the separation of the categories of inmate. It looks, therefore, as if these two, like those at Black Notley and Wethersfield, were now closed and their inmates transferred to either Braintree or Bocking workhouses. They were both sold off in 1838 when the new Union Workhouse opened.

Calculation of poor rate per head

The sub-committee looking into the finances of the parish workhouses in 1836 also came up with some figures which showed how much per head of population was being spent on the poor of the fourteen parishes. Braintree's population was 3422 and Bocking had 3120. The smallest parish was Panfield with only 316 people. The total population for the fourteen parishes was 15,097 in 1836 with an total annual poor rate of £13,440. This worked out at 18 shillings per head of population. This information gave the Guardians some insight into how much it was costing them to fund the poor at present and hopefully by the provision of just one Union workhouse in the future savings would be made.

Contract to build flour mill

In early 1836 there were still no plans to build the new workhouse and so the Guardians were still prepared to spent some money on improvements. The minutes record a resolution to erect a manually operated (flour) mill at the Braintree parish workhouse similar to the one in existence at Dunmow. Tenders were invited. The contract was eventually awarded at a cost of £82 to include a ladder and meal bins with the work to take five weeks. The minutes said that some minor alterations would be needed to the Braintree workhouse but the mill could be incorporated into the existing building. The most popular design used in workhouses was a multi-handle corn grinding machine where rods passed through the wall of the grinding mill which were turned manually by the inmates in the next room.

Braintree and Bocking parish workhouses

The masters and matrons (the wives) of Braintree and Bocking workhouses were summoned to the Guardians to discuss the running of their workhouses and to have their salaries reviewed. The minutes also record that the Guardians took over the Braintree workhouse from the parish at a rent of £35 per year. In the case of Bocking workhouse the survey found that many parts of the structure were in a condition not suitable for the inmates and that Bocking parish had to put the property in order before the Guardians would take it over and start paying rent to that parish.

March 1836
Parish workhouse attendance rules

Not all paupers lived in the parish workhouse and we have seen previously that out relief was paid to local residents to care for those less fortunate. Able bodied paupers though invariably had to attend the local parish workhouse to work at basket making and other local skills. In 1836 we see the Braintree Guardians laying down some attendance rules. All paupers who did not live in the workhouse had to be at work in the workhouse by 6am and work to 6pm with a half hour break for breakfast and one hour at midday.

1837/38
The new Union Workhouse

The Braintree Board of Guardians invited four architects to submit plans to build the workhouse. The contract was eventually awarded to William Nash of Royston who had a good track record as he had designed the workhouse in his home town of Royston and also those for Buntingford, Halstead and St Ives. The workhouse was built to accommodate up to 300 inmates to the west of Braintree on the Rayne Road. Construction took place during 1837/38.

Braintree Union Workhouse built 1838

Braintree Union Workhouse built 1838

March 1838

At the Guardians meeting on the 5 March one of the Guardians was asked to go and inspect the new workhouse to see if it was fit for occupation. Mr Dixon reported back that in his opinion the first floor rooms were now quite aired and ready for occupation but the rooms on the ground floor had been left open in damp weather and were not ready yet but in one week the whole new workhouse would be satisfactory. Notwithstanding the foregoing assurance the Guardians the following week were talking about putting locks on the doors which obviously had not been done previously.

Bocking and Finchingfield parish workhouses

We now see the Guardians arranging to sell the fixtures and furniture of the Bocking parish workhouse. The parish workhouse at Finchingfield was also being sold in March 1838 with the auction sale price being £194.

Problems at the new workhouse

It looks that as soon as the inmates had moved in problems cropped up immediately concerning 'the construction, fittings and arrangements of the new workhouse'. It is not clear from the minutes what these problems were but the architect, Mr Nash, was called back to sort out the problems.

April 1838

Emigration of the Breed family

Life in the new workhouse was obviously not to the liking of Catherine Breed and her child as she asked the Guardians if she could emigrate to Canada. Application declined.

Furniture for the Guardians rooms

Arrangements were made for furniture to include tables, chairs, fire irons and matting or carpet be supplied for the Guardians Board Room, the clerk's office and the visitor's room.

Appointments at the new workhouse

Master & wife	John & Eliza Turner	£80 year
Porter	John Larkin	£20
Schoolmistress	Eliza Turner	£16
Nurse	to be appointed	£16

It looks as if the master's wife also took on the role of schoolmistress. The Guardians also allowed the Turners to have with them in the workhouse their two youngest children. Their other children were presumably old enough to be out to work. The Guardians discussed appointing a chaplain to the workhouse. The motion was put to the vote but the proposition was lost by 14 votes to 8. A few months later the matter was raised again and a chaplain was appointed to the workhouse.

May 1838
Admission of vagrants
The Guardians decreed that no vagrants be admitted to the workhouse after 8pm and that the diet of vagrants be bread and water only, except in cases of absolute necessity. Any vagrants would not be charged out to their parish like the ordinary inmate and so the Guardians were only going to spend to spend the minimum on these casual visitors.

Means test for pauper's next of kin
The Braintree minutes record various cases through the years of paupers' relations being taken to court. There were many cases where relations were proceeded against for not maintaining their kin if they were financially able. A family could not just place an old or infirm relation in the workhouse. It looks as if the Guardians always did some research into the pauper's family, if there was one, to see if they could maintain them before admittance to the workhouse. There was an instance where the Guardians at Braintree ordered the churchwardens and overseers of the poor of Braintree town to take measures to obtain a Mr Clark's pension as he would not maintain his wife.

June 1838
Turning the mangle
The visitor's book was brought to the attention of the Guardians as a visitor had seen a man in the laundry turning a mangle. It was ordered that the practice be avoided, 'except when there is an insufficiency of able bodied woman for the work'!!!

Coronation celebrations - Queen Victoria
The Guardians sanctioned the provision of plum pudding and a meat dinner and a pint of beer for each inmates in respect of the forthcoming coronation of Queen Victoria.

September 1838
Catherine Breed
We saw in April that Catherine Breed had asked if she could emigrate to Canada with her child. This request was declined as the Guardians were very strict with this type of request as they required to know details of who will look after the emigrants when they get to their new country and what will be their ability to earn a living wage. We now see Catherine being taken before the Magistrate for assaulting the Matron and generally misbehaving herself. Maybe one of the reasons for the earlier

decline was that the Guardians felt that Catherine Breed would not make a good Canadian citizen.

Confinement of inmates
John Patmore and Philip Totman had complaints brought against them for leaving the workhouse saying they were going to church and returning drunk having visited a public house. They were both confined to the workhouse for two months.

Leave of absence
A rather unusual minute appeared in September which had not occurred before. Two boys in the workhouse, Charles and James Harrington, who the minute said were in poor health, were allowed leave of absence for three weeks to visit friends in Finchingfield. Possibly the conditions in the workhouse were not favourable for these two brothers and maybe the Guardians thought that a short time away from the workhouse may improve their health.

November 1838
'Discontented spirit'
These were the words used by a visitor in the visitor's book when referring to the able bodied men. The master was interviewed but could not confirm that this was the case with the able bodied men. Anyone in a Union workhouse in the 1830s was not going to be a particularly happy person.

December 1838
Lunatics deaths at Hoxton asylum
The clerk reported the death of one of their inmates who had been transferred to the asylum at Hoxton. He said that this was the fifth occasion recently when inmates from Braintree had died at the asylum after only being there a very short time. The clerk had set in motion certain enquiries as to the respectability of this establishment with which he would report on later. The Essex Lunatic Asylum at Brentwood was not built until 1853.

January 1839
Parish poor rate
The Guardians set the following poor rate on their parishes partly proportionate to the rateable value of the parish in respect of the cost of running the workhouse and paying the salaries and partly proportionate to how many of the parish residents were accommodated in the

workhouse or on parish out-relief. Whilst the first part of the poor rate in respect of the running costs meant that each householder that was rated the same paid the same irrespective if his parish was large or small, the second part of the rate charge was harder on residents of a parish which had a high level of unemployment and consequently more reliance on financial assistance.

	£		£
Braintree	600	Black Notley	80
Bocking	500	White Notley	80
Finchingfield	400	Great Saling	55
Wethersfield	350	Pattiswick	50
Stisted	100	Rayne	90
Shalford	65	Bradwell	35
Cressing	95	Panfield	75

As far as the above figures are concerned the amounts chargeable to each parish are fairly relative to their respective populations which means that no parish had a higher incidence of unemployment than the next and consequently no parish had a relatively higher number in the workhouse or on out-relief. There are various letters to the Guardians at this time from the parishes requesting that their parish be re-valued for rating purposes. Previously the parishes were setting their own rate internally but now that the Union workhouse was working out how much they had to pay for their poor rate the parishes were querying whether their parish was correctly rated and the parishes were calling for a revaluation.

Christmas 1840

The *Essex Standard* reported in its first edition in January 1841 on what some of the local Union Workhouses supplied for their inmates Christmas lunch. The Braintree workhouse supplied roast beef and plum pudding with a pint of (weak) beer for each adult and a half a pint for each child. The Guardians also supplied pipes, tobacco and snuff. The newspaper was very disparaging in its article and inferred that society was being over generous in its attitude to paupers.

The census of 1841

The first national census after the Union workhouse opened was in 1841 and the data shows a staff of six with the master and matron having a five year old daughter living with them.

Master	John Turner	45
Matron	Eliza Turner	45
	Esther Turner	5
Porter	John Larkin	60

| Nurse | Susan Weavers | 50 |
| Schoolmistress | Ann Smith | 40 |

The Turners were still master and matron since 1838 but Mrs Turner had given up her duties as schoolmistress and Ann Smith had been appointed. John Larkin still held the position of porter.

There were 96 male inmates and 60 women inmates making a total of 156. The census showed the previous occupation of the paupers and whilst there were many male agricultural workers and females in domestic service there were a number of occupations which reflect the spinning and weaving industries of the Braintree and Bocking area. The following occupations cropped up quite regularly:

| Wool | comber | spinner | weaver | silk winder |

Other interesting occupations were:

| Tallow chandler | maltster | straw plaiter | ropemaker |

By 1851 the combined population of Braintree and Bocking had increased from 7100 in 1841 to 8100, an increase of 14%, but the inmate population of the workhouse now stood at 276 compared with 156 in 1841 an increase of 80%. Since the workhouse was built a new dining hall had been built as had a chapel and there was now room for 400 inmates.

Over the next 50 years the number of inmates fell from 276 to 214 excluding staff.

The census of 1901

Males	128	The total included 12 staff and 24 children under
Females	98	14. The percentage of children to total number of
		inmates was 8%
Total	226	

In the 1841 census 39% of the inmates were children which had dropped to only 8% sixty years later.

The workhouse sick

Many inmates of the workhouse were sick, and if they were not when admitted they invariably became unwell mainly due to the Spartan conditions that existed in all of the Essex workhouses. The commonest of causes of sick persons being brought to the workhouse were tuberculosis or consumption but as can be seen in almost every Essex workhouse cases of smallpox were always a problem. Workhouses were not built with specific infirmaries and the sick were just housed in a separate ward no different from the others. A visitor to a workhouse in the West Country in the 1860s said the 'the infirmary is an accident of the (work) house .....not its main object'. Eventually, as readers will see, separate infirmaries were built especially to cater for the sick and to isolate infectious cases.

Smallpox in 1904
Mention was made in the Billericay Union chapter of the cases of smallpox in the 1880s and this was still a problem at the start of the twentieth century. A case was reported to the Guardians of an inmate with smallpox in 1904 and consequently the man aged 65 was transferred to the Braintree Hospital Board's hospital at Black Notley. The man had only been in the workhouse for seven days before the symptoms developed. Previous to admission to the workhouse the man had been to the towns of Chelmsford, Colchester and Halstead and he had slept the night before admission at his sister's house in Bocking, Braintree. It looks as if the man was of no fixed abode and according to Union workhouse rules it was decided that the Braintree workhouse would bear the cost of his hospitalisation.

Local Government Act 1929
This Act applied not only to Braintree Union Workhouse but to all 17 of the Essex Union Workhouses and all Union workhouses throughout the country. Basically the Act brought to an end the Board of Guardians of each Union on the 31 March 1930 and on the 1st April transferred all the assets and liabilities of the Essex Unions to Essex County Council. In Braintree's case their last meeting was held on the 24 March 1930 which did not conduct any official business but was basically a 'thank you' to all the staff for their services over the years. Mr Bartram, the chairman, had been a Guardian for 51 years and chairman since 1917. The minutes recorded the names of all the officers and their length of service and it is noted that there were 22 salaried officers employed at the workhouse in 1930. The workhouse master was now referred to as the labour master and in addition there were nurses, catering staff through to a needle mistress, a laundress, an engineer and a shoemaker. The 'outside officers' numbered 14 and included four clerks, six district medical officers, three relieving officers and a boarding out visitor. In the final

years the total number employed by the workhouse both in the workhouse and outside was 36.

Post April 1930

Nothing really changed at the workhouse for the first few years after Essex County Council took control. Government benefits saw fewer able bodied adults being admitted with the majority of inmates being the old and infirm, some unmarried mothers and a nursery of young children. Most of these children were invariably referred to in the Admission Book as 'bastards'. The old workhouse buildings eventually took on the role of St Michaels Hospital.

Chapter 4

CHELMSFORD AND ITS ENVIRONS

PARISH WORKHOUSES

The following 26 parishes were grouped together in 1834 following the Poor Law Amendment Act to form the Chelmsford Union. Before 1834 each parish may have had its own poorhouse or workhouse.

Great Baddow, Little Baddow, Boreham. Broomfield, Buttsbury, Chelmsford, Chignall St James, Chignal Smealy, Danbury, Good Easter, Fryerning, East Hanningfield, South Hanningfield, West Hanningfield, Ingatestone, Margaretting, Mashbury, Pleshey, Roxwell, Sandon, Springfield, Stock, Great Waltham, Little Waltham, Widford, and Writtle.

At the first meeting of the new Union Guardians in 1835 it was decided by the Poor Law Commissioners that the following five parishes would be added to the Chelmsford Union:

Great Leighs, Little Leighs, Rettendon, Runwell and Woodham Ferres

The government undertook a survey of parish workhouses in 1777 and the following parishes in this area had a workhouse open in that year. The survey listed Stock and Buttsbury as having separate workhouses but in fact the two parishes had a combined workhouse.

Chelmsford	Broomfield	Springfield
Gt.Baddow	Danbury	Stock/Buttsbury
Lt.Waltham	Gt.Waltham	Fryerning
Roxwell	Writtle	Gt Leighs
S.Hanningfield	Woodham Ferres	

Chelmsford

In 1639 there was a parish property which housed 18 men and women which was located in the St Marys church and New Street area. This very early accommodation for the poor of Chelmsford was some 40 years after the first Poor Law which passed the responsibility for the poor from the church to the parish. It is quite probable though that this early property was owned by the church but after the Poor Laws of 1597/98 the cost of running the poorhouse would have been the responsibility of Chelmsford parish. A later Poor Law of 1697 required paupers to have a parish badge sewn upon the shoulder of the right sleeve with letter 'P' for pauper and also a letter denoting their parish. For Chelmsford, as to be expected, the lettering was 'CP'. By 1713 Chelmsford parish was using many properties to house the poor and these were as follows:

5 houses behind the churchyard
4 almshouses in New Street
2 almshouse rooms by the Blue Boar in Duke Street
2 cottages in New Street
4 almshouses near Quaker meeting house in Baddow Lane

There were also the Mildmay almshouses which had been used previously by the parish to house the poor but in 1713 they were occupied at this time by the residents appointed by the Mildmay charity. In 1716 it was decided to pull down all the accommodation in New Street and build a new brick building. Trustees were appointed and they borrowed £200 to build the new workhouse on the site of the New Street almshouses and Church House (4-6 New Street). The building was 110 feet wide and 17 feet deep and had fourteen rooms with a yard and garden at the rear. The final cost was nearer £600 with £300 being borrowed. Like the Orsett workhouse, later in the text, the inmates were referred to as the 'Family'. The formal government act giving parishes permission to build a workhouse was not until 1723 and consequently Chelmsford's workhouse was one of the first built in Essex. An inventory of the workhouse was carried out in 1745 which describes the brick building as being over three floors with a cellar comprising in total 14 rooms. The top floor was referred to as the 'Garrets' and were probably very small low ceiling rooms. The master's apartment was four rooms over two floors. The ground floor rooms for the inmates were described as the Great Room and the Little Room. On the first floor the rooms were described as the Great Chamber South, the Next Chamber and the Next Chamber North. The Great Room, which was the day room for the inmates, contained eleven spinning wheels. In 1745 the number of inmates totalled 30.

Chelmsford workhouse was obviously well run which one would hope be the case for the county town of Essex. In the early nineteenth century committees were being set up to check on various aspects of the running of the workhouse and one in 1817 produced a sample menu for the week.

	Breakfast	**Dinner (lunch)**	**Supper**
Sunday	Soup from bones	Beef, suet pudding	Bread & cheese
Monday	Soup from meat	Bread & cheese	Bread & cheese
Tuesday	Milk pottage	Cold meat & veg.	Bread & cheese
Wednesday	Milk pottage	Beef & veg.	Bread & cheese
Thursday	Soup from meat	Pork with veg.	Bread & cheese
Friday	Milk pottage	Ox cheeks & veg.	Bread & cheese
Saturday	Ox cheeks soup	Soup from bones	Bread & cheese

Pottage was anything that could be put in a pot. It was either vegetables on their own or with meat and in this case milk would have been added to form a thick soup. If vegetables were on the menu then bread would not be served but the inmates would probably have had small (weak) beer. Another committee was set up by the vestry in 1818 to produce a report on the situation concerning the poor of the parish both in the workhouse and also on out-relief.. The workhouse was still in New Street and in 1818 there were 27 males and 34 females grouped into five 'Classes'. The inmates were classified as follows:

Infirm, deaf, lame, blind, bedridden or of unsound mind	12
Handicapped in some way but capable of light work	11
Able to work within workhouse	17
Employed outside workhouse including children over 10	9
Children at school or having minor duties at other times	12
Total	61

The report also said that a further 60 men, women and their children were all being looked after by the parish either in houses owned by the parish or in the parish almshouses. There were three almshouses on the side of the churchyard, two poor houses next to the charity school in New Street, five parish almshouses in Baddow Lane and the Mildmay almshouses in Moulsham. There was an unusual arrangement among these properties where the custom was that a place in one of the poorhouses or almshouses could be passed on from one generation to another. This unfair practice was soon put a stop to after the vestry had seen the report. Despite the number of paupers in the workhouse and those living in the parish poorhouses and almshouse it seems as if there was still a demand for social housing for the less well off as in 1818 the parish vestry rented sixteen cheap cottages in Clapham Square off Springfield Lane. The prospective tenants were vetted for their ability to pay the rent which ranged from one to three shillings a week. In addition to the 61 in the workhouse and a further 60 in the various properties mentioned about the vestry was looking after in excess of 550 men, women and children throughout the town by way of out-relief. In 1820 Chelmsford built its own infirmary which was said to be the only parish workhouse with its own separate infirmary. As Chelmsford was the county town it was sure to have had a large income from its Poor Rate and could probably afford this expenditure. In 1823 an application was made by some of the old women in the workhouse that they be allowed half a pint of beer a day and four pence a week allowance. Two weeks later the vestry agreed that six aged women could have a pint, not a half, of beer per day together with the four pence allowance they had requested.

Great Baddow

The parish workhouse was built in 1790 and the parish records for April show the payment of three bills totalling £98 for building the workhouse. The governor was paid a salary of two pounds two shillings up to Easter 1790 which means that the workhouse probably opened a month or so earlier. The location of the workhouse was in Vicarage Lane which was previously called Workhouse Lane. In 1800 the parish purchased 27 spinning wheels and lent these to the poor of the parish in order that they could earn for themselves an income from spinning. This was a good strategy by the parish vestry as possibly some of these 27 families may have ended up in the workhouse and ultimately cost the parish a lot more.

As a further way of reducing costs and ultimately the parish poor rate, selected paupers were 'farmed' out to local farmers and there is an agreement with Thomas Sullings in 1804 that he would take paupers at the rate of three shillings and six pence a week.

During the reign of George 111 further Acts were passed concerning the setting up of workhouses but it was not until 1813 that a public meeting of the residents of Great Baddow was held when 76 residents agreed to set up a workhouse and adopt the rules and regulations for the running of workhouses as outlined in the government's Act. The residents also agreed that whoever was appointed governor of the workhouse would receive a salary of £21 a year. The application for the workhouse went to the local justices, who replied saying, 'We..........consider the parish of Great Baddow aforesaid to be of magnitude sufficient to have a workhouse provided within it (the parish) for the reception and employment of the poor'.

Just prior to the control of the workhouse being transferred to the new Chelmsford Union in 1834 the parish vestry commissioned a review of the running of the workhouse in 1833 and set up a sub committee for this purpose. The problem was, like all parish workhouses in Essex, the cost of running these establishments was escalating and the committee was asked to recommend ways that the costs could be kept down and ultimately to ensure that the poor rate did not rise any faster than the rate of inflation. Their long report ran to five pages and among the recommendations was one to sell the existing workhouse together with its land and build another more convenient building where the inmates could be housed in accordance with their classification. Nothing happened of course as within a year the new Chelmsford Guardians had their own ideas for the Great Baddow workhouse.

Boreham

There are various references in the Boreham records of poorhouses and workhouse in the parish with the first reference being in the late sixteenth century when the churchwarden's accounts refer to the parish poorhouse. At the end of the sixteenth century in 1592 there is again a reference to a house for the poor people of Boreham. This property was probably just a cottage owned by the church and possibly run by the parish where the poor were accommodated probably on a rent free basis. The inmates would have an allowance to feed and cloth themselves.

The next mention is in 1714 when the conveyance of a property called Averyes referred to part of the property as being used as a workhouse. The property seemed to be a terrace of cottages all referred to as the same name. There was no need at that time for the individual tenements to have a name or number and the block would just be referred to under one name. In 1724 the records name the workhouse as having four occupants and by 1782 the parish register refers to the master of the workhouse as being James Rice. A reference in 1897 describes the old workhouse as being called Abreys and at that date had been converted into ten cottages. It is unclear what proportion of the ten was the workhouse in the 1800s but it is unlikely to have just been the original cottage of 1714 and probably the workhouse expanded into some of the other cottages. When the Union Workhouse Committee was commissioned to inspect the existing workhouses in 1834 there is no mention of the Boreham workhouse. It rather looks therefore as if the workhouse closed prior to 1834. The cottages were demolished in 1955 and a new property on the site is called Avery's Rest Home. There is a reference to a further workhouse in the Waltham Road which later became known as Henning Hall. This building was most likely the successor to the 'old workhouse' and would have closed in the 1800s.

Buttsbury and Stock

The Buttsbury and Stock Parish Workhouses in Common Lane, Stock

The first mention of a parish workhouse was in 1757 when court papers were drawn up and signed by the tenants of the Manor of Imphey Hall in Buttsbury consenting to grant a licence for the erection of a workhouse on Stock Common. This document was followed up a year later when the Lord of the Manor of Impiety granted to the churchwardens and overseers of the parishes of Stock and Buttsbury four acres of waste land on Stock Common for the purpose of erecting a workhouse. The rent of the land was to be five shillings years and the two parishes would contribute equally towards the cost of building the workhouse. Both the parishes would raise a rate of one shilling in the pound towards the cost of building which was payable yearly until the whole cost was repaid. In the seventeenth century Stock Common was a considerable size but the Enclosure Acts saw all commons reduce in size including Stock Common although in 1760 four acres were still being rented for the purpose of the workhouse. There were further enclosures up to 1815 by which time the workhouse plot would have reduced considerably.

The government survey of parish workhouses in 1777 quotes both parishes as having a workhouse and both having a capacity of up to 10 inmates. There are inconsistencies with the figures for Essex in this survey and probably the return by the parish quoted the joint parishes of Stock and Buttsbury and the compiler presumed wrongly that each parish had a workhouse.

The workhouse was converted into cottages when the property was no longer required by the Chelmsford Union and the building remains today in this form. The location of the workhouse cottages is in

Common Lane which was previously called Workhouse Lane. The cottages still stand and whereas they were originally converted into five cottages in the 1840s they are now only three. The old workhouse building can be found on the right hand side of Common Lane from the Mill Road end.

Fryerning

A deed dated 1816 describes Brook House as previously being a public house called first the Three Nuns, then the Ship and then the Coach and Horses and then a private house part of which was being used in 1816 as a parish workhouse. The vestry minutes of 1825 refer to discussions for altering and improving the workhouse. The minute said 'that we the parishioners consider the said (work) House inconvenient for an increase of the poor and that we are also desirous of employing a man and his wife to manage the same'. The object seemed to be that it would be cheaper for the parish and the poor rate to accommodate new paupers in the parish workhouse rather than pay them out-relief. This of course was true and was the reason that workhouses were set up in the first place. There is no further information on this proposal but later in the year the vestry were proposing that property belonging to Fryerning Hall should be purchased for the use of the poor. It is possible then that Fryerning did not have a workhouse master and wife but just used various cottages in the parish to house the poor without a workhouse master.

In 1834 there were seven males and one female in the workhouse who were all described as being old and infirm. The Fryerning parish workhouse does not get a mention as one that was inspected by the Union Workhouse Committee in 1834 and so it looks as if the eight inmates were transferred to one of the other workhouses as soon as the committee was formed.

Ingatestone

A row of cottages that were used as the parish workhouse are still sited in the High Street on the same side as the church, and opposite Norton Road, just along from the Crown public house. Ingatestone workhouse does not feature in the government survey of parish workhouses in 1777 but it was open by at least 1784 as Thomas Caton was placed in charge of the poor of the parish at the rate of two shillings and four pence per inmate per week. Later in 1796 a resolution was passed for a workhouse matron, Mrs Sullen, be appointed for one month and receive three shillings and six pence per inmate 'to find them sufficient meat, drink, washing, mending and fuel'. Presumably this was a trial period and as there was no further reference to the job then she probably got the position on a permanent basis. Two years later in 1798 Mrs Sullen was still the matron but her allowance per inmate was reduced to three shilling per inmate

Ingatestone Parish Workhouse as it is today

Mr Sutton the overseer of the poor conducted a survey of the inmates in the workhouse and drew up a list of the clothing requirements in December 1811. He mentioned the names of 18 inmates and their requirements ranged from a new cap or shirt or stockings down to new shoes.

An inventory of the workhouse carried out by the parish vestry in 1823 describes the various rooms and their contents. There seems to be five rooms used as bedchambers together with the keeping room (day room), the kitchen or work room, the bakehouse, the scullery, the pantry, the coalhouse and the outside yard. From the list of utensils it does not seem as if there were more than a dozen inmates at this time. An earlier inventory in 1810 specially named one of the work rooms as the 'Spinning Room' which had six spinning wheels in use but by the date of the later inventory these had all been discarded.

Ingatestone retained its parish workhouse right up to the establishment of the Union in 1835. At this time it only had eight inmates, seven men and one woman who were all old and infirm. By 1836 the property was no longer being used as a workhouse although it had been planned to transfer all of one category of pauper into the Ingatestone workhouse but this does seem to have taken place. Although still owned by the parish the workhouse was now controlled by the Chelmsford Union Workhouse Guardians. In 1836 the property had been converted back into cottages with three being let to Mr Alexander Hogg and one used by the relieving officer to give out the allowances to those on out-relief and also to weigh out the flour for the poor.

Roxwell

The parish had a workhouse by at least 1725 and it may have existed even earlier. The location was in Roxwell Street and although the site was previously known as Gladwyns it has not been possible to pinpoint the exact location. It was the practice of the parish to appoint a senior inmate as Governess, who was usually a widow, and this system ran until 1784. During this period there were up to 20 inmates under her control. It was unusual for inmates of parish workhouse to get a treat at Christmas but this is what happened at Roxwell in 1734 when Thomas Bramston the principal landowner laid on a treat for the inmates in December of that year. The detailed list of items purchased appears to be more than the inmates of the workhouse could consume and possibly other poor residents on out-relief were invited. The list included:

18 gallons of brandy	34 dozen lemons	36 pound of sugar
6 gallons of wine	36 gallons of beer	83 pound of beef
bread, salt, butter, tobacco and pipes, candles, firing (wood)		

Thomas Bramston also arranged for the mending of windows, cleaning the house and the supplying of music. In addition the cost included the payment of servants to prepare and serve the meal and the supply of doorkeepers to keep out gatecrashers. The cost to Mr Brampton was £21 which was the equivalent of many thousands of pounds in 1734.

In the year 1767 the Essex Quarter Sessions tried the case of Martha Penny who was alleged to have taken a coin commonly referred to as a 'French Penny' and worth about ten pence which was in the care of the workhouse mistress. The money had been earned by the inmates and was kept in a locked cupboard in the workhouse. Apparently witnesses saw her take the key which was hung up in the room. There is no record of the outcome of the case but a guilty verdict would almost certainly have resulted in a custodial sentence.

During 1784/5 the workhouse was subject to much improvement culminating in the appointment of a Governor who was not an inmate. This first official workhouse master, who previously held the appointment at Gestingthorpe, only lasted a year and he was given notice by the parish. The workhouse continued to function up to the time that the Chelmsford Union was established in the 1830s and was then converted into three cottages. By 1841 these were in a poor state of repair and the parish decided to sell them off.

Springfield

An inventory of the workhouse of 1813 lists eleven rooms which roughly equates with the eventual five, two up, two down tenements. The rooms were named as follows:

The House (dining room)	Governor's room	pantry	Buttery
5 bedrooms	kitchen	lower new room	

It looks as if, by the number of beds, that the workhouse could house about 20 inmates. The building was converted back into five tenements at the end of its life as a workhouse in 1838 which gives an idea of the size of the property. The parish vestry passed a resolution in 1830 that no person living in the workhouse shall admit any person as lodger into the workhouse and also should any inmate have a member of their family come into the parish who requires accommodation then sanction must first be obtained from the parish before they are admitted. One would have thought that the governor of the workhouse would have exercised this control himself and things must have got out of hand if he was letting other persons reside in the workhouse without permission. The workhouse was sold off by the parish in 1838 which would have been soon after all the inmates were transferred to the new Union workhouse in Chelmsford.

Great Waltham

In 1762 the parishes of Great Waltham and Little Waltham made an agreement whereby two named poor residents of Little Waltham be fed and clothed in the Great Waltham workhouse for the sum of seven pounds sixteen shillings a year.

It rather looks as if the following arrangements refer to a new workhouse. The residents of Great Waltham met on the 4 December 1818 to approve an Agreement for fitting out the parish workhouse and agreeing a salary for various parties. The Agreement named Mr Leonard Thompson Good eve, Mr John Snow and Mr William Adams as appointed Guardians of the poor and Mr James Byford, Mr Jeremiah Westlegard and Mr Peter Golding as Governors of the poor house. The Guardians were to be paid a salary of £50, £25 and £12 respectively. The Governors were to be paid the sum of £20 each. It seems rather unusual for the three Guardians to be paid a salary and also for three Governors to be appointed. Usually a workhouse was run by a master/governor who would normally be assisted by his wife. To have three men appointed was unusual. Maybe there was a workhouse master in addition to the above personalities but this would have increased the salary bill even more.

In 1811 there were eighteen inmates who fell to twelve by 1823 and there were only eight by the time the workhouse closed.

Writtle

Writtle workhouse was built in 1717 in Bridge Street adjacent to the River Wid. The formal government act giving parishes permission to build a workhouse was not until 1723 making Writtle's workhouse one of the oldest in Essex. The government survey of parish workhouses in 1777 stated that Writtle workhouse could accommodate up to 100 paupers but this figures seems to be much too high and a figure of less than half this number, say 40, seems more appropriate.

Sir John Comyns of Hylands died in 1740 and some years previously he gave to the Writtle workhouse two pieces of land totalling seven acres near to, as described by the churchwardens later, as 'the New Bridge in the road leading from Chelmsford to Roxwell and adjoining to the lands of the farm called Reeds in Writtle'. In recognition of the gift the churchwardens printed a morning and evening prayer for the governor to read to the inmates daily. The prayer encouraged the inmates to go to church, obey the commandments, respect authority and refrain from 'lying, swearing, evil speaking and stealing'. The long prayer ended with the Lord's Prayer.

The Essex Record Office has a record book, presumably written up by the workhouse master, of all the names of the inmates on a monthly basis covering the period 1793 to 1808. During this period the average number in the workhouse was as follows:

1793	25	1802	32
1796	39	1805	37
1799	32	1808	34

The workhouse master kept a weekly sheet of what the inmates were doing on a daily basis. In June 1810 there were 32 inmates and their daily chores were as follows:

Garden work	1	Sick and infirm	6
Making faggots	2	Road work	1
Making sacks	2	Pregnant	1

Hemp spinning	3	Housework	3
Turners ?	4	At mothers	1
Winding	2	Working away	2
Needlework	1	Children	3

In 1821 the census recorded that there were on the 28 May a total of 34 persons living in the workhouse made up of 21 males and 13 females including children. This total would have included the master and matron who normally lived on the premises. A parish survey of the workhouse a year earlier made mention of three garret bedrooms, eight ground floor rooms together with a cellar and a yard. An earlier inventory of the workhouse in 1803 recorded that there were 12 spinning wheels and 6 carding stocks in the workshop but by the 1820 inventory the workshop had been renamed the 'Ward' and the spinning and carding equipment had gone. This room was probably now the infirmary.

Writtle's parish workhouse seems to have been retained by the parish for seven years after the Union workhouse was built in 1837 as it was not sold off until Jan 1844. Although the paupers would have been transferred to the new Chelmsford workhouse in 1837 the parish probably retained the property for other purposes although eventually the proceeds would have had to go the coffers of the Union.

THE CHELMSFORD UNION WORKHOUSE

All the parishes which made up the Union had one representative on the Board of Guardians with Chelmsford having four representatives and Springfield, Great Waltham and Writtle having two each. These last three parishes are all on the outskirts of Chelmsford and had larger populations than all the remaining small villages. This gave a total of 32 Guardians representing 26 parishes.

The first meeting of the new Chelmsford Union Guardians was held on the 15 August 1835 at the Black Boy Inn in Chelmsford. Subsequent meetings were held at the Shire Hall, Chelmsford.

Of the 31 parishes that made up the Union it is surprising that 14 had a parish workhouse in 1777 with this number falling to only a handful by the time the Union was established in 1834. The new Union Guardians at one of their first meetings set up a Workhouse Committee to inspect the existing workhouses and also to look at any other workhouses/poorhouses in the Union's area. The existing workhouses were located at:

Chelmsford   Great Waltham   Writtle   Ingatestone

The committee presented their report to the Guardians a month later which recommended that the above four existing workhouses were suitable to continue housing the poor. Springfield, Great Baddow and Buttsbury (Stock) were also available for use. These latter three were obviously not being used as a workhouse at the time but had been used previously for this purpose as all three appear in the list of workhouses for 1777. The committee did make some recommendations concerning the cleaning of the establishments and also that all the drains be cleaned. There was also a recommendation that an infirmary be established for the sick.

The report went on to recommend to which workhouse the various class of pauper is sent:

Great Baddow, Springfield, Writtle and Ingatestone:
   class 1 paupers - the aged and infirm of 60 years and upwards
   class 4 paupers - the infirm and under 60
Chelmsford
   class 2 paupers - able bodied males and youths of age 13 and upwards
Buttsbury (Stock)
   class 3 paupers - boys aged 7 to 13
   class 6 paupers - girls aged 6 to 16
   (the Report recommended that the Buttsbury poorhouse be known as the 'Asylum for Children' and not the 'Workhouse'.)
Great Waltham
   class 5 paupers - able bodied females and girls 16 and upwards

The very comprehensive report stated that the total number of paupers was 350 and that they could all be accommodated in the seven workhouses as outlined above. As the seven workhouses were in the ownership of the respective parishes rents were agreed to be paid by the Union with £60 to be paid for the use of the Chelmsford workhouse down to only £15 for the Great Baddow workhouse reflecting the size of each building. The second report by the Workhouse Committee said that improvements and alterations had been made or were in the course of being made to the various workhouses and that the situations were now as follows:

Springfield   presently occupied by 12 men and 8 women
      now ready for 13 men and 19 women in pauper classes 1 and 4
Great Waltham and Chelmsford were also now ready for occupancy
      (no present occupancy figures were quoted)
Writtle and Buttsbury were still under repair

It was anticipated that the Buttsbury workhouse could accommodate up to 60 children which seemed rather high. There was no mention of the Great Baddow and Ingatestone workhouses but a subsequent report indicated that Great Baddow could accommodate up to 32 aged or infirm males and females. By November 1835 all the seven workhouses had had their alteration and improvements completed and all the inmates had been sent to their allocated workhouses according to their class. Considering that the committee was only appointed in the August this was a great achievement.

The workhouse was built in 1837/38 on the west side of Wood Street in the standard design as recommended by the Poor Law Commissioners. The site was previously described as the Chelmsford Barracks Ground. The design was a central cross of buildings surrounded by other ancillary buildings enclosing the exercise yards the whole looking like a great big box. The workhouse was built to accommodate 400 inmates. The Board of Guardians met for the first time in their new board room in June 1838 and the appointment of the various officers was made in the August of that year. The inmates from the old parish workhouses were transferred into the new Union workhouse at weekly intervals during September 1838.

In 1886 the workhouse was almost completely destroyed by fire. Most of the Essex workhouse was not functioning to full capacity and the inmates would have been spread around the other local Union workhouses. New buildings were erected on the same site which was eventually opened in 1889. Some of the original buildings were incorporated into the rebuilt workhouse and when completed the workhouse could now accommodate 435 inmates.

The Union Workhouse minutes of the 1840s

For specific detail of Chelmsford Union Workhouse we will look at the 1840s when it should have been running smoothly after any teething problems of its building during 1837/38 were ironed out. Weekly meeting of the Guardians were still the norm and they were elected or re-elected on an annual basis. Like today in clubs and associations, those attending the meetings were duly recorded by name and it is interesting to note from what sector of society the Guardians came and how many turned up for the weekly meetings. People of course had to work and to attend a meeting every Monday morning would not be possible for every

The rebuilt Chelmsford Union Workhouse of 1889 after the fire of 1886

one. By the 1840s the number of Guardians had increased to 36 and at that time there was on average an attendance of 50% for the Monday meetings. At the annual election of the Guardians there was placed against each name their occupation and for the 36 Guardians the occupations were as follows:

| Farmers | 26 | Gentlemen | 6 | Tailors | 2 |
| Surgeon | 1 | Stone Mason | 1 | | |

As the majority were farmers and the gentlemen probably did not work, although they probably also had farm interests, one can see that it was possible for the attendance on a weekly basis to be possible for these self employed local residents.

The medical officer

The Guardians appointed a number of medical officers to cover the whole area. There would usually be one appointed to cover the inmates of the workhouse and probably three or four more to cover the poor that were on out relief in the rural parishes. The medical officer was paid an annual salary to care for the sick and infirm but it looks as if this was just for routine medical assistance and he was paid extra amounts for more difficult work. There is recorded in the minutes various examples where the Guardians authorised special payments and the norm seemed to be a fee of £1 for setting a fractured arm, £3 for a fractured leg and £5 for a leg amputation.

It was quite a feather in the cap to be appointed the medical officer of a Union workhouse with its annual salary boosting the income from the private work of the local residents. I have noted though that various Essex workhouses have questioned occasionally the conduct of medical officers towards inmates and I am sure that the workhouse sick did not always receive the treatment they deserved. There has been recorded many cases when the medical officer did not attend to a sick pauper either in the workhouse or out in the country when he should have done. The reason was usually that he had to attend to a private patient who always seemed to come first. Although there was a certain prestige in being appointed one of the medical officers for the Union workhouse it is clear that the novelty seemed to quickly wear off as the Guardian's minutes for all of the Essex workhouses record that they were always accepting the resignation of a medical officer after a relatively short time. Whilst on the one hand the medical officer was well paid for his responsibilities he was always at short notice being called upon by the Guardians to attend a pauper patient which invariably conflicted with the demands of his private clientele.

A wing of Chelmsford Union Workhouse which is now St Johns Hospital

The census of 1841

The first national census after the Union workhouse opened in 1838 was in 1841 and the figures are as follows:

Males	99	The total includes 7 staff and 82
Females	104	children under 14. The percentage of
		children to total number of inmates was
		42%
Total	203	

It is interesting to note that when the Guardians first took over the parish workhouses and had conducted their survey they concluded that the 350 existing paupers could be accommodated in the selected parish workhouses. Now after only a few years the number of paupers in the new Union workhouse was only 196 excluding staff. The Union workhouse was a much stricter regime than the parish workhouse and one can see that after the financial examination of the paupers many did not qualify to enter the Union workhouse and others may have left shortly after admission having found out what conditions were like.

December 1843

Complaint against medical officer

The Guardians had brought to their attention the conduct of the medical officer that covered Fryerning towards a pregnant woman. The board member for the parish of Fryerning said that the doctor had in his care a woman in labour and had left her in the care of the workhouse cook. The cook delivered the child but unfortunately had cut the umbilical cord too close to the baby's body which had resulted in the loss of a large amount of blood. The statement said that the doctor had not been to see the woman and child until the day after the birth and that the child had not been washed and dressed for three days after the birth. The medical officer was asked to attend the weekly meeting and stated that he had seen the woman in the morning of the day before she gave birth and had left her in the care of the cook. He said that he was sent for later in that day and saw the woman again in the afternoon. One of the paupers, Mary Keys aged 26, confirmed that the doctor had attended as he said. She also said that the child was washed and dressed as soon as possible after the birth. Another witness confirmed that the child was dressed again the day after the birth and the doctor attended that day.

It seems that the doctor came twice on the day before the birth but was not in attendance on the birth day. The Fryerning Guardian said he did not attend until the day after the birth and the witness confirmed this but he was not there on the birth day. The Board said that they wished to investigate the situation further and postponed the matter until next week. The following week a letter was received from the cook resigning her position but no reason was given in the minutes. Maybe she felt that playing the role of midwife was not part of her duties as a cook or possibly she felt that as she had put the baby's life in danger by her actions she felt that a change of scenery was the best course of action.

Two weeks later the Guardians reviewed the case again and came to the conclusion that the doctor 'was exonerated from all blame and that the woman and child had received proper attention whilst in the (work) House'. There is no doubt that the medical officer was not present on the day of the birth but it does seem that the mother and child received adequate attention notwithstanding the cook's unfortunate mistake. Union workhouses usually had a nurse, who may not have been qualified, on the staff and it was probably usual practise to leave straight forward confinements to in-house staff without the need for a doctor to be in attendance.

Following the resignation of the cook, an advertisement were placed in the Chelmsford Chronicle and eventually after the interviewing stage a lady was employed at a salary of £40 a year whereas the previous incumbent enjoyed a salary of £48 a year.

January 1844
Casual & vagrant paupers

The government body, the Poor Law Commissioners, continued to control the administration of Union Workhouses and in January 1844 issued a directive concerning the work to be undertaken by casual and vagrant paupers. As the name suggests these were paupers who passed through the workhouse and maybe only stayed overnight or for a maximum of a few days. These casual paupers were not accommodated in the normal male or female wards but usually in a special ward adjacent to the main gates of the workhouse. The facilities for these casuals would have been even more basic than for those permanent inmates as the Guardians did not wish to encourage them to stay for anything more than a day or two. The new directive said 'that in return for food and lodging the casuals be made to perform work that could include the picking of oakum, digging in the workhouse garden, pumping water, sweeping the yards or any sort of work the master may decide'. This directive was only applicable to adult persons not suffering from a temporary or permanent infirmity. Oakum picking was a very common occupation in workhouses which was the picking to pieces of old ropes which would then be taken away and remade. Many workhouses were often referred to as the 'Spike'. This reference is to the tool that was used to separate the old ropes which was just a slim spike of pointed metal.

April 1844

Smallpox epidemic

It came to the attention of the Guardians that several cases of smallpox had occurred in the parishes of Chelmsford and Springfield and that the disease was spreading. The Guardians wrote to the Poor Law Commissioners requesting permission to employ local doctors to vaccinate all the inmates. Permission was given and four local doctors were contracted to give vaccinations to all inmates at the rate of one shilling and sixpence per injection. It is evident from the minutes of all the Essex workhouses that the Guardians seemed to have a general responsibility for the prevention of the spread of infectious diseases in the area for which they were responsible. Apart from the situation above, which was specifically in respect of their own inmates, one often sees Guardians getting involved in sewage and health problems near to their workhouse.

Proceedings in bastardy

This was heading in the minute book in April 1844 which said that a statement had been made to the Board of Guardians in which they were satisfied that Walter Doe of Great Dunmow, labourer, was the father of an illegitimate child of which Susan Hammond was delivered in the Union House on the 19 March 1844. This child was now chargeable to the Parish of Great Waltham (presumably Susan Hammond's parish). The minutes went on to say that 'it was resolved and ordered that the notice now produced of our intended application to the Magistrates for an order on the said Walter Doe to reimburse the said parish (Gt Waltham) for the support and maintenance of the said bastard child be signed by the Guardians here present'. The Chelmsford Guardians would charge Great Waltham for the keep of the child and the Magistrate would issue an order for Walter Doe to reimburse that parish accordingly.

Dismissal of porter

The workhouse had just employed a new porter although we are not sure of his exact duties. All workhouses had a porter's lodge by the main gates and presumably his job was to control the comings and goings of inmates, staff and visitors. He was on the salaried staff and consequently he was ranked along with the nurse and the cook and possibly his duties were more than just a gatekeeper. The advert stated that he had to be 'diligent'. After a couple of months the master of the workhouse reported to the Guardians that 'the affliction of the porter impairs recollection and memory so as to render him quite inefficient for the duties of his office'.

This man got the sack and the Guardians advertised again for a new porter who was to be a single man at a salary of £20 per year with board and lodging and washing facilities in the (work) House to be included.

The workhouse vagrant and admissions blocks near to the main gate

Special case of relief to able bodied paupers

This was another heading in the minute book in this year when the Guardians agreed that Mary and Elizabeth G......?, (surname unreadable) the two eldest daughter of Henry G......?, be admitted into the workhouse and that the case be reported to the Poor Law Commissioners. Presumably children that had parents and were not orphans were not usually admitted into the workhouse on their own and sanction needed to be sought from the Commission. At first glance the above minute did not appear to be too unusual until the ages of the children were revealed. The report went on to say that the father belonged to the parish of Writtle and that he had a wife and seven children. Mary and Elizabeth, the two children being admitted, were aged seven and six years old and that the other five children were all under six years old. The wages coming into the family unit were ten shillings a week. Presumably ten shillings a week in 1844 was insufficient to support a family of seven and Henry and his wife had made the devastating decision to place the two eldest children in the workhouse. There was no further comment in the minutes on this case and presumably the Poor Law Commissioners gave their approval for the admissions.

Also in 1844 a similar case saw a father, George Brazier, who had eight children apply for Eliza, aged nine, and Benjamin, aged six, to be admitted to the workhouse. The eldest child was 13 and the youngest aged one. The eldest was most likely to be at work and bringing a small wage into the family unit as he still lived at home. The total weekly family income was eleven shillings and sixpence. One again permission from the Poor Law Commissioners would be sought.

May 1844
The matron's children
It is clear that the rules and regulations concerning who could be admitted to the workhouse were strict as evidenced by the two examples above. A case later in the year concerned one of their own staff. It had been brought to the attention of the Guardians that the matron had been in the habit of having one or more of her children living with her workhouse which was contrary to the regulations. Other examples of the appointment of a master and matron do not refer to children as the accommodation is usually just for the husband and wife. Presumably if there were children and they were not allowed in the workhouse they would have been boarded out unless the master and matron did not actually live in the workhouse which would have been very unusual. The matron admitted allowing one or more of her children to come into the workhouse and eat workhouse rations and also agreed the period over which this had happened. It was decided that the matron be charged for the maintenance of one child from December 1843 to May 1844 at double the rate for the rations of a child. The matron was admonished but did not lose her job. She was though allowed to have one child, Caroline aged 17, live with her until mid summer in 1844 subject to the payment of double rations. This seems to be fairly harsh justice as she had to pay back the cost of double rations for six months when obviously there were on some occasions only one child eating rations. For the next month or so she was also being charged double for the food that Caroline was to eat. This fine was probably better though than losing her job.

Special case of out-relief
For this final extract from Chelmsford's minutes I have pinpointed a case where the Guardians had been financially generous compared with the case of the matron above. The master had reported to the Guardians that Charles M......?, (surname unreadable) aged 11, the bastard child of Charlotte M......?, a pauper still remaining in the Union with two other bastard children, could obtain work in the parish of Boreham at a wage of two shillings a week. The Guardians felt that this wage was

insufficient to maintain the boy although the Board was of the opinion that it was desirous that this pauper, and all other paupers of this age, should be sent out to work. Consequently it was agreed that to enable the boy to take up the employment and to give him sufficient income to provide for board and lodging that the Guardians would allow out-relief of a further two shillings a week. From the boy's point of view he would on the one hand be separated from his mother but on the other hand he would be leaving the workhouse and have an income of four shillings a week to make a start in the big wide world which he may never have seen before if his early years were spent in the workhouse.

The census data of the late 1800s
Towards the end of the nineteenth century the number of inmates for most of the Essex workhouses peaked between 1871 and 1891 although the figures for Chelmsford do not peak until 1901. This later date seems to be the case for other areas of large population like Colchester and Romford and especially West Ham.

Chelmsford

Number of inmates on census night:

1841	196
1871	269
1891	246
1901	285

Vagrants 1891
The census recorded 12 casual vagrants on census night, eight men and four women, which are included in the above figure of 246.

Their ages, occupation and place of birth are as follows:

Male	Occupation	Place of birth
56	French polisher	London
45	Engine fitter	Manchester
45	Agr. labourer	Saxmundham
42	Agr. labourer	Norfolk
36	Agr. labourer	Colchester
41	Agr. labourer	Portsmouth
51	General lab.	Lancashire
40	General lab.	Dover
Females		
66	Pipe maker	Monmouth
40	Factory hand	Lancashire) mother &
18	Factory hand	Lancashire) daughter
67	Needlewoman	Suffolk

The twentieth century
The census of 1901

Males	183	The total includes 12 staff and 46 children under 14. The
Females	114	percentage of children to total number of inmates was 16%
Total	297	

There were 196 inmates in 1841 which increased to 285 in 1901. The number of children though dropped considerably from 42% of the total to only 16%. Following the take over by Essex County Council in 1930 many of the 1889 buildings remained and now form part of St Johns Hospital. The present maternity block is the one surviving part of the original 1837 workhouse which was then used as the kitchen block.

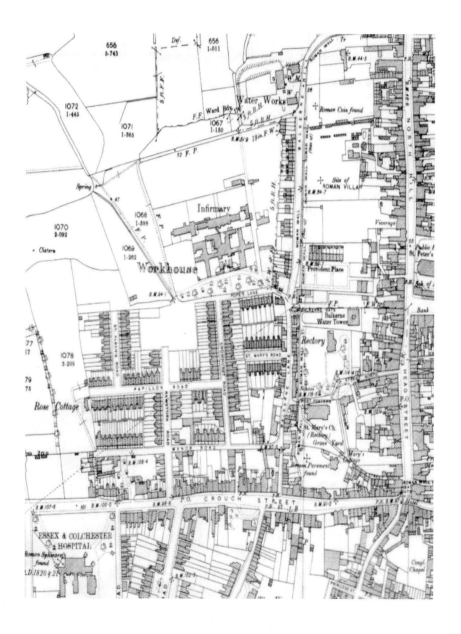

Map of Colchester 1897 showing the Union Workhouse and the Infirmary off Balkern Hill

Chapter 5

COLCHESTER AND ITS ENVIRONS

PARISH WORKHOUSES

The following 16 parishes in the above area were grouped together in 1834 following the Poor Law Amendment Act to form the Colchester Union. Before 1834 each parish may have had its own poorhouse or workhouse. Thirteen of the parishes are within the town of Colchester and the other three were adjacent rural parishes.

Colchester parishes: All Saints, Holy Trinity, St Boltoph, St Giles, St James, St Leonard, St Mary at the Walls, St Martin, St Michael-Mile End, St Mary Magdalen, St Nicholas, St Peter and St Runwald. The three rural parishes were Berechurch, Greenstead and Lexden.

The government undertook a survey of parish workhouses in 1777 and the following nine parishes in this area had a workhouse open in that year.

St Boltoph	St Giles	St James
St Martin	St Mary at the Walls	St Nicholas
St Peter	All Saints	Lexden

It was mentioned in the first chapter that a parish was only responsible for its own poor and if someone came from another parish they would have to bring a certificate with them confirming their situation. If this was the case then the parish could provide for them and charge the parish from where they came. An interesting exception occurs in Daniel Defoe's *Moll Flanders* written in 1722 when Moll recalls that at the tender age of three she was abandoned in Colchester by gypsies and taken in by the officers of the parish. Not being a resident of Colchester the parish took the case to the magistrates to decide what to do. The compassionate magistrate decided to order the town of Colchester to look after the child and Moll was placed in the care of a nurse who also kept a small school. Colchester paid for her keep until she was eight when the magistrates decided that she should then go into service and no longer be a drain on Colchester's poor rate.

In 1725 Colchester formed the Workhouse Corporation of Colchester to cater for all the poor of the town in the Colchester parishes listed above. The ruling body were 45 Guardians who were elected by the population. The Corporation levied a poor rate on the townsfolk to pay for the upkeep of the poor. Funds collected by the poor rate were passed on to two appointed 'Payers' whose job it was to relieve the poor according to their circumstances. Any amounts paid out would have to be supported by a voucher to be handed over to the treasurers in order to prevent any fraud. In 1725 one of Colchester's workhouses had one part for children and another as an infirmary for the old and sick. It is recorded that there were about 40/50 children in the workhouse but no mention of the number in the infirmary. The children were put to work carding and spinning wool which would be sent to the local bay-makers who produced course woollen garments. Money earned by the children could be retained. There was a workhouse master whose salary was £20 per annum and for the infirmary there was a nurse to look after the inmates. The report indicates that the old and infirm were given an allowance to look after themselves together with any other money they could earn by carrying out the same work as the children. It looks, therefore, as if the workhouse master was only responsible for the children and the old and infirm were looked by themselves as a group.

Surprisingly this sophisticated arrangement for the whole of the town of Colchester did not last for it appears that in about 1750 the Corporation was dissolved and it was then left to each parish within the town to look after its own poor and levy its own poor rate. By 1777 there were nine parish workhouses within the town and these are recorded in a government survey of that year. The names of the parishes and the maximum number of inmates each workhouse could accommodate were as follows:

All Saints	28	St Boltoph	35	St Giles	30
St James	24	Lexden	34	St Martin	12
St Mary(Walls)	30	St Nicholas	14	St Peter	20

By this time the 'Payers' would have been substituted by the overseer for the poor for each parish. The nine workhouses could house 227 inmates which was a large increase on the situation in 1725. By the 1790s those in the workhouses and those on out-relief were still increasing in number as the war in Europe involving France and Spain had affected the export of baize and this industry was now in decline. Colchester's poor were assisted by the many Friendly Societies in the town. Members paid in one shilling a month and when sick received up to ten shillings a week and slightly less for the aged.

Colchester, All Saints

All Saints parish took one six room house in 1753 and converted it into a workhouse. In 1777 the workhouse could accommodate up to 28 inmates. By 1801 the parish vestry were talking about creating a further parish workhouse and records show that a further property was in use for this purpose by 1822. Despite there being two workhouses in existence in 1822 these did not survive for much longer as they had both been closed prior to 1834 when the Colchester Union was established. Any paupers at closure would have been transferred to one of Colchester's other workhouses with All Saints paying for their board and lodging.

Colchester, St Boltoph

St Boltoph parish maintained a workhouse from at least the 1770s as one was mentioned in the government survey of that year which could accommodate up to 35 inmates. The property was six cottages in Moor Lane which was previously called Priory Street. At the end of its life in the 1830s the numbers varied from 17 to 27 inmates.

Colchester, St Giles

St Giles parish also established their workhouse in the 1770s and it could accommodate up to 30 inmates in 1777. This parish also took paupers from St Leonard's parish and the site could have been the large warehouse in Stanwell Street which was mentioned as such in 1833.

Colchester, St James

The parish converted three existing building near East Bridge in East Street into a workhouse in 1755. At the 1777 national census it could accommodate up to 24 inmates. A few years later in 1789 the parish vestry passed a resolution to rent a malthouse from John Dunnage for use as a workhouse but it is not clear whether this came to fruition. The parish appointed a new master in 1802. Samuel Hedgthorn was given a salary of thirty guineas a year together an allowance of one shilling and six pence per inmate to feed and cloth the paupers. In 1810 the parish overseers received a notice to quit the workhouse or pay an increased rent. This could be referring to the malthouse mentioned above.

In 1826 the parish converted the pantry in the workhouse as a secure lock-up for a deranged woman. Usually parishes sent their inmates 'of unsound mind' to the lunatic asylum at Bethlehem in London or the Holly House lunatic asylum in Hoxton, Middlesex. The parish would have had to pay the institution for the maintenance of the person and possibly the parish felt that it would be cheaper to make their own arrangements within the workhouse. By 1834 the numbers in the workhouse were down to only 14 but nevertheless the workhouse was chosen by the new Union Guardians to continue until the new Union workhouse was built.

Colchester, St Leonard

The Victoria History of Essex records that St Leonard's parish maintained their own workhouse from at least 1768 although there is no mention of one in the government survey of 1777. Maybe it opened and closed again before 1777 but the Victoria History also states that the workhouse was in existence again as late as 1834 on the south side of Hythe Street opposite Knaves Acre.

Colchester, St Martin

The St Martins parish workhouse is believed to have been in Hospital Yard, Angel Lane and had been established in about 1770 with the number of inmates not more than 12 by 1777.

Colchester, St Mary at the Walls

In Crouch Street the old St Catherine's hospital had been used by the borough of Colchester as one of their borough workhouses in the late sixteenth century. Following the break up of the Corporation workhouse arrangements in about 1750 this building was used by St Mary at Walls parish as their parish workhouse as a record is in existence of an inventory of the workhouse dated 1753 which is probably when the parish workhouse came into operation. When the workhouse closed by 1834 the number of inmates for that year only averaged eight persons which is probably why the new Colchester Union did not use it as short term accommodation until the new Union workhouse was built.

Colchester, St Nicholas

There were a number of almshouses on the north side of Bucklerbury Lane and by 1748 these were taken over by the parish and converted into the St Nichollas parish workhouse. When Elizabeth Finch was moved into the St Nicholas workhouse in 1774 an inventory was taken of her possessions which indicated that she had previously worked as a weaver as her possessions included a bay loom and a quill wheel which was used for winding yarn. Although the circumstances of her removal to the workhouse are not known her possessions indicated that she had seen better days as they included the following:

2 beds, 1 pair curtains, 7 sheets, 3 blankets, 4 pillows, 4 pillow cases, 2 bolsters, 2 coverlets, 1 pair drawers.
3 tables, 1 looking glass, 12 pictures, 16 plates, 9 basins, 4 tea pots, 16 cups and saucers, 2 silver spoons, 3 pewter measures, 1 bird cage.
Elizabeth also had a comprehensive stock of kitchen utensils.

The government survey of workhouses of 1777 recorded that St Nicholas workhouse could accommodate up to 14 inmates and this small workhouse survived until 1834.

Colchester, St Peter

St Peter's parish workhouse was established by at least 1777 as it features in the government survey when up to 20 inmates could be accommodated. The location was North Street. In 1820 the actual number of inmates was 31.

Colchester, Holy Trinity

Holy Trinity parish established their own parish workhouse/poorhouse as soon as the Corporation workhouse system mentioned above collapsed and it is believed to have been in existence from about 1750. The location was believed to be a property on the north side of Eld Street. There is no record of this workhouse in the government survey of 1777 and possibly it was classed as a poorhouse without a master or guardian as opposed to a full parish workhouse. There is also no record of a workhouse being in existence in 1834 when the Colchester Union was established which bears out to some degree that Holy Trinity parish probably only maintained a house for the poor of the parish as opposed to a workhouse.

Colchester, Holy Trinty
Colchester, St Leonard
Colchester, St Michael, Mile End
Colchester, St Mary Magdalen
Colchester, St Runwald

Of the thirteen parishes in the main town of Colchester eight had a parish workhouse at some time but the above five parishes did not maintain a workhouse although they may have maintained a parish poorhouse which did not have a resident workhouse master or governor. In St Mary Magdalen parish four houses on the north and south sides of Magdalen Street were being used by the poor of the parish in the 1800s. On sale in 1837 they were described as a workhouse but it is more than likely they were houses owned by the parish and used to house poor families where some work was carried out. With regard to St Leonard's parish there are conflicting records as to whether there was a workhouse or not in the 1800s as the new Union Guardians do not make mention of it when they conducted their surveys in 1834. Possibly there was one in 1834 but the Guardians had already dismissed it as unsuitable for further use and made no mention of it in their reports.

Lexden

A parish workhouse was established in Spring Lane in 1751. At the time of the government survey of parish workhouses in 1777 the Lexden workhouse could accommodate up to 34 inmates. The workhouse was still functioning in 1834 when it came under the control of the new Colchester Union but it did not feature in their plans for the future. It was sold off in 1835.

Combining the parish workhouses in 1818

As early as 1818 the parishes of the town of Colchester had considered combining their workhouses due to the expense and inefficiency of eight separate institutions within the town. The suggestion was that they would convert part of the garrison hospital into a shared 'house of industry'. Nothing more came of the suggestion and the individual parishes carried on running their own workhouses until the Poor Law Amendment Act was passed in 1834 which saw the start on the Union system of workhouses where parish workhouses were grouped together into a Union.

THE COLCHESTER UNION WORKHOUSE

The first meeting of the Colchester Union Guardians was on the 21 October 1835 in the Assembly Rooms at the Cups Hotel. After the appointment of officers the first job for the new Guardians was to inspect the existing parish workhouses. One of the Guardians visited the workhouses in the parishes of St Boltoph, St James, St Mary at the Walls, St Peter and St Giles. This Guardian recommended that three of them, St Mary At the Walls, St Giles and St James could accommodate up to 150 persons and it was recommended that rather than each workhouse has a mix of paupers that they be separated into groups according to sex and age. The report concluded that in his opinion that there was no suitable accommodation in any workhouse for a governor (master) and matron. The total number of inmates spread around the parish workhouses in 1835 was only 79 and these could be easily accommodated in the selected three workhouses which could take up to 150 inmates. The workhouse at St Nicholas was subsequently inspected and it was decided in the end by the Guardians to use all six workhouses and that the paupers be divided up as follows:

St Mary at the Walls	Able bodied men, able bodied women and young men
St Giles	Aged men
St Peter	Aged women
St James	Young children and girls
St Boltoph	Use to be decided
St Nicholas	Use to be decided

Lexden workhouse was quite a large workhouse which could have accommodated up to 34 inmates in 1777 and although still open when the inspections took place it did not feature in the Guardians' plans for the future. It looks, therefore, as if up to 150 paupers could be accommodated in three parish workhouses according to the sub committee of Guardians although the Guardians as a whole felt that all six inspected were suitable for use.

The Guardians soon changed their meeting place to the Committee Room in Lion Walk and their next major task was to examine those paupers from the parishes who were in need but not residing in the workhouse. Their job was to check and confirm what out-relief they should get which had previously been agreed by the individual parish vestries. One of the sub committees again visited the parish workhouse at St Mary at the Walls and decided what expense was necessary to bring the workhouse up to standard. Included in their report were details of the inmates who at this stage had not been redistributed according to the recommendation above. There were 15 inmates ranging from a 5 year old orphan to Hannah Hockley aged 79 who was described as being 'helpful'. There were only twelve beds in the inventory but it appears that of the 15 inmates two were only day inmates. The other parish workhouses visited, now some for the second time, were recorded as follows:

> St Giles workhouse was visited next where there were 12 paupers and 14 beds.
> St Boltoph had 7 paupers and 10 beds.
> St Nicholas had 7 paupers and 7 beds
> St James had 20 paupers and 30 beds
> St Peter had 17 paupers and 30 beds
> St Martin - considered not suitable for the use of the Union. Only 5 paupers
> Lexden - 7 beds but no mention of the number of paupers

No mention was made of the All Saints workhouse, which was open in 1777, but it looks as if this one closed prior to 1835.

It looks as if the Guardians changed their minds again as to which workhouses would be used as the clerk was requested to write to the parish clerk of the following four workhouses to say they would take them over for the use of the Union:

St Peter   St James   St Boltoph   St Giles

The first report recommended three workhouses would be suitable but thereafter six parish workhouses were selected for use. Now only four were written to. Possibly St Marys and St Nicholas needed work done on them before the new Union would take them over and this work would have to be paid for by the parish. It does appear though that St Marys and St Nicholas were dropped from the list as the Guardians went ahead with various appointments to the other four. The following appointments as superintendents (workhouse master or matron) of the under mentioned workhouses were made:

St Boltoph	Susan Lester (from St Marys)
St Peter	Mr Hummon and his wife (from St Nicholas)
St James	John Read and wife (from St Peter)
	Ann Bell as schoolmistress
St Giles	Mary Ann Cant

It looks now that finally the above four old parish workhouses would be used as temporary accommodation for Colchester's paupers until the new Union workhouse was built.

The site chosen for the new Union workhouse was nine acres on Balkerne Hill just outside the boundary of the Roman wall that circumvented historic Colchester. Although the Union workhouse was only pulled down a year or two ago it must have been an imposing sight at nearly the highest point in Colchester. The architect chosen was John Brown who designed a number of workhouses although no others in Essex. He was responsible for three built in the same period in Norfolk. The Board of Guardians knew that they had to build a workhouse large enough to cater for the paupers in the existing workhouses within the sixteen parishes and also to allow for any increase in numbers during the following decades. Back in 1777 the nine parish workhouses within the Colchester area could accommodate up to 227 inmates although in the 1830s the actual number had fallen to under 100.

The standard design as recommended by the Poor Law Commissioners was either buildings arranged in a cruciform within outer buildings or a 'Y' shaped design also surrounded by other buildings. The design for Colchester was to be a double cruciform (crosses side by side) with either an outer wall or other buildings surrounding the two cruciforms. Where the two east/west cross wings came together in the middle the architect placed the administration block at this point. The girl's school was in the far west of the western cruciform and the boys school was to be found at the eastern end of the eastern cruciform. Consequently the boys and girls were as far apart as could be. Like all the other Essex workhouses a separate infirmary was eventually built whereas for a start the sick would have been in a ward within one of the main cruciforms. The infirmary was built in 1848 to the north of the other buildings although it was extended on more than one occasion.

The new Union workhouse was built in the period 1836-37 and the old parishes workhouses were sold off as soon as the inmates were transferred. When the inmates were transferred from the old parish workhouses there were 133 in number.

The census of 1841

The first national census after the workhouse opened was in 1841 recorded that there were 130 inmates and six staff. It is surprising that in 1777 the nine parish workhouses within the town could accommodate up to 227 inmates although when the Guardians were surveying the existing parish workhouses in 1835 there were about 90 inmates spread over seven parish workhouses. Of the nine in 1777 only St Martin and All

Saints workhouses do not get a mention by the Guardians in the 1830s. The 1777 data was the maximum the workhouses could hold and not the actual. The 1841 census figures for inmates are as follows:

Males	85	The total included 6 staff and 70 children under 14. The percentage of children to total number of inmates was 54 %
Females	51	
Total	136	

The Guardians minutes 1844-1846

July 1844
Arrest of William Goding

The Guardians reported that a warrant had been issued for the arrest of William Goding for deserting his child. It looks as if, because of the desertion, the child had been taken into the workhouse and as William Goding was living in the parish of St Martin at that time the parish was being charged for her keep. Mr Goding was arrested and sentenced to 21 days in prison with hard labour. Apparently the Godings did not come from Colchester as the next entry in the minutes was for an Order of Removal for the child to be sent to her place of settlement which unfortunately was not named (probably her parish of birth). That parish in turn would have placed the child in their Union workhouse.

Joseph Sewell an insane pauper

Joseph Sewell came from St James' parish in Colchester and was presently residing in the Whitechapel workhouse although the Colchester Union would be paying for his keep and this amount would be chargeable out to St James through their poor rate. Someone from Colchester was instructed to go and collect Joseph and take him to a lunatic asylum called The Retreat. It had been agreed with the asylum that Colchester workhouse would pay the asylum five shillings per week for his keep chargeable to St James' parish.

September 1844
Lunatics Return

Every year an inspector visits the workhouse to complete his Lunatics Return, on behalf of the Poor Law Commissioners, of those of unsound mind in the institution. These are inmates that, whilst not having the need to be transferred to a secure institution, are classed as being of unsound mind but are not harmful to others in the workhouse. These inmates are allowed to mix with other inmates. Whilst the minute did not mention the number of those of unsound mind the report did specifically refer to two inmates. The inspector had obviously now reassessed Emma Ponder who was now considered to be 'dangerous to those around her' and that she should be sent to an asylum. With regard to Sarah French the inspector reported that 'accidents have occurred both to herself and others and also acts of violence have occurred and as these acts are so repetitive ……she ought to be removed'. The Guardians had the opportunity to respond to remarks made and in the case of Emma Ponder they said she 'was not in a fit state to be removed' and with regard to Sarah French they recommended she stay where she is as she was not considered to be dangerous to herself or others. A difference of opinion existed in these two cases. The Commissioners responded to the claims of the Guardians but said that with regard to Emma Ponder that they had a medical officer's report which said that as soon as she is fit enough to travel then she should be removed to a lunatic asylum. With regard to Sarah French the Commissioners said that they agreed with the inspector's report that she was 'a dangerous lunatic' but if the Guardians wished to keep Sarah in the workhouse they would be laying themselves open to problems from relatives of anyone that Sarah harmed. The Commissioners recommended that she be transferred to an asylum.

October 1844
Out-relief
The clerk produced to the Guardians the cost of out-relief of the various parishes in respect of clothing and provisions. The return also listed the number of persons on out-relief in each of the Colchester parishes which were as follows

All Saints	2	Magdalen	8
Berechurch	5	St Martin	10
St Boltoph	41	St Mary at the Walls	20
St Giles	14	Mile End	8
Greenstead	2	St Nicholas	33
St James	30	St Peter	23
St Leonard	8	St Runwald	16
Lexden	18	Trinity	10

Total on out-relief	248

Each parish was charged the amount spent on food and clothing for their residents on out-relief. In addition the parish was charged with a proportion of the cost of running the workhouse relative to the rateable value of the parish and not in relation to the number of inmates they had in the workhouse. The two calculations were charged out to the parish as their poor rate which they collected in from their residents.

October 1844
Corporal punishment
It had been brought to the notice of the Guardians that the schoolmaster had inflicted corporal punishment on the child George Miller but had not entered the punishment in the appropriate punishment book. The schoolmaster was called before the Guardians and 'admonished'.

October 1844
Medical officer's report
The medical officer responsible for the workhouse sick reported to the Guardians that Andrew Watson who had been placed in the Probationary Ward had refused to take his medicine for a foot infection. The workhouse master also reported that Andrew had broken down the door of his ward.

November 1844
Complaint from another parish
The Guardians received a complaint from St Mary Magdalen parish that they had been charged for 46 days of out-relief for Ann Johnson (the grandmother), her children Ann and Sarah and their children but they were not residents of that parish. The Guardians looked into the matter and found that the costs should have been charged out to St James' parish. An adjustment would be made when the next poor rate was being calculated.

Medical officer's report
We saw in September 1844 that the inspector appointed by the Commissioners made recommendation regarding the mental state of the inmates and this type of recommendation could also be made by the appointed medical officers. The surgeon appointed to care for the inmates within the workhouse reported that in his opinion Robert Balley should be immediately removed to an asylum and that Sophia Cadman should be withdrawn from the workhouse and placed in the care of some fit person in the parish of St James. Apparently the parish vestry at St James had been consulted on the matter and agreed with the course of action. The cases of Robert Balley and Sophia Cadman had not been mentioned when the inspector visited in September and probably they were taken into the workhouse after his visit. This is borne out by the visit of Robert's mother at the next board meeting when she said that she

could not contribute to Robert's stay at the either the workhouse or the asylum to which he was being transferred. As soon as an inmate is accepted into the workhouse the Guardians contact the relatives to try and extract a contribution towards their keep.

December 1844
Relaxation of workhouse rules
All the various classes of inmates had their exercise yards within the walled boundary of the buildings. Most workhouses also had quite large pieces of land outside the walls which were used as gardens, allotments or for keeping pigs. The Guardians at Colchester agreed to let fit paupers wander the grounds of the workhouse between the hours of 10am to 12 noon. The Guardians also agreed to place three moveable settles (benches) capable of seating six persons each for use in the grounds. Later in the year the privilege was extended and aged inmates were allowed to walk the grounds at 10am and in the afternoon. Notices were to be placed in the appropriate wards to this effect. At 10am in the morning and 2pm in the afternoon the porter, the yardsman or the miller would ring the yard bell to indicate that the aged inmates were free to wander the grounds. At 11.30 am and 5pm the bell would be rung again to summon the inmates back to their wards. One of the porter's duties was to take the names of those leaving the workhouse for one reason or another and check them back in afterwards.

January 1845
Privilege withdrawn
Paupers are usually allowed out of the workhouse on a Sunday invariably to go to church. Jonathan Taylor returned after his Sunday day out and was reported to the Guardians as being disorderly on his return He was probably the worse for wear as he had probably been drinking. His punishment was that he could not leave the workhouse on the four following Sundays.

Health hazard
Mr Newman one of the medical officers who was responsible for the parish of Mile End reported to the Guardians that Clay Lane was in a bad and impassable state due to an accumulation of water and vegetable matter which could result in a health hazard. It has been seen on various occasions in the Essex workhouse minutes that the Guardians get involved in health matters which were not their official responsibility until 1872 when the Public Health Act was passed. This act passed sanitary matters to the Unions where there was no urban sanitary

authority. Mr Newman's report was also copied to the Corporation of Colchester and they probably took the appropriate action.

February 1845

George Cater released

The Cater children had been abandoned by their father and were now in the workhouse. There was no mention of the mother. A warrant had been issued for the arrest of the father, George, who had now been apprehended. He appeared before the Magistrate on the charge of deserting his family. He agreed to take his children out of the workhouse and maintain them. On this understanding he was released from custody. The court and the workhouse Guardians would have checked that he had a job to go to and had enough income to maintain the family.

March 1845

Mr Bromley the messenger

Mr Bromley was employed, as the name suggests, as a messenger for the Guardians but his duties also entailed the transferring of lunatic inmates to the asylum, transferring inmates from one workhouse to another and also apprehending relations of inmates on who warrants for arrest had been issued. His request for travelling expenses regularly appears in the accounts. One wonders what type of person got a messenger's job as on the one hand the duties purely as a messenger would not have been onerous whereas the responsibility for transferring inmates from one place to another would have been a much greater.

May 1845

Smallpox

The house surgeon's report recommended that in view of the increasing number of smallpox cases in the workhouse the patients be allocated a separate exercise yard. In later decades the Essex workhouses were building separate infirmaries to cater for the sick and especially for the care of those with infectious diseases. In the 1840s though all those that were sick were catered for within the main workhouse complex which meant that those with infectious diseases were never far from the normal inmate. A separate infirmary was built in 1848 which was a lot earlier than most Essex workhouses.

The Gibbons family

William Gibbons, his wife and seven children were all in the workhouse. The eldest child was ten years old. He had now applied to leave the workhouse and to take with him his wife and five of the children. He explained to the Guardians that he had now been offered work at ten shillings a week and his eldest son one shilling a week. He felt that he could maintain a family of seven on this wage but would have to leave two children in the workhouse. No ages were mentioned in the minutes of the other children except that the two to be left were girls named Rosina and Matilda. The Guardians checked the circumstances of the request and agreed to let seven of the family leave the workhouse. The minute inferred that possibly the father would come and collect the other two girls when finances allowed.

June 1845
Appointment of new porter
The master's son, William Roy, had been temporarily appointed as gate porter. A Guardian's resolution at the June meeting was that Roy should not be offered the job on a permanent basis. The motion was not seconded. The matter was discussed and eventually two of the Guardians proposed and seconded that William Roy be offered the job. The vote was not unanimous as some Guardians objected as William was the son of the master. The Commissioners were written to for their opinion who agreed that he could be offered a permanent appointment notwithstanding the family link as he had carried out his duties for three years on a temporary basis without there being any complaints about his work.

September 1845
Vagrants in court
Tramps and vagrants were accommodated in a separate ward usually near to the main gate. They usually stayed a day or two and were required to work to offset the cost of their board and lodging. Three tramps, Messrs Arnold, Smyth and Cook refused to work and consequently they were summoned before the magistrate who gave Arnold 21 days hard labour and the other two 14 days hard labour each. I do not think that they would have refused to work if they came to the Colchester workhouse again.

November 1845
Stolen onions
The master complained that Arthur Norman, an aged inmate, had stolen onions from the Union vegetable patch. The evidence was that onions had been found in a cupboard wrapped in Mr Norman's handkerchief. Mr Norman contended that a relation, William Norman of North Hill, had given him the onions on his last Sunday visit. The story was checked

and could not be substantiated. The Board decided to segregate Arthur Norman for the time being until they decided on the action to be taken. The outcome was that Mr Norman was deprived of the right to leave the workhouse on the next two Sundays.

January 1846

Complaints

The master reported that he received information that Joseph Newman, the yardsman, had 'been criminally connected with a female indoor pauper named Sarah Wilson aged 14 years'. It was subsequently discovered that the schoolmistress knew about the incident for nine days prior to it being reported by the master. Apparently the child reported the 'maltreatment' to the schoolmistress but she had taken no action at the time. The schoolmistress was called before the Guardians and 'expressed great sorrow' for her non communication of the incident. She was admonished and reminded of her responsibilities to the children in her care. James Roy, the master, decided to tender his resignation as a result of the incident and in his resignation letter he said that could no longer 'keep peace and order in the Union House'. The 'maltreatment' of Sarah Wilson turned out to be carnal knowledge by Joseph Newman who was aged 70 and previously he had been the porter before being demoted to yardsman. Unfortunately the minutes at the time were silent on what happened to Mr Newman but he was undoubtedly discharged and most probably summoned to appear before the magistrates for his offence. Later it transpires that Joseph Newman did appear in court but the case was dismissed for lack of evidence. Joseph Newman lived with his wife in the workhouse and as yardsman he was as much an inmate as an employee. They were both asked to leave the workhouse and placed on out-relief.

March 1846

Appointment of new master and matron

The Poor Law Commissioners confirmed the appointment of Mr and Mrs William Hooper as the new master and matron at a joint salary of £100 a year. Their letter went on to refer to Mr and Mrs Rudd, the schoolmaster and mistress, who had both been the subject of complaints over the last few months. Mrs Rudd was the schoolmistress who had omitted to report the incident concerning Sara Wilson. The Commissioners warned the Guardians that should there be any further complaints against the Rudds then they would be dismissed.

1874

Although I was concentrating on the period 1844-46 for interesting snippets on life in the workhouse I came across some information about children from the Colchester workhouse that were sent to Canada in 1874. In Peckham, south London, Miss Maria Rye had founded a home called the Maria Rye Emigration Home for Destitute Girls. The popular emigration destination in the 1870s, in addition to Australia, was Canada and this home took in girls who were mainly orphans who would eventually be immigrated to Canada. It looks as if many of the workhouses in southern England had been asked if they had suitable candidates for emigration as the list of children for a particular group in 1874 included girls from 16 workhouses in the southern counties together with those from the home in Peckham. The girls from Colchester were:

Jane Sexton	Orphan	Aged	13
Alice Knights	Orphan	Aged	9
Annie Hutter		Aged	17

Annie Hutter was not described as an orphan and presumably she was, because of her age, now an adult and that title was dropped. The rules of the home did say though that should any girl have known parents then their permission had to be sought. The ship was the Sarmatian and it sailed to Canada in June 1874. The expense to the Colchester workhouse was £8 for each girl plus the cost of transportation to Peckham. It would have cost Colchester a lot more to have provided board and lodging to these three girls if they stayed in the workhouse for some years and consequently workhouses were always keen to let children or families emigrate as they were to let young adults take apprenticeships or go into domestic service in this country. On the face of it those children who emigrated should have been in for a better life in their new country but in the nineteenth century conditions in the developing countries were very harsh and invariably the children were sent to farms and into domestic service in outlying areas where facilities were very basic. In fact the UK government even as late as 1909 excluded children under 14 years from emigrating to Canada as the educational facilities in country areas were found to be inadequate.

Into the twentieth century

By the end of the nineteenth century the Guardians still needed more space and so extra buildings were erected to the south of the site where the Union owned land which was at that time the main drive to the workhouse. On this land a laundry was built in 1896 and this was followed by a new Casual Ward in 1898, a porter's lodge and a new administration block which held the Guardian's board room. Whereas most of the other Essex workhouses had peaked out with their number of inmates in the period 1860/80, Colchester, like other large towns, was still taking in more paupers which were probably prompting the building projects at the end of the nineteenth century. The census data for 1901 shows that the numbers were nearly reaching 300 which was the peak for the Colchester workhouse.

The census of 1901

The number of inmates

Males	179	The total includes 15 staff and 51 children under 14. The percentage of children to total number of inmates was 18%
Females	112	
Total	291	

The work of the Guardians came to an end in 1930 when the workhouse came under the control of Essex County Council. The workhouse after 1930 changed its name to the Colchester Public Assistance Institution and later it became St Mary's Hospital. The hospital closed in 1993 and in 2003 the site was developed for housing.

Chapter 6

GREAT DUNMOW AND ITS ENVIRONS

PARISH WORKHOUSES

The following 25 parishes in the above area were grouped together in 1834 following the Poor Law Amendment Act to form the Great Dunmow (Dunmow) Union. Before 1834 each parish may have had its own poorhouse or workhouse.

From 1834 the new Union workhouse for the area was to be located at Great Dunmow (Dunmow) and the Poor Law Commissioners decided that 25 parishes surrounding Great Dunmow would make up the Dunmow Union. Great Dunmow's population at the time was just under 2500 with the smallest parish being Morrell Roding with only 32 residents. The parishes were:

Great Bardfield, Little Bardfield, Bardfield Saling, Barnston, Broxted, Great Canfield, Little Canfield, Chickney, Great Dunmow, Little Dunmow, Great Easton, Little Easton, High Easter, Felsted, Hatfield Broad Oak, Lindsell, Aythorpe Roding, High Roding, Leaden Roding, Margaret Roding, White Roding, Stebbing, Takeley, Thaxted and Tilty.

The government undertook a survey of parish workhouses in 1777 and the following seven parishes in this area had a workhouse open in that year.

Great Dunmow	Bardfield Saling	Felsted
High Easter	Stebbing	Thaxted
Hatfield Broad Oak		

Great Dunmow

The parish workhouse was built at least by 1777 for the government survey of that year shows that the workhouse could accommodate up to 50 inmates. The workhouse may well have been in existence for up to 50 years previously. Essex workhouses came and went according to demand and if the parish could not afford a workhouse master and his wife then the premises may have just been a parish poorhouse where the inmates looked after themselves. The location was on the east side of Dunmow High Street between numbers 43 to 61. The workhouse comprised three properties which still stand today and covered 53 yards (49 metres) of the High Street opposite the present day war memorial. The parish vestry met at Dunmow Town Hall and the following are extracts from the minutes for the years 1805 and 1806.

Vestry minutes 1805

It was agreed that a shade be erected in the poorhouse yard 'for employing the non-employed poor of the parish'. The vestry are probably referring here to the able bodied poor who are on out-relief and come to the workhouse daily to work. Every two or three months the vestry sanctioned clothing grants for those on out-relief and the list usually ran to over 30 grants a time ranging from shoes to sheets to shirts to breeches and stockings. Thomas Hawes of Great Waltham obtained the contract to supply food to the workhouse at the rate of three shillings and six pence per head for one month.

Dunmow Parish Workhouses occupied 43/61 Dunmow High Street

Vestry minutes 1806

The vestry agreed that Mr Wybro senior and his wife should be placed in the workhouse with their youngest son and their daughter until the son and daughter are provided with other situations by the parish officers and the governor of the workhouse. No mention is made of the age of the children but it looks as if they are coming up to the age where they could be put out to work on a farm or in domestic service. At the following meeting of the vestry the overseer reported that the Wybro family refused to go into the workhouse. Consequently cash out-relief was cancelled to this family. Unfortunately the minutes are silent on the eventual outcome but if out-relief was cancelled then they would have no alternative but be admitted to the workhouse.

Mr S Philback agreed to accept the pauper James Tiler as an apprentice for a period of seven years. The condition was that James would receive clothing for his apprenticeship from the overseer of the parish.

Mrs Samuels agreed to take the pauper daughter of Mrs Paveling as a domestic servant for one year with an allowance of £2 for clothing.

When the parish workhouse was sold in 1840 the auction was held at the Saracens Head Inn on the 27 October. The workhouse was a substantial building and was sold off in three lots which divided the property up into three cottages. Lot 1 had High Street frontage of just under 50 feet and previously contained the dining hall, the matron's room, the kitchen, the bread room, the coal place, the shoe place together with outside sheds in the yard where there was a water pump. Lot 2, which also had frontage to the High Street, was just over 50 feet and contained the men's keeping room, the mill house, the engine house and outside sheds in the yard. Lot 3 had High Street frontage of 60 feet, the entrance gateway and contained the governor's office and the boys room together with the usual yard and sheds. The auction also contained the sale of four cottages on Dunmow Down owned previously by the parish with the sale proceeds for the benefit of the new Dunmow Union Workhouse indicating that they were previously parish poor houses as opposed to a workhouse with a workhouse master.

High Easter

The first mention of a workhouse in High Easter was in 1740 when the name appears in a baptismal register. In 1743 the overseers accounts refer to eleven persons being on out-relief and four paupers in the workhouse. At this time the four paupers would have probably been allocated a cottage owned by the parish and would have to fend for themselves with a small weekly allowance. There would not have been a workhouse master or governor for such a small number of inmates. As the eighteenth century progressed the number of poor increased and the government survey of 1777 recorded that High Easter workhouse could accommodate up to 33 inmates. By this time the parish would have provided larger premises and almost certainly there would have been someone in charge who would have lived in.

High Easter Parish Workhouse was converted into five cottages when sold off and are now two properties

Four years later in 1781 the parish built a new workhouse and it would appear that the site was the same as the previous building as the rent for both properties was the same. The first governor (master) of the new workhouse was appointed at a salary of five shillings a week. There was no daily allowance for the number of inmates which means that all the food, drink and provisions must have been supplied by the overseers of the parish. This system was changed in 1789 when the governor received two shillings and six pence a week per inmate out of which he had to provide everything that the overseers were providing previously. He would still have received his own weekly wage. A wife is not mentioned in earlier records but in 1789 the church buried Margarita Searle, mistress of the workhouse. Possibly she was the governor's wife but as she does not appear in any of the workhouse accounts she may have been unrelated and just held an unsalaried position and lived away from the workhouse. In this period of the late eighteenth century there were between 20 and 25 inmates living in the workhouse but by 1800 the number had risen to 35 but by 1807 the number had dropped to 26. Memories of the latter days of the workhouse (1830s) record the ground floor as having a doctor's dispensary at one end and the matron's room at the other. It seems that by the nineteenth century the workhouse was run by a matron. There were three middle portions between the two end rooms which were used as one long day room and work room. Upstairs there were four bedrooms.

The style of the building being five rooms wide with similar rooms upstairs lent itself to conversion into five cottages when the workhouse was sold off in 1835. The location of the old workhouse was on the south side of the main road through the village some 2/300 metres east of the village centre. The workhouse is now only two properties but one retains the black weatherboarding which would have originally covered the whole building.

Felsted

The cottages now known as Little Garnets and Nanty's at the bottom of Garnets Lane by the water tower were previously part of the parish workhouse. Prior to modern development the road was known as Workhouse Lane and also Chase way. It looks as if the workhouse was much bigger when it finally closed in the late 1830s than it is today.

Felsted Parish Workhouse in Garnets Lane

As it is known that the workhouse had been converted into seven cottages by the 1850s. The sale particulars of 1858 state that there were seven cottages being copyhold of the Manor of Felsted and producing rent of nineteen pounds thirteen shillings a year. The cottages were probably built in the 1600s about the time the Poor Law Acts were introduced in 1597. There is no exact date for when the property became the parish workhouse as it may have been just a parish poorhouse previously where Felsite's poor were housed to look after themselves with the benefit of out-relief.

Felsted appointed three overseers of the poor. The village was divided into three sections - Town, Middle and Common 'quarters'. The Town quarter covered the village centre and westwards to the border with Little Dunmow, the Middle covered Bannister Green and surrounding 'Greens', with the Common quarter being that part of the parish now in Rayne and the area around Willows Green.

Felsite's vestry appointed in August 1777 a new 'Master of the Workhouse' and the details are contained in an Agreement which stated that John Cornell of Stebbing was to have not fewer than twenty persons for which he would receive £3 a week for their maintenance to include meat, drink, clothing, washing, lodging and firing (fuel). For women taken in labour he would receive one pound ten shillings in each case for a period of twenty eight days and thereafter three shillings and sixpence per week for mother and child for as long as they stayed. The parish provided bedding, brewing utensils and spinning wheels and the master was allowed a further five shillings a quarter for brooms, mops and pans. On the face of it £3 a week in 1777 to feed and cloth 20 paupers seems satisfactory but the master received no salary and his own food and clothing and that of his family came out of the same sum. An unscrupulous master would make sure he looked after his own family and one could image the paupers getting a raw deal. John Cornell appeared not to receive any further assistance for numbers over 20 inmates whereas an Agreement of 1821 paid William French three pounds ten shillings a week (an improvement) and also three shillings and sixpence a head for numbers in excess of twenty. It looks as if the overseer's policy, and probably not just in Felsted, was to make living in the workhouse an unattractive proposition. This policy would hopefully keep the numbers down for if numbers increased there was the obvious increased cost of maintenance which would lead to an increase in the poor rate.

The overseer also had the responsibility of looking after the paupers who became sick, which was probably often, and female inmates in childbirth. Felsite's records show that the overseer of the poor had an Agreement drawn up in 1777 with Mr John Rayners, surgeon of Dunmow, to attend to the sick in the parish workhouse for a fee of sixteen guineas a year. Childbirth was usually left to the village midwife with the doctor only being consulted in difficult cases. In 1782 Mr John Tweed received only twelve guineas a year with an additional fee for attending women in labour. Maybe Mr Rayner's fee included childbirth. In 1797 Mr Hagger received the same fee with a further guinea for any broken bones attended to.

The workhouse existed until the late 1830s until the formation of the Dunmow Union.

Hatfield Broad Oak

The parish workhouse was established at some time prior to 1777 as the government survey of that year stated that the workhouse could accommodate up to 60 inmates which was a high number for a small parish. The actual number is not known. The parish records contain a letter from Elizabeth Trudge in 1801 applying for the post of governor of the workhouse. She says in her letter that she presently holds the same post at Ingatestone workhouse but was not happy with the financial arrangements. She invited the parish to make enquiries for a reference with Ingatestone parish but she asked for a prompt reply as she had another place pending. The workhouse closed at some time prior to the 1830s as it was not open when the new Dunmow Guardians were appointed in 1835.

Stebbing

The overseers of Stebbing parish entered into an agreement in 1728 for the building of a workhouse. The builder was Esdras Overall of Stebbing who was to be paid £20 for building two lower rooms of which one was to be 20 feet long by 18 feet wide and the other 18 feet long by 18 feet wide together with a large brew house (presumably in the rear yard). The floors to be covered in white bricks and there was to be a double chimney between the two rooms. The brew house was also to have a chimney 'fit for a large copper and oven'. The (bread) oven was to be capable of baking two bushels of wheat. Upstairs he was to build 'chambers and garrets and another room for the master'. The instructions went on to say that the floors of the bedrooms were to be of oak and the floors of the garrets to be of elm with all doors to be made of oak. The roof was to be tiled.

A very formal document was drawn up in 1768 when the Manor of Stebbing at its Court Baron confirmed the use of the property as a workhouse and this was agreed by John Joslin junior who was presumably the leaseholder of the land on which the workhouse stood. An inventory of the workhouse in 1775 indicated that there were now six bedrooms and two garret rooms. It is not clear if there had been extensions to the 1728 building or whether the large rooms had just been subdivided to create more bedrooms for differing sexes and ages.

Just prior to the termination of the parish vestry running the workhouse they entered into a new agreement with William Philpot, shoemaker, for the government of the workhouse in 1832. The allowance to Mr Philpot was linked to the price of flour at the time. When flour cost between ten and fourteen shillings a bushel he would receive three shillings and six pence per head for adults and two shillings and six pence for children. There were increased allowances as the price of flour went up and conversely if the price dropped.

In 1777 the optimum number of inmates was 30 although there were not necessarily that number in the workhouse in that year but a record of 1794 seems to indicate that the workhouse population was only 18 inmates. It is quite probable that the number of inmates by the 1830s was under 30 and maybe, therefore, the building had remained virtually unchanged since construction apart from a dividing of both the ground floor and upper rooms.

Thaxted

The records held by the Essex Record Office for parishes are invariably incomplete as through time many have been lost prior to being deposited at the Record Office. For Thaxted though, the overseers account book exists for the period commencing 1696 through to 1716 whereas for many parishes there are few vestry parish records going back as far as the seventeenth century. An Act of Parliament of 1696 stated that every pauper should wear upon the shoulder of the right sleeve of the uppermost garment a large letter 'P' together with the first letter of the name of the parish in red or blue cloth. Thaxted consequently complied with this new law and passed a resolution at a public vestry in April 1697 'that all persons which receive collection (out-relief) shall wear the badge or else will not allow the collection to be paid'. The first mention of the Thaxted parish workhouse (poorhouse) appears in the overseers accounts for the year 1711 although this property was probably built the previous year. The location was probably near to the old Vicarage in Newbiggen Street.

The vestry minutes record that on the 20 April 1722 it was agreed to build a new workhouse. Probably the one being used for this purpose from 1710 was only a cottage owned by the parish and used as a poorhouse without a workhouse master and there was now a need for larger premises. A further minute dated 1726 confirms that the building

Thaxted Parish Workhouse at 44/48 Newbiggen Street

of the workhouse is complete. The location of the new workhouse was almost certainly on the site in Newbiggen Street of the old one.

Many parish records for the overseer of the poor just record the total amount being spent weekly or monthly for those on out-relief or in the workhouse. The Thaxted records itemise everything and it is interesting to note that in the 1720s it was usual for the workhouse to be supplied with malt and hops to make their own beer which would have been very weak beer which would have been drunk daily. Appearing in the accounts for this period was a charge of six shillings for a coffin for Mary Poultor and one shilling and sixpence for digging the grave.

It rather looks as if the accounting for the parish had become lax since the detailed accounts previously for in 1725 the vestry decided that all workhouse bills would not be paid unless a proper account was presented for payment. This particular minute related to the overseer's accounts as the vestry would have to account to the ratepayers for all expenditure which would eventually be recouped by way of the poor rate.

The Thaxted workhouse must have been larger than the average Essex village workhouse as the government survey of 1777 stated up to 50 inmates could be accommodated. A few years later in 1782 there must have been a problem in the village of Clavering as the Thaxted vestry passed a resolution agreeing that those residents of Clavering who were dissatisfied with their weekly out-relief allowance would be sent to the Thaxted workhouse at the expense of Clavering parish.

The workhouse was sold by public auction in February 1841 in three lots and was described as having a frontage to the High Street (44/48 Newbiggen Street) of 99 feet in total extending to over 100 feet to the rear to include the yards of the three properties.. One side of the premises abutted Back Lane East and one side abutted Vicarage Lane. This large parish workhouse boasted all the standard rooms for men and women and an indication of its size is reflected in the accommodation for the workhouse governor which consisted of four rooms, two on the ground floor and two bedrooms above. The sale particulars even mention that part of the workhouse at the southern end comprised 'a newly erected substantial brick and slate infirmary'. This seems to have been built in the yard of the southernmost section of the workhouse.

THE GREAT DUNMOW UNION WORKHOUSE

Of the 24 parishes in the Union, Great Dunmow and Thaxted, being the largest parishes, were allocated three representatives each on the Board of Guardians with Felsted, Hatfield Broad Oak and Stebbing having two each making a total of 31 Guardians.

The Dunmow Guardians had their first meeting in March 1835 and when they took over there were parish workhouses in the following locations:

Great Dunmow	Gt Canfield	High Easter
Felsted	Stebbing	Thaxted

Since the 1777 survey the workhouses at Bardfield Saling and Hatfield Broad Oak had closed but one had opened at Great Canfield. All the parish workhouses were sold soon after 1840 when the Union Workhouse opened. The architects for the new Union workhouse were George Gilbert Scott and William Bonython Moffatt who designed the Essex workhouses at Billericay, Tendring and Witham. The layout was similar to all the other workhouse although the style was mock Tudor as can be seen from the photographs.

The interesting feature of the Dunmow workhouse was the long front building which contained the porter's lodge, the Guardians' Board room and the chapel. In the archway that leads through to the main blocks high up in the wall is a large metal spike. Workhouses were often called 'the spike' after the tool the inmates used to unravel oakum (old ropes). The workhouse cost about £8,000 to construct and was built to accommodate up to 350 inmates. A separate infirmary was built in 1871 to the south of the main blocks. The location of the workhouse, which has now been converted into apartments, was the on Chelmsford Road about half a mile out of the town towards Chelmsford opposite the road to the Rodings.

Things did not go well with the selection of a site and even when one was chosen and agreed upon there were still objectors and letters to the Poor Law Commissioners and even a petition to Parliament. In June 1838 the Guardians formed a building committee to look for a site. First of all the committee recommended a site owned by Lord Maynard a very very large local landowner. Unfortunately Lord Maynard would not sell the field. In the meantime the committee recommended that a workhouse capable of accommodating 350 inmates should be built together with an infirmary and vagrant wards to take the total up to 380 paupers.

The next piece of land selected was owned by a Dunmow charity but there was so much discussion by the charity trustees and so many objections raised that the building committee decided to drop the recommendation and look for a further plot which was owned by an

(Great) Dunmow Union Workhouse in the early twentieth century.
This old postcard has been printed the wrong way round

The entrance to the workhouse and the Guardians and administration rooms has changed little today

individual where the title to the land was unquestionable. The committee were keen to acquire a piece of land as near to the town as possible and especially near to Dunmow's places of worship. The best option was a field owned by a Mr R Taylor and he was prepared to sell three acres of the field at the price of £540. The only problem was the distance to the parish church which was on the other side of town.

Mr J Barnard, one of the Guardians, was totally against the selected site and even personally wrote to the Poor Law Commissioners on the matter. This direct approach upset the Guardians and they then wrote to the Poor Law Commissioners to bring them up to date with what had happened so far. Their letter recounted the approaches to Lord Maynard and the Dunmow charity, pointing out that Mr Barnard was one of the trustees of the charity who objected and who in turn had offered three acres of his own land as a site for the workhouse at a cost of £1,000 with the Guardians to pay all his legal fees. They mentioned, of course, that they now preferred Mr Taylor's land which would only cost £540. Whilst acknowledging that Mr Taylor's land was some way from the parish church they also pointed out that Mr Barnard's land adjoining the Stortford Road was no closer to the church. All the above discussions and correspondence had taken place within the months of June, July and August 1838.

Mr Barnard, who lived at Canfield Hall, wrote again to the Poor Law Commissioners this time enclosing signatures of other Guardians objecting to the chosen site and saying that there would have been more signatures had time allowed. Mr Barnard also owned a house called Olives which could be seen from the proposed workhouse site (NIMBY - not in my back yard!!). Mr Barnard said that the proposed site was 'low, marshy, and consequently much exposed to damp and fog in the winter season'.

Mr Barnard was really upsetting the Guardians again and being one of their number the meetings must have been very tense. So, once again the Guardians wrote to the Poor Law Commissioners to set the record straight. They pointed out that 23 out of the 31 Guardians signed the resolution agreeing to the 'Taylor' site. The matter was raised five more times (presumably by Mr Barnard) and on each occasion the original proposition was confirmed by a majority. Mr Barnard, recounted the Guardians, canvassed certain Guardians to support his letter to the Poor Law Commissioners saying that the site was unsuitable and he asked every supporter to attend the next meeting of the Guardians. He put forward a resolution along the lines of his above letter saying that the site was damp and unsuitable. The resolution was seconded. When it came to the vote his resolution was thrown out by fourteen votes to two. What had happened to all those Guardians who had signed his letter to the Poor Law Commissioners?

The Guardians could have left the matter there but they decided to obtain a professional opinion on the selected site, which is where the workhouse was eventually built, with particular reference to the drainage situation and also the health aspect in view of the rather foggy and damp nature of the area. The report said that the land drained away to the extent of 13 to 14 feet and water was taken by a ditch into the River Chelmer. The field, whilst admittedly wet and foggy in winter, was no more so than other rural fields in the Dunmow area. The report also included the opinion of various doctors in the town as to what effect the conditions would have on the inmates. They said that the conditions were not ideal but health problems would not be any worse than in other parts of Dunmow.

Finally, when construction had started and the foundations were in, the Guardians called back the architects for their opinion on the site compared with the one that Mr Barnard was supporting (his own land). Messrs Scott and Moffatt said in their report 'that there was nothing to cause a suspicion of unhealthfulness'. In conclusion they said that of the 40 Union houses that they have been architects for they knew of very few sites that are preferable to that chosen for the Dunmow workhouse.

The Union workhouse opened in 1840 and the number of inmates at the 1841 census was as follows.

The census of 1841

Males	77	The total includes 5 staff and 82
Females	91	children under 14. The percentage of children to total number of inmates was 38%
Total	168	

Guardians' Minutes 1842/43

I have looked at the Guardians' minutes over the winter of 1842/43 to see what particular problems cropped up for the Guardians in the early stages of the workhouse's existence.

December 1842
Complaint regarding provision of out-relief

The Guardians received a letter from the Revd. William Smith, Rector of Little Canfield relating the case of Sarah Gunn living in his parish. He explained that Sarah is allowed three shillings a week and one shillings for an attendant who is her mother.The mother receives two shillings a week in her own right but other widows in the parish received two shillings and six pence . These sums would have been paid for by the Union in the form of out-relief. The Reverend went on to say that had it not been for charitable people in the village they could not manage. The family requested additional out-relief. The Guardians had made enquiries and the clerk to the Guardians was requested to write to the Rector pointing out that the case of Sarah Gunn had frequently been before the Guardians and requests for medical assistance had never been refused. On the financial side the clerk wrote that Sarah Gunn receives three shillings per week in cash together with three loaves per week and also mutton to the value of one shilling and two pence per week. Firing (wood) to the value of five pence has recently been added to the weekly allowances (it is December). Also one of Sarah Gunn's sons earns two shillings a week which he brings into the family home although the Guardians did acknowledge that the family unit also included three further single sons. Consequently the Guardians felt that no further out-relief was justified at the present time. The Revd. Smith wrote back a week or so later apologising for being misled by the family as to the extent of relief received but reiterated that he felt that the family income was insufficient.

(Great) Dunmow Union Workhouse which is now apartments
but which was built in the mock Tudor style

Vandalism by inmates

Also in December 1844 the porter reported to the Guardians that two inmates, Messrs Bottle and Cooke, had broken down a wall dividing the able bodied men's ward and a store room and had stolen some potatoes. The porter was ordered to prosecute the two men for the offence. There is no record of what the 'prosecution' entailed unless it meant that the case was reported to the local magistrate or possibly the matter was dealt with internally.

Complaint regarding delivery of corpse

Another case concerning a local parish vicar was that of the Revd
William Lampet of Great Bardfield who complained that a corpse had
been delivered to his church and that no prior notice had been given from
the Dunmow Union. As no prior arrangements had been made a
considerable time elapsed before burial could take place which
inconvenienced all concerned. The clerk was asked to write to the Rev
Lampet advising him that it was the usual practise for the workhouse
master to advise the clergy of the parish church of the death and to make
arrangements for the delivery of the body. It was regretted that this had
not happened in this case. No action appears to have been taken against
the workhouse master.

January 1843

Complaint against the overseers for Lindsell

Three members of the Bowtele family, who were now inmates of the
workhouse, complained to the Guardians regarding their treatment by the
two overseers for the poor for the parish of Lindsell. The family of three
had been given notice to leave their rented accommodation in Lindsell
where they had lived for the previous six years. On the expiry of the
eviction notice the family left the property which was the 2nd January.
Apparently the property was owned by a Mr Franklin who was one of
the two overseers for the poor for Lindsell. Towards the end of the day
of they 2nd they went to Mr Franklin's house and he said that they should
go back to where they had come from for one more night. Consequently
they returned to the house for the night. The next morning they were
visited by the constable for Thaxted who asked them why they had not
left the house. They told him about the previous night's circumstances.
The constable ordered them out of the house as their extra day had
expired and Mary Bowtele and the constable went to Mr Franklin's
house. Mr Franklin said that he had not allowed them back into the
house for any longer than the one night and that they should now go to
the village green.

They took some of their personal possessions with them from the
house, put them on the green, and they stayed there all night (it was
January). They returned the next day to Mr Franklin and said that they
had slept on the green. They begged him for some water from his
brewhouse and Mary also said that her brother was an idiot and was very
ill. There is no mention in the minutes as to who was the third member of
the family. Mr Franklin ordered them off his premises but Mrs Franklin
gave them some tea. Mary then went to the house of the other overseer,
Mr Ambrose, and applied to him for lodgings. He said he could not give

them any. The family did not have a written order and so they could not be admitted to the workhouse. The three of them stayed that evening in a cart lodge where they were found by one of the churchwardens who found them lodging for the night. On the next day they applied to the relieving officer (a workhouse appointed officer) who gave them funds and obtained temporary accommodation for the family.

The two overseers were sent copies of the statement by Mary Bowtele and asked for an explanation within one week. The overseers appeared before the Guardians the next week and only disputed the tea incident which they said was given by Mrs Franklin's niece and not Mrs Franklin. Mr Franklin said that the last time Mary Bowtele called he offered to give the family an order for admittance to the workhouse but the order was not given (no reason given). Mr Ambrose said that he was only an acting overseer and when Mary called he was about to leave for Braintree market and he asked the family to wait until he returned but they did not choose to wait. (this would have been some hours).

The Guardians were obviously concerned at the actions of the overseers, which they did not dispute, and consequently they decided to submit the facts of the case to the Poor Law Commissioners. Although the minutes make record of a reply from the Commissioners there is no record of what they said. I would have expected the overseers to have been severely reprimanded for their inhuman behaviour but it is clear that the three Bowteles were very shortly admitted into the workhouse which, in their case, was a lot better than spending a cold night on Lindsell village green.

February 1843

Fire in the laundry

On the 4th February of 1843 the Guardians convened a special meeting between the regular weekly meetings to consider statements concerning a fire in the laundry room. Statements were taken from Mrs Jackson who was in charge of the laundry, Mr Simpson the workhouse master, Miss Gardner the schoolmistress and Ellen Perry another lady on the staff. In addition statements were taken from three female inmates, Susan Caville aged 13, Mary Burls aged 14 and Sarah Page aged 13.

Mrs Jackson said that she left the laundry at 6.40pm leaving lines of washing hanging up to dry. She had examined the plate on top of the flue and checked that no linen was touching the hot flue and that the nearest linen was two to three inches away. She said she checked that everything was safe in the laundry with the fire in the ironing stove being nearly out which was left to go out. The fire for the drying flue was stoked up with four shovels full of coal. She left the laundry and locked the door.

Miss Gardner said in her statement that she gave the key of the laundry room to some girls to get hot water to clean the schoolroom floor. She did not supply them with a light (candle) for although it was dark they could usually see by the glow of the laundry room furnace. The girls were gone ten minutes.

Susan Caville said that she and the other girls went to the laundry room, unlocked the door and proceeded to get the hot water. They did not need a light as the furnace door was not quite shut but she remembers hearing a roaring noise from the furnace. No one touched the furnace but she can also remember that when they opened the internal door into the copper room they could feel a draught. There was no fire at this time and the girls left. Mary and Sarah confirmed Susan's statement.

Ellen Perry said that she was the first to notice the fire at about 8.30pm. She saw fire and black smoke coming from the laundry. She contacted the workhouse master. Mr Simpson the master went to the laundry and found the door locked and when he looked through the window the glass was too hot to touch. Mrs Jackson came and unlocked the door and Mr Simpson said that he could not see anything other than the furnace that could have caused the blaze. The seat of the fire appeared to be the top of the furnace. There were rope lines over the furnace containing articles of linen. The fire engine was summoned (a hand pumped machine owned and operated by the workhouse staff.). The fire engine proved to be ineffective and so the staff and inmates passed buckets of water in a line to the fire until it was under control. No one was hurt and the master wished to thank the staff and the able bodied inmates who helped for their efforts.

The Superintendent of Rural Police arrived with three of his men after the fire had been quelled and he was also impressed with the organisation that had taken place to get the fire under control. I suppose that if a similar fire had started in a village community there would not have been someone like the workhouse master on hand to organise everyone so quickly. On hearing all the evidence the Guardians concluded that the cause of the fire was an accident. Probably something fell off of one of the drying lines on to the very hot furnace to start the fire or one of the girls accidentally in the semi-darkness knocked something off one of the drying lines. The minutes go on to record that a claim was being made to the Essex and Suffolk Equitable Fire Insurance office in respect of the damage to the laundry.

March 1843

Medical officer reprimanded

Elizabeth Perry, wife of Willam Perry, of the parish of Takeley complained that she was in receipt of an order for the doctor to attend her child but the doctor did not attend for nearly a week. Presumably the Perry family were an out-relief and consequently the medical officer for the Takeley area was responsible for their health. When the doctor did visit the child he said that really there was no need for a parish visit and that he would not visit again but would send some powders. Mr Hodson, the doctor, was asked to attend the next meeting of the Guardians the following week to give an explanation.

Mr Hodson did not attend but wrote saying that he did see the child again after sending the powders. Presumably he visited again after the Perry family had complained. He said in his letter that he did not say that a visit was not needed in the first place but said 'that from the circumstances of the father he was not a fit person to be a parish patient'. It is not clear how this statement relates to the sick child but it does seem that the doctor was not keen to visit this family in view of his relationship with the father. The doctor went on to say that he could not personally attend due to 'professional engagements'. Mrs Perry did confirm that the doctor called again after the receipt of the powders.

The clerk to the Guardians was asked to write to Mr Hodson advising him that the Board wished him to understand that it is his duty as medical officer to attend upon all the paupers within his district on him receiving an order for that purpose and that he is not justified in withholding his attendance under any circumstances. The medical officer did attend the Perry child but there is obviously more to this story than we can be read in the minutes. This is another case, and there are many in the minutes of the various Unions, where a medical officer gives more time to his own private patients than to the paupers in his care.

April 1843

Case of William Webb deceased.

The clerk to the Guardians read out a letter from the Poor Law Commissioners concerning a complaint from the Rev. Thomas Jee, Vicar of Thaxted, who had written direct to them concerning the late William Webb of his parish. The Reverend's letter said that Mr Webb 'was carried to the Union almost in a dying condition and that he died in about a fortnight afterwards and it appeared that his removal was unreasonable and improper. It (the removal) could not have had the sanction of the Union. It was an act of thoughtlessness and unfeeling as well as (being) unreasonable and unnecessary'.

The Board conducted an enquiry into the transfer to the workhouse and Mr Webb's condition on entering up to the date he died. The minutes ran into three pages of statements including the relieving officer at Thaxted who arranged for the order for Mr Webb to be admitted to the Union. Although he said that Mr Webb was ill he was walking up and down during the days before admittance. The medical officer saw the prospective inmate prior to admission who confirmed he was fit enough to travel from Thaxted to Dunmow. The medical officer went on in his statement to say that his chances of survival were better in the workhouse than if he stayed in Thaxted. The porter at the workhouse confirmed that he admitted Mr Webb and he walked to his ward. The medical officer also commented on Mr Webb's health during those two weeks saying 'Webb was in the last stages of consumption and I do not think that his danger increased by his removal to the workhouse. Mr Webb never said anything on the subject of his removal'. The Union nurse, Mrs Allen, said in her statement that Mr Webb had every attention during his 15 days before he died and did not complain about being in the workhouse. The nurse said that his mother was sent for prior to death and that she came to see him.

The Board resolved that it was their opinion that the charges by the Revd. Jee were unfounded. A copy of the evidence was sent to the Poor Law Commissioners. It is clear that the Guardians were thorough in their investigation.

The census of 1881 and 1891
I have taken the census figures for 1901 for the other workhouses as a

A metal bar high up in the entrance porch representing the 'the spike', the popular name for a Union Workhouse and the tool used by inmates to unravel oakum

date for comparison purposes but the census records for the Dumow area.at the Essex Record Office did not contain this information. I have consequently taken the census data for 1881 and1891 including a breakdown of the staff and previous occupation of the inmates for 1881.

The census of 1881

Staff	Inmates	
Master, Matron + 3 children	No occupation	78
Schoolmaster, wife + 3 children	(men & women)	
Porter, Laundress + 3 children	Agricultural lab.	25
Cook, wife and 1 child	Carpenters	2
Schoolmistress	Thatchers	2
Nurse	Bricklayers	2
	Tailor	1
Staff and families 20	Miller	1
	Stonemason	1
	Cattle driver	1
	Pig dealer	1
	Domestic servant	1
	Lunatics	9
	Blind	3
	Children	15
	Orphans	49

Number of inmates 191

Of all the Essex Union workhouses Dunmow had the most number of families of staff resident in the workhouse. There was eight appointed staff in 1881 and twelve wives and children. The mix of pauper inmates though was typical of the occupations seen in all the Essex workhouses.

The census of 1891

Males	103	The total includes 8 staff and 37 children under 14. The
Females	47	percentage of children to total number of inmates was 26%
Total	150	

The census figures for 1881 are at their peak at 213 inmates but still well below the maximum of 350 for which the workhouse was built. Thereafter numbers fell to 142 inmates in 1891 excluding the same eight staff. The trend for children, like the other workhouses, has been a fall from 38% in 1841 to 30% in 1881 and down to 26% by 1891. On the census night for 1891 the figures record that the Dunmow workhouse had eight casual vagrants staying at the time. The records recite their occupation and place of birth.

Shipyard labourer - Liverpool

General labourers - Dover (2)

Coach painter - Manningtree

General labourer - Wisbech

General labourer - Ipswich

In addition to the six above there was also a Mr and Mrs Price who were described as a general labourer and wife from Middlesex.

The twentieth century

At the outbreak of the 1914-18 war the inmates of the Dunmow Union were moved to the Braintree Union Workhouse and the army took over the workhouse but not the infirmary. The Sherwood Foresters had part of the workhouse and Belgian refugees were given another part. Later the workhouse was used as a prisoner of war camp. Like some of the pauper boys from the Romford Union a number from the Dumow Union were sent, when they were old enough, up to Grimsby as apprentices on the fishing trawlers. Trawlers from this part of eastern England were commandeered for use as mine sweepers during the war and unfortunately two of the ex-Dunmow boys lost their lives when their trawlers were blown up. Essex County Council took over the running of Essex workhouses from 1930 and in 1932 the property was sold for conversion into flats and remains so today. The Dunmow Union Workhouse looks different from the majority of Essex Union Workhouses and although the plan is similar to the standard design used throughout the county it is easy to not recognise this substantial building as a Victorian workhouse due to its mock Tudor Gothic styling.

Map dated 1880 shows Epping Union Workhouse just south of Epping Plain
(see page 134)

Chapter 7

EPPING AND ITS ENVIRONS

PARISH WORKHOUSE

The following 17 parishes in the above area were grouped together in 1834 following the Poor Law Amendment Act to form the Epping Union. Before 1834 each parish may have had its own poorhouse or workhouse.

Chigwell, Chingford, Epping, Great Parndon, Harlow, Latton, Little Parndon, Loughton, Magdalen Laver, Matching, Nazeing, Netteswell, North Weald Bassett, Roydon, Sheering, Theydon Bois and Theydon Garnon

Later the parishes of **Buckhurst Hill and Epping Upland** were added.

The government undertook a survey of parish workhouses in 1777 and the following parishes in this area had a workhouse open in that year.

Epping   Chigwell   Harlow   Theydon Garnon

Epping

There are three almshouses beside the Thornwood Road alongside The Plain and it is thought that this was the site of one or more parish poor houses. There was also a poorhouse on the site of the Gates Garage near to the Half Moon public house. Records also refer to a poor house standing beside the Rose and Crown ale-house in 1757. The parish records mention in 1763 an allowance to the workhouse master, Mr Snook, for tea costing one pound sixteen shillings - a lot of tea in those days. It does seem, therefore, that at least one of the parish poorhouses or workhouses was large enough to justify the appointment of a workhouse master. This is borne out by the government survey of parish workhouse in 1777 which recorded that the Epping workhouse was capable of housing up to 20 inmates which would have needed someone to run the establishment. Although a number of properties were being used by the parish in the eighteenth century as homes for the poor the records do not say which one had a workhouse master.

It seems that there was more than one poor house or workhouse in Epping and a document in the Essex Record Office drawn up by the parish vestry and the manor of Epping Bury recites in 1774 that two cottages were owned by the manor one of which was used as the parish workhouse. This small cottage was probably only a house used by the poor of the parish on a rent free basis as there were only two occupants James Haslam and Jeremiah Gaywood. The property was described as being 'for the lodging, keeping, maintenance and employing of the poor, aged and impotent'.

Later in the century in the latter 1780s a three story brick building was purchased on the corner of Station Road to be used as a workhouse. There is a story that the last master, Thomas Godfrey, in the 1830s led a woman down the High Street with a halter round her neck and sold her off in the street for two shillings and six pence. The workhouse was sold off in 1837 when the Union Workhouse was built on the Plain.

Chigwell

The first mention of a workhouse came in 1728 when the parish vestry commented that they were becoming unable to maintain those poor parishioners on out-relief and consequently decided to establish a workhouse. The parish records are not specific as to the outgoings of the overseers to pinpoint the date of building but a minute of 1729 does refer to the workhouse and one must assume that it was built soon after the 1728 reference.

There is a deed in the Essex Record Office dated 1762 granting a lease on the parish workhouse and an adjacent small piece of ground which appears to be on land owned by or adjacent to Luxborough farm, Chigwell. This lease probably refers to the Chigwell Row workhouse which was located at the southern end of Gravel Lane near to the crossroads where All Saints church is now located. The government survey of 1777 records the Chigwell (Row) workhouse as capable of housing up to 33 inmates. The workhouse was being used right up to the time that the new Epping Union Workhouse was built. A room in the workhouse was used for church services for the Chigwell Row residents from 1841 with the services being transferred to the schoolroom in 1860. All Saints church was built in 1867.

Harlow

The manor of Harlow Bury drew up a document in 1746 referring to a property called Wyburs which had been converted into two tenements by 1746 and was previously the workhouse. This property was probably two cottages rented by the parish as rent free accommodation for the poor of the parish. It seems as if these cottages were no longer used as a poorhouse/workhouse in 1746 and the parish had made other arrangements.

There is no specific description in the document as to where these cottages were but other properties and land mentioned were all in the area of the old Market Place. Parish records are few and far between for Harlow parish and I have not been able to locate the whereabouts of a subsequent workhouse which was definitely in existence in 1777 when the government survey stated that the workhouse could accommodate up to 20 inmates. This latter workhouse was still functioning in 1836 when the new Epping Union took over parish workhouses.

Theydon Garnon

The parish had a workhouse from at least 1773 as the vestry minutes record the payment of goods supplied to the workhouse. In the following year the minutes record the appointment of a new workhouse master following the death of the. predecessor Mr Jepp. Mr Edmund Robinson was to be the new master at a salary of thirteen guineas a year. There are some crossings out in the minute but it seems that either he or the inmates and probably both were to be allowed one pint of ale per day but the parish would not bare the charge of any tea or sugar. Tea and sugar was expensive and most inmates of workhouses drank weak beer. The vestry minute book also records that at a vestry meeting in April 1776 the vestry were threatening to prosecute Richard Palmer a bricklayer of Epping for building cottages for the use of the poor of the parish without the statutory requirement for four acres of land attached to the property. This minute gives the impression that the vestry were not aware of what was going on and maybe Richard Palmer was building the cottages as a speculative venture hoping to lodge the poor of the parish and charge out the cost to the vestry. Unfortunately there are no further references to this development. In 1777 when the government survey took place the Theydon Gagnon workhouse was capable of housing up to 30 inmates.

When Mr Robinson above was appointed the new master of the workhouse the source of reference was a minute in the vestry parish records. In addition to the vestry minutes, Theydon Garnon is also fortunate in having survived an overseers file which includes letters from residents asking for relief which are often written by others as the applicant was not always able to write. Included in this file of papers are two letters one of which appears to be applying to take inmates out of the workhouse and the other for the post of workhouse master. One letter which is dated 29th March has no year mentioned but it is probably 1828. The letter of application asks the church wardens and overseers of the parish to consider William Jessop Junior and his wife for the position of 'farming' workhouse inmates at the rate four shillings and three pence per week per inmate. This does not mean that the Jessops would take the inmates to their farm but would take on the care and maintenance of the inmates within the workhouse and provide their food and maintenance at the specified rate. The other letter is dated 13th July 1828 and also comes from William Jessop. It seems that since his March letter the parish had been making enquiries and had asked for further information. This time Mr Jessop offers to look after up to ten inmates at a certain price per day with a graduated lesser rate as the number increases. Mr Jessop invites the parish to make enquiries at Orsett and West Thurrock workhouses where he was previously was employed. He says that they will find out that he did 'a wrong thing' there by letting his son run the (work) houses for him and there seems to have been a problem with this arrangement. Whether Mr Jessop got the job or not is not recorded but with the problems at his previous establishments it rather looks as if he would not get the job.

When the new Epping Guardians took over in 1836 the workhouse does not get a mention and it seems that it had either closed some time between 1828 and 1836 or if still open in 1836 the inmates were transferred to one of the other parish workhouses and the workhouse closed.

THE EPPING UNION WORKHOUSE

Of the 17 parishes listed previously they all had one representative on the Board of Guardians with Chigwell, Epping, Harlow and Loughton having two representatives each making a total of 21 Guardians. To these 17 parishes was added Buckhurst Hill and Epping Upland in later years.

The Epping Poor Law Union was formed in January 1836 with the initial 21 Guardians. One of the first resolutions was to re-organise the three existing parish workhouses in the Union area. The one at Chigwell was to be used in future for women and children and that at

Harlow would be accommodated solely by able bodied men. The third, at Epping, would be used, if there was a need, to house the aged and infirm. The Poor Law Commissioners had recommended the segregation of sexes at any existing parish workhouse if it was practical.

1836

Purchase of land for new Union Workhouse

Having sorted out the existing parish workhouses as to their structural condition and the segregation of sexes the next major job was to find a piece of land in the area on which to build the new Union Workhouse. The plot chosen was a piece of waste ground on the common called East Plain which was on the south side of the Chelmsford Road. Part of the plot was in the manor of Epping Bury and part was in the manor of Hemnalls in Theydon Garnon. Consent was obtained from the two Lords of the Manor to enclose two acres and build a workhouse to accommodate 300 paupers. Subsequently difficulties were encountered with the two lords of the manor over the purchase and so an appeal was made to the Rev. G W Daubeny to see if he was willing to sell part of one of the Mill Fields. This land was just to the rear of the original proposed purchase which is why there was a long drive from the road to the workhouse crossing the land owned by the two lords of the manor. The two acres purchased was part of a five acre field which was in the parish of Theydon Garnon and was acquired in November 1836.

Initially, the architect chosen to design the workhouse when the Guardians were talking to the two lords of the manor was Sampson Kempthorne. By the time that the different piece of land was eventually purchased in November 1836 it was decided to start again with a new architect and so Mr Kempthorne was discharged from his post and his bill settled. It is surprising that Mr Kempthorne was not given the contract to design the workhouse as it was he who drew up the design for a Union workhouse for the Commissioners in 1836 and his plan was included in the original documents that were sent to all the new Boards of Guardians. New plans were drawn up though for a workhouse to accommodate 220 paupers by Mr Lewis Vulliamy with an initial costing of £4000. Things did not go smoothly. First of all a tender by a builder from Camden Town was accepted which he withdrew in March 1837. A Mr Thomas Smith had his tender accepted in the same month but there were delays in the start of building. Eventually building work did start and by May 1838 the Guardians took possession and the workhouse officially opened although all the work had not been finished. The first master and matron were Charles Littlechild and his wife who were in these positions at the Harlow parish workhouse.

The main workhouse buildings have been pulled down but the
two infirmary buildings remain

Vulliamy's design was for a three storey building in the shape of a cross with the master's Parlour in the centre. From this vantage point he could look down on the four various exercise yards which were divided up for men, women, boys and girls. From the front entrance hall at the end of one of four arms of the cross further buildings extended all the way round around the sides of the cross wings so that the exercise yards were boxed in. On the ground floor one passed from the entrance hall through the reception area and then into the school room and dining hall before reaching the master's parlour. From the master's parlour off to one side ran the kitchens and from there into the women's infirmary. On the other side of the cross were a day room and workroom and then the men's infirmary. Continuing straight on from the Master's parlour there was a further dining room and the chapel and this room led into the 'dead house' where those that passed away were kept temporarily. The rooms and buildings, some of which were only single storey, which went all the way around the cruciform design, were used as stables, wash houses, bake-houses, workrooms and storehouses. The accommodation for the inmates was on the upper floors.

June 1838
Complaint by Hannah Ruskin
Hannah Ruskin a pauper girl in the workhouse complained to the Guardians that Charles Littlechild the master had 'attempted to take improper liberties with her'. The girl was interviewed in the presence of the master and his wife. The girl, said the minutes, changed her statement somewhat and in the absence of any supporting statements the Guardians could not place any reliance on her statement and dismissed the case.

August 1838
The Visiting Committee report
This was probably the first report made by the Visiting Committee after the new workhouse opened. They remarked on thirteen items some of which are listed here:

> The committee found the (work) House well ventilated.
> The small pox prevails in nine cases of children
> The few men able to work are kept at work
> The schoolmistress is attending to her duties
> The children are clean and appear well attended to
> The dietary recommendations are duly observed
> Prayers are read by the master there being no chaplain
> The provisions were found to be of good quality

When the committee came a few months later they found the drains under the master's room defective - presumably there was a smell. They also found that a girl was in solitary confinement and had been so for the past fortnight. They called for a report on the circumstances.

October 1838
Double and single beds
It had come to the notice of the Guardians that some of the men in the Men's Ward were sleeping in double beds. It was decided to exchange

these beds for single beds from the Women's Ward. It is not clear what the occupancy was of the double beds!!.

November 1838

The Barker children

The Guardians were disappointed that following the desertion of the three Barker children by the mother, Mary Barker, that no order for her apprehension and arrest had get been authorised. This matter should have been brought to the attention of the Guardians by the master and he had obviously forgotten to advise the Board. Presumably the three children had been brought into the workhouse after the disappearance of the mother and nothing had been done about finding the mother.

Advertisement for a porter

The Guardians asked the clerk to place an advertisement in the local paper for a porter. The first porter had only been in the job for six months and presumably working in a Union Workhouse was not to his liking. Going through the minutes for all the Essex workhouses it seems that those occupying the position of porter, schoolmaster or nurse invariably did not stay more than a year or so as the Guardians were always placing advertisements for replacements. The advertisement said that the Guardians were looking for an able bodied young man who was able to read and write and also willing to teach the children in the workhouse the trade of either a tailor or a shoemaker. The salary would £20 a year with board and lodging. The job was offered to George Humerstone a shoemaker from Epping.

Religion for lunatics

Inmates were allowed out on Sundays to go to church but in the case of lunatics, who were not allowed out, the Guardians agreed that if a request was forthcoming then they would arrange for a minister to visit the workhouse on a Tuesday.

December 1838

New road to workhouse

Mention has been made before that the workhouse was built farther in from the road than was intended originally as arrangements fell down to purchase the land immediately adjacent to the road. We now see in the minutes that the Union workhouse had upgraded the road to the workhouse which crossed waste land, presumably owned by the lords of the manor mentioned above, and the nominal sum of one guinea was paid to the owners of the land. Correspondence regarding the right of way over the waste land appeared to drag on with the Guardians replying to a recent letter saying that whilst they were agreeable to paying a guinea a year as rent for the right of way they did not wish there to be any other conditions placed on this right.

Boys for service in the navy

The Guardians were always trying to get their young boy and girl inmates work or apprenticeships as this would get them out of the workhouse and they would no longer be a drain on society. The Guardians had been sent a request to see if any boy inmates would be interested in service in the navy and the clerk was asked to write to find out the criteria as to age and size of boys required.

January 1939

The Ware family of Newport, Essex

The clerk was ordered to write to the officers of Newport saying that the Epping Union had been supporting William Ware and his family on out relief to the extent of four shillings and four loaves a week. The family were all suffering from small pox and must have been staying with someone they knew in the Epping area. The clerk was to ask if Newport would sanction this allowance, which would mean that Newport parish would be charged for their board and lodging, or otherwise arrangement would be made to send them back to their home parish.

The census of 1841

The workhouse opened in 1838 and the first national census after opening listed the following:

Males	69	The total includes 4 staff and 56 children under 14. The percentage of children to the total number of inmates was 41%
Female	71	
Total	140	

1846

The infirmary

Mention is made at various workhouses of the problems of isolating cases of contagious diseases as the infirmary was invariably all part of the main workhouse complex. Epping took the decision in 1846 to build a separate two storey infirmary. This small building had two wards on the ground floor and two on the upper floor separated by a nurse's room.

This building was subsequently used as a laundry when another separate infirmary was built in 1876.

Contagious diseases

Diseases like typhus, smallpox, diphtheria and measles were prevalent all over the country in the nineteenth century and the workhouses suffered probably more than most with their poor drainage and water quality. There was no mains drainage at the Epping workhouse and it relied on 13 cesspools which were built into the design of the building. For fresh water the source was a pond and well in the basement of the building. This water was supposed to have been filtered by a devise installed into the pump but it was not very effective.

1847
Change of name of governing body and new rules

The design of all workhouses was one where the sexes were segregated and even the children were separated from their parents as soon as they were of school age. The Poor Law Commissioners were the controlling body of all the workhouses from its inception in 1834 until 1847 when its named changed to the Poor Law Board. Basically it was only a change of name but the new Board did bring in one change that was well received by one category of inmate. The separation of husband and wife was a rule that was not well received by married couples and I suppose that this was just one of the deterrents to being admitted to a workhouse. In 1847 the rule was changed to allow married couples over the age of sixty to share a separate bedroom. In practice few workhouses took this new concession on board and where couples were separated it was usually only by a curtain in a large room made up of a number of aged couples.

Despite the name changing from the Poor Law Commissioners to the Poor Law Board all the clerks at the Unions still referred in their minutes to the body as the Poor Law Commissioners. The Poor Law Board was itself succeeded by the Local Government Board in 1871.

1848
Design weaknesses

The design by Vulliamy had as its weakness, as mentioned above, the provision of water and the operation of the cesspools both of which were not efficient leading of course to contagious diseases. These shortcomings were noted by the Poor Law Board in 1848 when their report to the Guardians stated that the building was badly built including the provision of water and the design of the drains. A cholera epidemic in 1854 led to the excavation of a new well in the green area to the north of the buildings. The workhouse was originally lit with candles which lasted until 1865 when gas lighting was introduced.

September 1848
New rules for tramps and vagrants
Union workhouses generally took in tramps and vagrants for a day or two before they moved on and made them earn their board and lodging by breaking up stones or other menial tasks. The Guardians at Epping passed a new rule that they would only admit tramps and vagrants in the following categories together with a rule new regarding a second appearance.

'That the master only relieve (tramps and vagrants in the following categories) the aged, the infirm, those of an enfeebled appearance and children under the age of twelve. That upon any of the above classes relieved a second time then they should be detained and carried before a magistrate and charged with vagrancy'.

November 1848
More tough measures by the Guardians
The Guardians resolved: 'that the allowances of tea and sugar given to the women in the washing department be taken off during the ensuing fortnight, they being dissatisfied with their allowances of bread'.

December 1848
Nuisance at Chigwell
Two residents of Chigwell wrote to the Guardians saying that two properties within the parish of Chigwell were 'in a filthy condition and a nuisance to the premises adjoining and required the Guardians to proceed under the Act passed in the last session of parliament concerning the removal of nuisances and prevention of contagious diseases'. Initially the assumption was that the Union Guardians must have had some interest in these two properties and possibly they were old parish poor houses or the old Chigwell parish workhouse which were now controlled by the Epping Union.

The Guardians set up a sub committee to inspect the properties and report back. At the following weekly Guardians meeting there was a similar request from residents of the parish of Chingford. It would be rather a coincidence if property owned by the Union in Chingford was in a poor condition and it now seems that Union workhouses had a general responsibility for health in its area and to ensure that property did not fall into such a state that might be the cause of an outbreak of infectious diseases. Roydon parish followed the next week with their own request for properties in their parish to be put in order and this time the Guardians in their minutes quoted the Nuisances Removal Act of 1848 as the act upon which the parishes were basing their requests for action. Later in the year Mr Andrews, who owned one of the Chigwell properties, was sent the bill for tidying the nuisance his property was causing.

February 1849

Ill-treatment of daughter

The Guardians picked up a report by the medical officer that a Mr Featherstone had brought into the workhouse his daughter Emily 'in a starving and emaciated state caused by the want of sufficient food'. The Guardians directed that the clerk should appear before the magistrates and if possible obtain a warrant for the arrest of Mr Featherstone on the grounds of ill-treatment of his daughter. A couple of weeks later the minutes recorded that Mr Featherstone had been committed for trial at Chelmsford Assizes for which he received two months imprisonment for neglecting his child.

March 1849

Inmates' money

As workhouse inmates had their board and lodging paid for, and as there were few opportunities to leave the workhouse, they had very little use for money. It had come to the attention of the Guardians that inmates were receiving letters which contained postal orders or cash. It was decided that the all letters addressed to the inmates, which were probably very few, be opened in the presence of the inmate and the master. Should the letters contain cash or postal orders then this money would be retained by the master and the Guardians advised in order that they can decide what should happen to the funds.

School inspection

The inspector reported that the schools had improved since his last visit but it would benefit the children if 'maps of England, the World and Palestine be furnished for each school'. There were two schoolrooms and whereas it would have been sensible for all the young children to be educated by the schoolmistress and the older children to be taught by the schoolmaster this was not the case. The boys and girls were separated and consequently the schoolmaster and schoolmistress had a full age range to teach from the age of five to thirteen. Surprisingly the Guardians did not agree with the provision of the maps and they wrote to the Poor Law Commissioners. Despite the authority now being called the

Poor Law Board all workhouses still referred to it as the 'Commissioners'. The letter said that they would not be taking up this suggestion in the inspector's report. The Commissioners replied and although the contents are not recorded it did prompt the Guardians to hold a special meeting to which all Guardians were asked to attend. Presumably the Commissioners, understandably, were in favour of the provision of maps but the Guardians passed a further resolution once again refusing the introduction of the maps. Of the 21 appointed Guardians 17 attended the special meeting. The reason given by the Guardians for the non provision of maps was that the expense was not justified as this would have to be passed on to the ratepayers.

February 1850
Reduction in salaries
The minutes during the month of February were taking up much time discussing the county rate and the general expenditure at the Union workhouse. Out of the blue one of the Guardians gave notice that he was to put a proposition at the next Guardians' meeting proposing that the salaries of the Union's officers be reduced by ten per cent with the exception of those for the schoolmaster and schoolmistress. At this next meeting 20 out of the 21 Guardians attended. An amendment to the proposition was tabled that, in essence, there should be no reduction in salaries. The Guardians voted in favour of the amendment that there should be no reduction.

May 1850
Unqualified medical officer
All the Essex Unions employed one medical officer to look after the patients in the workhouse and various others to care for those on out relief living in the parishes. These medical officers would all have had their private patients in the area where they live. One gets the impression by the turnover of medical officers that the extra work was more trouble than it was worth and it was more lucrative to stick to the private work. The Guardians minutes record on numerous occasions a year the appointment of new medical officers and the checks that were made as to their qualifications. In May 1850 the Guardians were considering the appointment of Mr Fearon to cover the Roydon area. When the application form was returned the Guardians noted that Mr Fearon 'was not qualified in any one of the four modes required by the Act'. Apparently Mr Fearon was previously employed by the Ware Union in this capacity. The Epping Guardians reported the situation to the Poor Law Commissioners. It later turns out that the residents of Roydon parish

were happy to have Mr Fearon as their medical officer notwithstanding his lack of qualifications. The Guardians reported the position again to the Poor Law Commissioners and sought their support for the appointment which was given.

1880s
Rebuilding programme
It was only forty or so years after the Epping Union Workhouse was built that there were major works which saw the remodelling of the entrance block in the north, the rebuilding of the southern wing which included another new infirmary, a dining hall and a chapel. To the west of the complex further new additions were built.

The twentieth century
The census of 1901

Males	83	The total includes 10 staff and 30
Females	65	children under 14. The percentage of
		children to the total number of inmates
		was 22%
Total	136	

The total number of inmates over the 60 year period had remained fairly static with the percentage of children though falling from 41% to 22%.

In 1911 a large infirmary was built to the east of the workhouse. The whole complex was renamed the Epping Institution after 1930 when the Union Workhouse was dissolved and Essex County Council took control. Eight years later in 1938 the old workhouse was renamed again and called St Margarets Hospital. The main workhouse buildings have now been demolished but some of the peripheral buildings and St Margarets Hospital still remain.

Chapter 8

HALSTEAD AND ITS ENVIRONS

PARISH WORKHOUSES

The following 16 parishes in the above area were grouped together in 1834 following the Poor Law Amendment Act to form the Billericay Union. Before 1834 each parish may have had its own parish poorhouse or workhouse.

Castle Hedingham, Colne Engaine, Earls Colne, Gosfield, Great Maplestead, Great Yeldham, Halstead, Little Maplestead, Little Yeldham, Pebmarsh, Ridgewell, Sible Hedingham, Stambourne, Tilbury-juxta-Clare, Toppesfield and White Colne.

The government undertook a survey of parish workhouses in 1777 and the following parishes in this area had a workhouse open in that year.

Colne Engaine	Earls Colne	Gosfield
Halstead	Castle Hedingham	Sible Hedingham
Pebmarsh	Ridgewell	Toppesfield
Gt Yeldham		

Compared with the other areas of Essex it is surprising that 10 out of the 16 parishes had a workhouse in 1777. Halstead was the largest parish with only a population of about 4000 with the other parishes only having a few hundred residents each. The decline of the wool industry in this part of Essex possibly contributed to the large number of parish workhouses.

Halstead

The Halstead parish workhouse was situated in Mill Chase, previously called School Lane and before that Workhouse Lane. Greenwood School is now on the site of the parish workhouse. The workhouse was the largest in the surrounding area as the population of Halstead was many times larger than any of the other parishes. The workhouse was established some time before 1777 as the government survey of that year stated that the workhouse could house up to 80 inmates which gives some indication of the size of the building although of course there may have actually been a lot less in residence in 1777.

The overseer's records in the Essex Record Office contain an interesting letter dated 1773 from the overseer of the parish of Earls Barton in Northamptonshire to the parish of Halstead. Apparently the widow of Lazarus Wooden and William Wooden, presumably her son, were paupers who were both bona fide residents of Earls Barton and were now under the care of the overseer of Halstead. The letter from Earls Barton agrees to pay a lump sum of five pounds four shillings for the board and lodging of the Wooden family up to date. Maybe the Halstead overseers had just found out that their parish of residence was not Halstead and were charging Earls Barton for past care. Presumably from now onwards there would be regular payments. There must have been a good reason for Halstead to take on the responsibility of these two paupers and possibly Halstead had a workhouse and Earls Barton did not.

There also exists the overseer's record of the poor rate by residents of the parish for the quarterly rate for the March quarter 1778. Three hundred residents paid rates at the rate of two shillings and sixpence in the pound of their rateable value which realised £421 for the quarter to pay for the running of the workhouse and to pay for those on out-relief.

There are few records of the progress of the workhouse between the late 1700s and the 1830s but when the new Halstead Union Workhouse Guardians had been established in 1835 they commissioned a survey a year later by Franklin & Son, auctioneers and estate agents, of the existing parish workhouses to see what they had inherited and what the inventory contained. The dining room of the Halstead parish workhouse had a 42 bench table which gives some idea of the size of the room and the number that could be accommodated in the workhouse. In addition to the usual kitchen, brew house and outbuildings there were bedchambers for the men and women and Halstead had a special nursery room for children. The surveyor took some measurements of the various parts of the workhouse which appears to be made up of several buildings. The descriptions were as follows:

Front	62 feet x 20	Side wing	80 feet x 21
Old building	52 feet x 15	Factory	62 feet x 10

Together with various other smaller buildings, a yard and a piggery

Castle Hedingham

Castle Hedingham's parish workhouse was probably built some time just prior to 1763 as the parish account book first mentions the workhouse on October 6th of that year when the parish paid a bill of nearly £19 for work done at the workhouse. The governor of the workhouse was paid a salary of eighteen pounds ten shillings a year which means that the parish paid separately for all the food, drink and necessaries for the inmates. The government survey of 1777 stated that the workhouse was capable of accommodating up to 65 inmates.

Parishes had to pay for the medical care of their paupers whether in the workhouse or on out-relief and the parish entered into an agreement with Bhatt Walker and John Parmenter in 1782 that they would be paid twelve guineas yearly to 'provide medicines' to the poor 'in all cases of surgery except midwifery'. The agreement concluded that the surgeons were not to administer assistance to 'families as reside in the parish without certificates which do not belong to the parish are excluded from the above agreement'. A later agreement with different surgeons specifically mentioned smallpox as a disease which came within their brief for which they were to treat as best as possible.

Compared with other Essex workhouse in rural areas Castle Hedingham workhouse was large in 1777 with up to 65 inmates but it did not survive until the Union was established in 1835 as it was not open in that year when the new Halstead Guardians took over the parish workhouses. The reason that the parish had a large workhouse probably relates to the decline of the spinning industry in the area, which was similar to the situation at Bocking, and probably by the nineteenth century those paupers had found other work and the workhouse was no longer needed. It seems that by the turn of the century the size of the workhouse had reduced drastically as an inventory of 1808 lists goods and chattels that could only be used by a handful of inmates.

Colne Engaine

The parish workhouse was open in 1756 as the overseer's accounts list payments to the workhouse and to the governor/master. In the same year the parish vestry drew up an agreement with William Andrews to be governor of the workhouse with his wife and son also to be allowed to live with him. The rate of pay was to fourteen shillings a month to look after the inmates. The arrangement for the termination of the contract was one month's notice either way. Some parishes gave the new governor an allowance for each inmate for weekly provisions but it seems in Colne Engaine's case the parish vestry paid for all expenses.

Surprisingly in 1761 the vestry decided to 'break up (close) the workhouse...for so long a time as we shall think convenient'. There followed in the vestry minutes a list of residents of the parish and what they were given from the workhouse. The items included clothing, beds, bedding, furniture and spinning wheels. It was not unusual for a parish to close their workhouse for one reason or another and reopen it again some time later which was what happened at Clone Engainge as we see that in 1777 it was open again and capable of accommodating up to 30 inmates. Of course having given away most of the contents in 1761 they would have had to refurnish the workhouse again. The overseer's accounts for 1786 record the appointment of John Spurgeon and his wife of Halstead as governor of the parish workhouse for one year at a salary of £12. In 1756 the governor received £8.40 a year and one can see the effect of inflation over a thirty year period. The vestry would be paying for the board and accommodation of the governor and his wife and the inmates but the arrangements was that Mr and Mrs Spurgeon would supply their own tea and sugar which were deemed to be luxuries in those days.

In 1795 the overseer's accounts record the goods and chattels owned by Ann Bacon when she was admitted to the parish workhouse. The inventory was taken on the day she was admitted and the items were possibly put in store in case she came out of the workhouse. Presumably though, Ann Bacon was a destitute widow and more than likely her belongings would be sold by the parish with the proceeds being placed in the Poor Rate fund. There are a few items which are not recognisable today but her belongings were as follows:

2 tables	9 chairs	1 hutch (chest)
1 skep (basket)	1 trunk	1 bedstead
1 flock bed	4 sheets	2 bolsters
2 pillows	1 cupboard	1 kneading trough
1 pail	1 pair of bellows	1 pair of tongs
1 washing kneeler	1 washing stool	1 tin kettle
1 linen drier	2 wooden bottles	2 glass bottles

These are the basics that someone would need although there is no mention of crockery, cutlery or pots and pans.

A government return in 1821 recorded that there were 16 adult and 4 children as inmates although it seems that the workhouse had closed again prior to 1835 as it was not open when the new Halstead Union Guardians were appointed.

Earls Colne

The first mention of a workhouse in the parish came in 1738 when an agreement was made with Joseph Cook to build 'a tenement or dwelling fifty feet in length and eighteen feet in width and in height eleven foot'. The construction was to be 'hefty oak timbers'. The cross beams were to be 'of good and sound elm'. The roof rafters were to be of oak and the collar beams were to be of sound elm. The agreement went on to say what thickness of timber was required for each type of beam and also that the stairs were to be made of elm boards. Mr Cook was paid "with good and lawful money of Great Britain".

The poor of Earls Colne prior to the building of the workhouse were accommodated in the workhouse at Halstead and Earls Colne parish would have been responsible for their keep. Some of the parish poor would have received outdoor relief or have been lodged with a local resident but presumably those that could not be accommodated in one of these two ways would have gone to the Halstead parish workhouse. Fortunately for the vestry at Earls Colne the parish was left £300 in the will of Mrs Mary Pointer for 'the use of the poor'. The vestry decided at their meeting on the 7th July 1740, two years after it was first discussed, to use £200 of this bequest to build a workhouse.

In 1777 at the time of the government survey of parish workhouse the Earls Colne workhouse could accommodate up to 42 inmates although it may not have had that many in that year. There are records though of the actual number being looked after in the period 1819 to 1829 which ranged from 20 to 30 inmates. Looking at the names of the inmates it is evident that they came and went quite regularly not stopping for very long unless they were ill or infirm. One family though is interesting as in 1819 there was Henry Strange, his wife and the children, Susanna and Hannah and William. By 1820 there was no longer any mention of Susanna and Hannah and possibly they had come up to an age where the girls had gone into service which was invariably the case for girls around the age of 13 or 14. From June 1822 William no longer gets a mention and maybe he had come of age and a position was found for him. The list for October 1825 list both Mr and Mrs Strange but a month later William Strange no longer appears and Mrs Strange is referred to as Widow Strange. Mrs Strange's name appears for a further period and there is no more mention of her after February 1826. She may also have died but possibly taken in by a relative. I wonder what happened to the children?

When the workhouse was taken over by the new Halstead Union a survey was undertaken by a local estate agent in 1836 which listed the rooms and their contents. There was the keeping room (the day room), the pantry, the kitchen, the coal house, a room which appeared to be the dining room, the housekeeper's room and chamber, the men's ward, the women's ward and a further room. This last room seems to have been used as a store room and the inventory lists 12 hundredweight of oakum. Oakum was old ropes invariably covered in tar which workhouses bought and unravelled and sold back to rope makers for reuse. One of the tools used to unravel the rope was a simple metal spike and many of the future Union workhouses adopted this nickname for the workhouse as they also invariably put the inmates to work with oakum.

By 1838 the new Union workhouse had opened and it was decided by the Earls Colne vestry to sell the parish cage and the workhouse. The selling of the cage was deferred but the sale of the workhouse went ahead in 1839 with the proceeds being sent to the Guardians to offset the cost of the new workhouse.

Great Yeldham

The workhouse was established by at least 1758 as the overseer's accounts mention expenditure at the workhouse. Of the bills paid it seems that part of the staple diet was turnips and milk as there are many bills for these items. One of the paupers was shaved and the barber's bill was one old penny.

The government survey of 1777 stated that the parish workhouse could accommodate up to 20 inmates although the actual number could have been lower in that year. An agreement was entered into in 1789 by the four parishes of Great Yeldham, Little Yeldham, Tilbury and Sturmer with John French of Little Yeldham to lease for seven years as a joint workhouse 'all that messuage or tenement of him the said John French situate and being in the parish of Great Yeldham now and for sometime past used as a workhouse for the poor of the parish of Great Yeldham with the yards and gardens'. This document is probably the renewal of a previous seven year lease.

Sible Hedingham

The first mention of a parish workhouse in Sible Hedingham was in 1745 when the churchwardens and overseers took a lease on two tenements in Church Street, which was at times called Tape Street. The location of the two cottages was, according to the lease, 'abutting to the west on Church Street and on the east to the land of Frances Brigg, widow'. The two tenements would have probably been of the two up and two down variety with possibly a small room in the loft. One would have thought that two properties of this size would not have held in total more than a dozen or so inmates but at the time of the government survey of 1777 the maximum capacity was 30.

Few records survive concerning the workhouse but Sible Hedingham workhouse was included in the survey by Franklin & Son to see what the new Halstead Union had inherited in 1836 and it is clear from the notes taken by the agent that the building was substantial. Either the workhouse had moved to new premises since the initial property in Church Street was leased or major extensions had been built at this location. The estate agent's survey listed one of the ground floor rooms as the 'Committee Room' which was unusual for a parish workhouse and probably this room was used by the overseers of the poor for the parish. The summary at the end of the survey lists up to twenty areas which was every room together with hallways and walk in pantries.

In January 1836, when the parish workhouse had come under the control of the new Halstead Guardians, one of the paupers got himself into trouble. Joseph Butcher was aged 23 and had a wife and three children. Misdemeanours by parish inmates after 1836 were initially brought before the new Halstead Union Guardians and Joseph appeared 'in a state of intoxication and conducted himself in a very disorderly and improper manner'. He declared that he was in a state of starvation which was not the case as he was adequately fed in his parish workhouse. The Guardians decided that he should be arrested for being drunk and disorderly and he was brought before the magistrate who was sitting at the Bell Inn, Halstead. He was fined five shillings for the offence but he was found to have over £1 in his pocket which was a large amount of money for a destitute pauper.

Toppesfield

Toppersfield workhouse was established prior to 1777 as the workhouse is mentioned in the government survey of that year as capable of accommodation up 30 inmates. Mrs Harrington was the workhouse mistress in 1812 and the overseer's ledger records that she was claiming for 11 inmates in the month of March at the rate of three shillings per inmate. At the end of the month the parish vestry made a special payment to Mrs Harrington in the sum of £3 up to Easter 1812 as the price of flour during the year had risen. This payment represents an extra two new pence rise per inmate on the three shillings a week she received. The weekly allowance per inmate was invariably linked to the price of flour and in many cases this was written into the masters/mistresses agreement. Later in 1812 the number in the workhouse had fallen to only seven but by 1813 the number had increased to nine. The workhouse was still open in 1823 and an inventory in this year lists four rooms on the ground floor - the ward (day room/dining room), a room next to the ward (room), the brew house and the buttery. Upstairs there were four bedrooms one of which was described as 'the bedroom over the shop'. There appeared to be sufficient beds and linen for up to 12 inmates. The workhouse was not open in 1835 when the new Halstead Union Guardians first met and with the numbers so low it is likely that the inmates were transferred to the Halstead parish workhouse some time previously.

THE HALSTEAD UNION WORKHOUSE

Map of Halstead Union Workhouse dated 1881

Of the 16 parishes that made up the Halstead Union, Halstead had four representatives on the new Board of Guardians and the larger villages of Castle Hedingham, Earls Colne, Sible Hedingham and Toppesfield has two representatives each with the remainder one each making a total of 23 Guardians.

The elected Guardians from the 16 parishes first got together in November 1835 but it was not until 1838 that the new Union workhouse was eventually opened in North Street and built to accommodate 300 inmates. One of the first jobs for the new Guardians in 1835 was to form a Workhouse Committee with the brief to inspect the existing parish workhouses that now came under the control of the Guardians. There were only three parish workhouse open in 1835 and these were in Halstead, Earls Colne and Sible Hedingham.

In January 1836 the Guardians transferred six inmates from Castle Hedingham parish workhouse to Halstead parish workhouse. The Guardian's minutes are not clear as to whether this was all that left at Castle Hedingham at the time or whether they just transferred one class of inmate to Halstead. The latter seems to be situation as later in January 1836 the minutes record that all three existing parish workhouses were now capable of taking extra inmates. The Commissioners recommended that until the new Union workhouse was built that the inmates be categorised into classes according to sex and age and spread around the existing workhouses accordingly. In the following month it had been decided to transfer all the infirm paupers to Earls Colne parish workhouse.

The Poor Law Commissioners in addition to providing all the Unions with guidelines on how the institution when built should be run also provided a model design for the building. The Commission's architect was Sampson Kempthorne and the Halstead Guardians accepted a plan submitted by William T Nash which was similar in design to Kempthorne's model which was basically two squares joined together. Although the Kempthorne design was a 'square' plan the majority of the designs of the other Essex workhouses favoured either the cruciform (cross) design or the 'X' shaped design or the 'Y' design. Which ever design was built, one of the objectives was to achieve a shape that allowed for separate exercise courtyards for the different categories of inmates. The location of the Union workhouse was a short distance from the town centre on the right hand side of the A604 road to Haverhill. At Halstead other ancillary buildings were built to the rear with the most important being the infectious wards in 1870 which became the basis of the new infirmary which was added to in 1893 and 1901.

1836
The Poor Law Commissioners' Second Annual Report

This government report includes various comments of clerks to the Guardians and one was by the clerk of the Halstead Union. He mentioned to the Commissioners that Ridgewell was one of the Halstead area's most pauperised parishes and a family ten, husband, wife and eight children, had recently been admitted to the workhouse (probably Halstead parish workhouse). As an example of the privations that the parish workhouse imposed, the family of ten only submitted to this regime for ten weeks which included ten hours a day working in the workhouse mill grinding corn. They all then left the workhouse but of course the Guardians would have made sure that the husband had a job to go to and the family were provided for even if out relief was to be given.

The census of 1841

The first census after the workhouse opened in 1838 listed the following:

Males	57	The total included 4 staff and 24 children under 14. The percentage of children to the total number of inmates was 26%
Females	41	
Total	98	

Although the Union workhouse was built to accommodate up to 300 inmates there were only 94 in 1841 excluding the staff three years after it opened.

Minutes of the 1850s

The following extracts are from the minutes of the 1850s and one of the major problems that faced workhouses in general and Halstead in particular was the isolating of typhus cases which initially were all housed with the other sick paupers in the infirmary which in the 1850s was not a separate building but all part of the double squared complex. The Guardians were well aware of this problem and this was brought to the fore in May 1853 which is recorded later in this section. Earlier in 1852 the Guardians decided to bring the problem of contagious diseases to the attention of the public.

Cholera precautions

The Guardians took the initiative to print 1000 hand bills which contained directions as to how to avoid cholera. Presumably these would be distributed through the sixteen parishes that made up the Union. The population of the area at the time was less than 20,000 and there were probably about 5,000 houses and so there was not a leaflet for each household but many people could not read anyway.

April 1852
Lunatics

Mention had been made in the first chapter that the Essex County Lunatic Asylum opened at Brentwood in 1853 and up to that date those that were mentally ill in the Halstead area were sent to the Hoxton Asylum. The minutes record that a cheque was sent to Hoxton in respect of the care and maintenance of James Evans and Sarah Prethloe lunatic paupers belonging to the Halstead Union.

May 1852
Appointment of a cook
A new master and matron (husband and wife) had recently been appointed to the workhouse and they had now asked the Guardians that in place of a nurse could they appoint a cook. The workhouse master pointed out that there was more of a need for a good cook than a nurse and that his wife was prepared to take on the responsibility of caring for those in the infirmary. The nurse, Mrs Traveller, agreed to this arrangement and was told that she could continue acting as the nurse for the time being. Presumably there was no official appointment for a cook at Halstead which was unusual as most workhouses employed such a person. A cook was appointed at a salary of £10 a year together with free board and lodging. The Guardians paid salaries quarterly and in 1853 the list of principal employees and their annual salaries appeared as follows:

Chaplain	£100	
Clerk to the Guardians	£100	
Relieving Officers (2)	£100	each
Master and Matron	£62	combined
Schoolmaster and Schoolmistress (husband and wife)	£65	combined
Porter	£15	
Nurse	£16	
Cook	£10	

The medical officer's salary is not mentioned but he is not employed the whole time in the workhouse. He would have had a salary for his responsibilities within the workhouse and there would have been various other medical officers responsible for the poor in the rural parishes. The salaries for these doctors were probably paid on an annual basis.

May 1852
Emigration of the Parmenter family
A Letter of Approval had been received from the Colonial Land and Emigration Committee agreeing that John Parmenter of Little Yeldham, his wife and three children could have passage to Adelaide, Australia. The family would receive a payment of three pounds ten shillings and it was agreed by the parish of Little Yeldham that they could be charged as part of their Poor Rate. Little Yeldham would happily agree to this one off payment as the Parmenter family would no longer be a charge on

their Poor Rate. It is not clear whether the Parmenters were all in the workhouse or in receipt of out relief and living in Little Yeldham.

A month later two more families thought that emigration would be a good idea and of course they would be transported half way around the world to start a new life and away from the workhouse or the stigma of being paupers and living off the parish. John Myer, his wife and four children, and William Hayes who also had a wife and four children, applied and received permission to emigrate. Both families were the responsibility of Halstead parish. Once again it is not clear whether all or part of the two families were in the workhouse but possibly at least someone from each family was an inmate. It was rather a coincidence that these applications should come so soon after the Parmenters had received permission to emigrate. In view of these two requests it probably means that at least one member of the Parmenter family was a workhouse inmate and the news had travelled around the other inmates. This time each family received £4 together with 'an extra £3 towards the expense of their outfits'. The total of £14 was charged to the Halstead poor relief.

July 1852
The porter
Henry Hudson, the porter, was reported to the Guardians for being drunk. The Guardians investigated the matter and the offence was confirmed. The porter was called before the Guardians and his resignation was requested. He was given four weeks notice to vacate his accommodation. At the expiry of the four week period the Guardians extended his period of notice until Michaelmas allowing him to continue in office provided he was of good conduct during this period. On the day of Michaelmas (29th September) the Guardians decided to let him stay in his job subject to there being no further problems. If the porter was reported again and the case was proven then he would be dismissed without notice.

Emigration policy
Two months after the Myer and Hayes families had emigrated to Australia the Guardians received a copy of a resolution by Halstead vestry that they had earmarked out of their Poor Rate £100 to assist any more families from Halstead parish that wished to emigrate.

September 1852
Stolen funds belonging to Ridgewell Parish
The clerk reported to the Guardians that the Union had not received the poor relief funds in the sum of £47 due from the parish of Ridgewell. The Guardians investigated the matter and found out that the overseer of the poor for Ridgewell, Joseph Chaplin, had collected the monies due but had used these funds for his own purposes. Mr Chaplin said that he intended to repay the monies out of the proceeds of his own crops but as it turned out he was unable to repay from this source. Consequently the Guardians applied to the local magistrate and obtained a warrant for possession of Mr Chaplin's effects. Apparently it transpired that the bailiffs took possession of sufficient goods to ensure that after all expenses the Union was reimbursed in full. The parish records for Ridgewell will record what happened to Mr Chaplin but it is very unlikely that he retained his position as overseer.

September 1852
Coffins
The Halstead Union minutes record at almost every meeting the approval of bills to be paid for the supply of food and provision and for the maintenance of the substantial Union building. An item which only cropped up occasionally was for the supply of coffins. The death rate of inmates was high as many were old and infirm when they came into the workhouse. Even the mortality rate of younger paupers was high mainly due to the poor medical expertise in the 1850s and consequently many died of illnesses that they would not die of today. The Union took delivery of three sizes of coffin and paid the supplier eight shillings for an adult coffin, four shillings for a coffin for an under 12 and two shillings for an under 5s coffin.

November 1852
Destitute wayfarers and wanderers
In November 1852 the Guardians wrote to the Poor Law Commission asking for their opinion on four cases of 'destitute wayfarers or wanderers' so designated under a recent Act of Parliament. As we have seen previously paupers in the workhouse are charged out to their respective parish and paid for by the local poor rate. The new Act allowed for tramps and the like to be paid for out of the Union's own funds if it can seen that the person has been away from their own parish for a number of years. The four tramps in question were now all in the Halstead Union Workhouse having returned to their own parish and from their being transferred to the workhouse.

The four cases were all fairly similar but that for Joseph Coller, aged 35 a batchelor, is typical. Mr Coller lived in a cottage in Castle Hedingham rented previously by his father. The father had died six years ago and the mother and son continued to live in the cottage for the next five years or so and managed to pay the rent. Their financial situation came to a point where mother and son became destitute and so the mother was taken into the workhouse and Joseph left the village to tramp the countryside selling door mats which he made himself from rushes gathered from the roadside. Joseph passed through Essex, Hertfordshire, Kent and London but was unable to afford proper lodgings and so lodged in outbuildings and stables. He became so destitute that he returned to Castle Hedingham six months later and from there was immediately transferred into the workhouse.

He stayed in the workhouse for two months and during that time Castle Hedingham was charged for his board and lodging. He left the workhouse and set off again selling his door mats sleeping once more in outbuildings. He was not away for long (it was November) and soon returned to Castle Hedingham and from there back into the workhouse again. Despite the hardships of the workhouse they were probably better than living in outbuildings during the winter of 1852. The Guardians told this story to the Commission and asked whether Castle Hedingham should be charged for his future keep or should it come out of Union funds.

Of the four cases the decision came through fairly quickly on two which said that the two men could be classified as 'destitute wanderers' and therefore Halstead workhouse would have to pay for their keep. For the case Joseph Coller and the other man the Commission wanted to know if either of the men had taken lodgings when they returned to their village. In both cases the Guardians replied that they had not taken lodgings which seem to be the crunch of the matter. The new law said that if the tramp returned to his village and was immediately transferred to the workhouse then the Union would pay for future board and lodging. If either man had taken lodgings before being transferred then the parish would pay. Both in the case of Joseph and the other man they had been transferred into the workhouse as soon as they arrived back in their village and so Castle Hedingham and the other parish did not have to pay for their future accommodation.

December 1852

Request for grant

The father of William Nash, aged 15, who resided in the workhouse and who originally came from Toppesfield approached the Guardians in

December 1852 for a grant for travel expenses for William to go and live with his uncle in Sheffield. The uncle had written a letter to the Guardians confirming that he would give William board and lodging. It is to be presumed that both father and son were inmates of the workhouse. The Guardians had obviously not come across this type of request before and so they wrote to the Commissioners for guidance. The reply was that the Guardians had no powers to grant travelling allowances but the only way that this could be achieved was for Toppesfield parish to pay out of their poor rates.

The following week there was a further approach and this time it came from William's mother and once again we do not know of her personal circumstances. The mother asked if William and his brother Lewis, aged 11, who we now know were both in the workhouse, could have travelling expenses to go and live with the mother's sister in Sheffield. It seems as if both William's father and mother came from the Sheffield area where their respective families still lived. Once again the Guardians said that they had no discretion to pay for travelling expenses but if these monies could be found from one source or another then the Union would pay for clothing for the two boys as there only clothes were workhouse uniforms which were not suitable for the outside world. Unfortunately the minutes do not say if this story had a happy ending.

February 1853
Complaint from workhouse master
The master complained to the Governors that the schoolmaster had refused to go with him on the rounds of the workhouse on Monday night - presumably this was the locking up procedure - and had also been insolent to him. The schoolmaster was summonsed to the Board and instructed to obey the request of the master but to report to them if he felt that the requests were unreasonable. This last bit about 'unreasonable requests' seemed a little odd when read but there was nothing further in the minutes over the next few months about both parties. Some months later though the master was found to be drunk and disorderly in the town of Halstead and had had a row with the schoolmaster. The Guardians investigated the matter and the master was dismissed. One wonders now whether the master was drunk at the time of the previous incident and the schoolmaster refused to do the rounds with him in view of his condition.

February 1853
The nurse
We had seen earlier in May 1852 that the nurse, Mrs Traveller, had been demoted when the matron took over her role although she was still paid

her salary of £16 a year. Mrs Traveller had now approached the Guardians for a testimonial as she was applying for the position of matron at Bedford Goal. This was readily given and the Guardians were obviously pleased that she was moving on as they had been paying her for nine months since May 1852 for a job that she was not doing although she was probably the assistant nurse to the workhouse master's wife who had taken on this role.

May 1853
Outbreak of typhus fever
The minutes record that the Guardians discussed the outbreak of typhus fever both in the workhouse and in the town and the medical officer reported that he felt it was not appropriate for the workhouse to take in any more paupers for the time being whilst the typhus was being dealt with. The following week the meeting was not held in the Union building but at the George Inn as the outbreak of typhus had worsened. The attendance at weekly meetings was usually just over half of the 23 elected Guardians but this particular week 19 of the Guardians attended. Maybe the Guardians felt that this important matter required their attendance or the George Inn was a much more amenable place for their weekly meeting than the forbidding workhouse and the possibility of catching something.

A deputation from the Local Board of Health also attended at the George and they asked the Guardians if a separate detached building could be provided as an infirmary for fever cases. The health authority also asked if two competent nurses could be employed from London to staff the suggested infirmary house. The Guardians said that would write to the Poor Law Commissioners for their approval of this expense.

The next week the Guardians met back in the workhouse and the minutes indicate that they did not get the approval they required but the Commission suggested that a separate part of the workhouse be used as a reception for fever cases. The Guardians wrote back to the Commission saying that there was no separate building within the workhouse that was suitable. The Guardians meanwhile called an extraordinary meeting when it was decided to use their small infirmary solely for typhus cases and move the other patients out. There is no record of a reply from the Commission to their last letter but they wrote again saying that they now had provided for 35 sick pauper cases and there were also 15 other persons with typhus who were being cared for within the workhouse complex. They re-iterated that they still felt that outside accommodation would be desirous.

There is no further mention of renting an outside detached property or the employment of extra nurses and presumably the Poor Law Commission would not approve this expense despite the further requests. Possibly the epidemic had reached its peak and the extra accommodation was no longer necessary. As was said at the start of this section Halstead's separate infirmary was not built until 1870.

The twentieth century
The census of 1901

Males	76	The total includes 8 staff and 14 children under 14. The percentage of children to the total number of inmates was 12%
Females	46	
Total	122	

Although the workhouse was built to take up to 300 inmates the actual number was one of the smallest in Essex in terms of the number of inmates with the total inmates only increasing from 94 in 1841 to 114 in 1901 excluding staff. Halstead also had in 1841 the lowest proportion of children of any of the 17 Union workhouses (26%) which fell to 12% by 1901.

1922
Closure of Halstead Union
The Halstead Union Workhouse was with Ongar, Dunmow and Witham the only four of the seventeen in Essex that did not last until 1930 when the Unions were abolished and the workhouses were incorporated into the more modern Essex hospital system. It was in 1916 that it was decided that the remaining 52 paupers in the Halstead workhouse would be accommodated in the Kedington (Suffolk) Union workhouse. During 1918 the old workhouse was used to house German prisoners of war who were working on local farms. Demolition of the workhouse took place in 1922.

The Lexdon and Winstree Union workhouse showing two of the accommodation
blocks joined to the central hub (see page 167)

Chapter 9

LEXDON, WINSTREE AND ITS ENVIRONS

PARISH WORKHOUSES

The following 36 parishes in the area surrounding Colchester were grouped together in 1834 following the Poor Law Amendment Act to form the Lexdon and Winstree Union. Before 1834 each parish may have had its own poorhouse or workhouse.

Abberton, Aldham, West Bergholt, Birch, Boxted, Brightlingsea, Mount Bures, Chappel, Copford, Dedham, East Donyland, Easthorpe, Fingringhoe, Fordham, Great Horkesley, Little Horkesley, Langenhoe, Langham, Layer-de-la-Haye, Layer Breton, Layer Marney, Marks Tey, East Mersea, West Mersea, Peldon, Salcott, Stanway, Great Tey, Little Tey, Virley, Wakes Colne, Great Wigborough, Little Wigborough, Wivenhoe and Wormingford.

The government undertook a survey of parish workhouses in 1777 and the following 17 parishes in this area had a workhouse open in that year.

Abberton	Aldham	Birch	Boxted
Bures	Copford	Dedham	Fordham
Gt Horkesley	Langham	Layer-de-la-Haye	W Mersea
Layer Marney	Stanway	Gt Tey	Wivenhoe
Gt Wigborough			

Like the Halstead area in the previous chapter, none of these rural parishes had a large population with Brightlingsea being the largest with about 1000 residents and all the others only having a few hundred inhabitants. It is surprising that Brightlingsea did not have a parish workhouse in 1777 although records show that one was established in the 1750s. Just under half of the 36 parishes had a workhouse which is a very high proportion reflecting the economic situation in the area in this part of the eighteenth century with the decline of the spinning and weaving industry.

Brightlingsea

Brighlingsea workhouse was probably opened in 1751 as a lease was granted to the parish for eleven years from this date. The location was on Hurst Green. The workhouse though does not appear in the government's list of Essex workhouses in 1777. It is possible that the workhouse was closed in 1777 or the overseer failed to complete the return for in a few years later the workhouse was functioning again.

A new Agreement in 1781 was made with the workhouse master who was to be paid £200 a year to feed and cloth the paupers in the workhouse. Mr John Burrows, the new master, was also obliged to give the inmates three hot meals a week and on the other days cold meat. For breakfast he was to provide bread and cheese. For those inmates who had to be transported to a magistrate for examination or transfer to another parish then this expense was to be payable by Mr Burrows. With regard to the medical care of inmates, Mr Burrows was to employ 'a surgeon and apothecary' at his expense which would include the mending of broken bones and attending to smallpox cases.

It was unusual for workhouse masters to be paid an annual amount to cover a multitude of expenses and the more usual arrangement was that made with another master in 1822. He was paid three shillings per inmate per week for food only with clothing and other expenses to be paid for by the parish.

Brighlingsea workhouse survived until the 1830s but did not feature in Lexden's plans for temporary accommodation for the poor pending the building of the Union workhouse. The Brightlingsea workhouse was converted into cottages in the late 1830s. The reason for not using the Brighlingsea workhouse was possibly because Brighlingsea was some distance from the other four that were to be used by the new Union which was partly borne by the fact that Brighlingsea was transferred to the Tendring Union at a later date.

Copford

In 1753 the parish sold two of their other parish poor houses and with the proceeds converted and enlarged a further house owned by the parish into a workhouse.

An inventory taken in 1816 showed that the property had four/five rooms downstairs and four rooms upstairs. On the ground floor there was the mistress's room, the work room, the kitchen, the brew house, the parlour and the pantry. Upstairs there were four bedrooms. In 1777 the workhouse could accommodate up to 30 inmates, which seems rather high, although the actual numbers ranged from only five to twenty two during the period 1813 to 1824. In the years running up to closure in the 1830s the numbers dropped to only ten inmates on average.

The cost of providing board and lodging to those in the workhouse was five shillings per head although this figure did fall to three shillings and nine pence per head by the time the workhouse closed. The total cost to the parish of running the workhouse was though only ten per cent of the total spent on poor relief.

Poor Rate Expenditure

Workhouse	10%
Regular out-relief payments	25%
Casual out-relief payments	65%

For those parishioners who were not actually residing in the workhouse but in receipt of parish relief it was usual for the acting overseer to pay these people every Monday morning at the parish workhouse. The workhouse existed until the late 1830s and was used as temporary accommodation for the paupers until the new Union workhouse was built.

Dedham

Dedham seems to have used two sites as a workhouse although the three timber framed cottages which were described as a former workhouse on sale in 1840 were possibly only poorhouses used by the parish to house pauper families. The cottages were sited on Dedham Heath and these are possibly those used from the 1670s for this purpose and held by the churchwardens at this time.

The parish subsequently converted a house on Crown Street in 1725 for a workhouse although this may have been the first proper workhouse with a workhouse master. The property was enlarged in 1730 with the help of money given by a benefactor, John Freeman, who was a churchwarden at the time. The other churchwarden was Jas Godherd whose initials were on the original building before enlargement by John Freeman. Presumably Mr Godherd paid for the building of the original property and Mr Godherd its enlargement.

An agreement with a new master in 1775 allowed him one shilling a week to feed and cloth his inmates. The inventory taken at the time showed that in the workroom there were 20 spinning wheels and 4 looms and there was a further room in the house for this purpose. The workhouse was large compared with other village workhouse and could accommodate up to 48 inmates in 1777. The large potential numbers reflected the current economic position with the downturn in the weaving industry. By the early 1800s the parish had diversified somewhat by setting up a sack manufacturing unit and a starching room. The spinning room was still in operation but not to the level of the previous century.

The 1800s also saw a fall in the number of paupers in the workhouse with the average being between 20 and 30. The workhouse existed until the late 1830s when the Lexden & Winstree Union was formed and used for a while until the new Union workhouse was built.

Langham

There have survived very few parish records for the parish of Langham and it has not been possible to establish when the parish workhouse was established. It was definitely in existence in 1777 as it is mentioned in the government survey of that year which stated that the workhouse could accommodate up to 25 inmates. This means that the size of the property must have been the equivalent of two or three cottages. The location was probably at Langham Moor where it is recorded that bread was distributed to those other parishioners on out-relief. The overseer invariably used the parish workhouse as his distribution centre. 'Workhouse Field' was close to Langham Moor which bears out the possible location.

By 1813 there were only 13 inmates in the workhouse but it did survive until 1834 when it was taken over by the Lexden & Winstree Union.

Great Tey

Great Tey did not have a parish workhouse but there are some interesting figures on the number of poor in the village.

	1729	1805
Rate payers	244	216
Weekly out relief	39	54
Occasional relief	33	256
Neither paid rates nor on relief	80	Nil

Whilst the data for 1729 was what one would expect from any Essex village in the early part of the eighteenth century, with 80 not paying any rates nor on poor relief and a further 70 plus on some sort of relief, the figures for 1805 show a completely different picture. The number of ratepayers and those poor on regular weekly out relief has changed little but those on occasional poor relief have increased considerably resulting in more than half the population having financial relief at some time or other. The reason for this situation in Great Tey, which mirrored the position in many Essex villages, was the effect of the wars on the continent. Trade with Europe was stagnant, wages were low and the price of bread was high due to the escalating price of flour.

Wivenhoe

There is a deed in the Essex Record Office which recites the granting to the poor of the parish of Wivenhoe a cottage for their use. The deed is dated the 13 April 1726 and the cottage lay between Wivenhoe Heath and Wivenhoe Cross. The cottage was converted into a workhouse. At this stage the cottage may have accommodated 10 or 15 inmates but in 1750 the parish decided to build a new workhouse but in the end extended the existing premises. There were between 20 and 25 inmates in the 1750s although in the government survey of 1777 the records show that the workhouse could accommodate up to 30 paupers. In the 1760s the parish appointed a new master who was previously a bay weaver from Colchester. The workhouse master and his wife were both to be competent in spinning and to teach the inmates. Spinning wheels were a standard part of any workhouse inventory. In the 1760s the records show that there were four weddings of workhouse inmates although it is not known if both parties were from within the workhouse. The parish paid for the expense of these weddings which may have been in their own interest if it meant that the parties would have set up home outside the workhouse and no longer been a burden on the parish.

By 1798 the number in the workhouse had fallen to a maximum of 16 although in the early part of the nineteenth century numbers rose again due to the effect of high inflation due to the wars in Europe. The workhouse master was allowed three shillings per inmate for food and clothing in 1807 although in later years the allowance per inmate fluctuated according to the price of flour.

The workhouse survived until 1834 when it came under the control of the Lexden & Winstree Union. When the new Union workhouse was built the parish workhouse was sold.

THE LEXDEN AND WINSTREE UNION WORKHOUSE

Lexden and Winstree Union Workhouse was situated on the west of Colchester on the London Road (the old A12) in the parish of Stanway and whereas the Colchester Union Workhouse looked after all the paupers principally within the confines of the town of Colchester, the Lexdon and Winstree Union Workhouse drew all their inmates from 35 rural parishes around Colchester.

Each parish provided one representative as Guardians with three justifying an extra representative by virtue of the size of their population-Brightlingsea, Dedham and Wivenhoe - making a total of 38 Guardians. The whole 35 parishes only had a total population of just under 20,000 in the 1830s with Brightlingsea being the largest with 1800 people and Mount Bures having about 260. Mount Bures incidentally is situated north west of Colchester abutting the Suffolk border and adjacent to Bures which is across the county boundary. The population of these 35 rural parishes changed very little from the 1831 census figures to 1930 when the workhouse was handed over to Essex County Council. Brightlingsea parish was subsequently transferred to the Tendring Union.

The new Guardians first met on the 2nd February 1836 at the Three Cups public house in Colchester although subsequently the Guardians met in the Colchester Union Board Room until their own board room was ready. After all the usual appointment of Guardians to various committees the Board first considered the existing parish workhouses and discussed the situation regarding those at Dedham and Langham. Later the workhouses at Copford and Wivenhoe were inspected to see if they were still suitable to take in paupers.

The Guardians' board room and the administration offices

The Union workhouse chapel

In these early days of the new Union the paupers that were on out-relief were asked to attend a meeting of the Guardians in groups so that their financial situation could be reviewed and their out-relief could be confirmed. As an example, forty five paupers from Dedham parish were ordered to attend the next meeting which was a special meeting out of sequence with the ordinary Guardian's meeting. It is not clear from the minutes whether these 45 residents were all on out-relief or included those in the parish workhouse.

The Guardians were now providing the food and clothing for all four of the parish workhouses which included cloth for making a uniform for males and females which would ultimately become the standard uniform in the new workhouse.

March 1836

Appointment of Workhouses Masters and Matrons

The following appointment was made:

Dedham	Master	Robert Dodd	Salary p.a.	£40
	Matron	Mrs Dodd		£40
Langham	Master	H Everitt		£26
	Matron	Mary Everitt		£26
Copford	Matron	Henry Hart		£26
	Matron	Mary Hart		£26
Wivenhoe	Master	George Philbrick		£30
	Matron	Martha Philbrick		£30

The salary must reflect the relative sizes of these parish workhouses which are now controlled by the new Lexden & Winstree Union. Back in 1777 Dedham parish workhouse was the largest of the four accommodating up to 48 inmates and it would appear that it was still the largest in 1836 with its salaries of £40. Langham could only take up to 25 inmates in 1777 and the indication is that it did not get any larger by 1836 and so the salaries were only £26 in 1836. In these first couple of months of their existence there were no plans yet in place for the new workhouse and so the Guardians had decided to instal a hand crank mill at the Dedham workhouse for the purpose of grinding and dressing corn. The cost together with associated equipment was contracted at a sum of £90.

May 1836

Having got all the administration matters sorted out the Guardians now involved themselves in the acquisition of a piece of land at Stanway for the new Union workhouse. The appointed architects were Messrs Foden and Henman and the building was constructed at a cost of £6,800. The location was on the south side of the London Road at Stanway which is 4 miles west of Colchester. The design could accommodate up to 330 inmates. The layout of the workhouse was rather unusual as the standard design, as employed in most of the Essex workhouses, was either a cruciform design inside a square or a 'Y' design inside a hexagon. For Lexden and Winstree though the design was an 'X' inside an octagon. The cross wings inside the outer wall were of three storeys with the outer wall buildings being single storey. The common feature though in all the Essex workhouses, whatever the design, was that the separate exercise yards for the inmates were enclosed by the outer walls. The administration block, the porter's room and reception rooms were on the northern side of the outer wall. This building though was of two storeys with the Guardian's board room and the clerk's office on the first floor. The master's quarters were at the hub of the cruciform with windows on all sides in order that he could see into all the exercise yards.

The workhouse opened in 1837 and the first national census after this date was in 1841 by which time all the four parish workhouses had been closed and the inmates were accommodated in the new Lexden workhouse. In the first chapter the four parish workhouses in the survey of 1777 are listed as capable of accommodating up to a total of 133 inmates. They may not of course have been working to capacity in 1777 but it does appear that paupers' numbers had dropped slightly by 1841.

The census of 1841 - Lexdon & Winstree Union Workhouse

Males	57	The total includes 7 staff and 38 children
Females	44	Under 14. The percentage of children to the total number of inmates was 40%
Total	101	

Twenty years on from the 1841 census the numbers had changed dramatically and the following statistics are taken from the April 1861 census. The census data shows that there were seven on the staff and 238 inmates. The 1860s were the peak period for the workhouse with the number of inmates falling thereafter. The staff was as follows:

Master	William Kingsbury	age 48	Married
Matron	Catherine Kingsbury	44	Married
Schoolmaster	Edward Griffiths	20	Single
Schoolmistress	Mary Ann Palmer	24	Single
Porter	Thomas Spooner	22	Single
Nurse	Lucy Grimwood	46	Widow
Cook	Jane Southgate	18	Single

One wonders what experience the 20 year old schoolmaster would have had before taking up the position and similarly the 18 year old cook. The schoolmaster and mistress had 56 children to teach ranging in age from six to fourteen and the cook, with assistants, was catering daily for well over 200 people.

The breakdown of the 238 inmates was as follows:

Orphans	56	(aged 6 to 14)
Single males	22	
Single females	29	
Widowers	19	
Widows	15	
Families	97	(husbands/wives/children)
Total	238	

The 'Families' were 26 family units ranging from just a husband and wife through to a large family of up to eight with the children all being under the age of six. There were a number, as to be expected in the workhouse, of single parent families ranging from a mother with up to four children or in one case a father with four children.

I have looked at the Guardian's minutes for the 1860s to get a picture of what sort of problems were being presented to the Board in this period.

November 1861
Out-relief
The minutes list the number of families in receipt of out-relief in this month and the reason they are in receipt of assistance. Thirty eight families were in receipt of benefit for the following reasons:

Husband ill   12   Wife ill   16   Children ill   10

One of the families listed above was the Harrison family of Pitsea. Eliza Harrison was 32 and had three children aged 10, 8 and 1 year old. The Guardians ordered that they be relieved as non-resident paupers with an allowance of three shillings a week and three loaves.

February 1862
Vaccination centres
The Union area was divided up into nine district and there was a medical officer appointed for each district. Vaccination against infectious diseases was now common throughout Essex and the workhouse Guardians set up addresses where local inhabitants could be vaccinated. Each district had at least two addresses where vaccinations took place and these were usually the medical officer's surgery and the house where out-relief was paid out. The Guardians also laid down some rules as to when vaccinations shall take place and how much the medical officer would be paid. Vaccinations would be conducted on the second Monday in April and the third Monday in October and on successive Mondays until there was no longer any demand. The rate of pay to the medical officer would be two shillings and six pence irrespective of whether the vaccination was carried out at the designated location or in the home of the recipient. The cost of the vaccinations would be added to that parish's rate bill.

March 1862
Salary increase for master and matron
The Guardians had written to the Poor Law Commissioners for permission to increase the salary of the master and matron to £100. Whilst agreeing to this proposal the Commissioners wished the salary to be split between the husband and wife at the discretion of the Guardians. It was agreed that the master would receive £65 a year and the matron £35 a year.

April 1862

Election of Guardians

The election of the 38 Guardians took place every year and it seems as if there was seldom any voting as usually the number of nominations equalled the number of Guardians required. Probably the nomination for any particular parish was sorted out at parish level and consequently the election at the Guardian's meeting was just a formality. For the 1862 elections though there were only 35 nominations with the parishes of Easthorpe, Layer Marney and Little Horkesley not providing a candidate. The Guardians met every week and although there was never a 100% attendance those elected to the position must either be retired or have had a job where they could take every Monday off. Off the 38 Guardians elected their occupations were as follows:

Farmers	21	Plumber	1
Clerks	9	Miller	1
Gentleman	1	Ropemaker	1
Builders	1	No nominations	3

By September the three vacancies had still not been filled and consequently the Guardians had the power to instruct the parishes to hold a public election to fill the places. Of the 35 elected representatives of the parishes the attendance at the weekly meeting was usually low with only about 12/14 attending on a regular basis notwithstanding that the majority were farmers and probably more able than most to attend. A year later when Guardians were elected in April 1863 Layer Marney and Little Horkesley had filled their places with farmers but Easthorpe still did not have a representative. Presumably the parish election did not bring forth a candidate.

June 1862

Inspector of Nuisances

Earlier in the month the Guardians looked into a case of 'inmate nuisance' but at that time did nothing about it. An Act had been passed in 1855 covering disturbances of this nature and the proceedings that could be taken against inmates. The Guardians decided to appoint an Inspector of Nuisances and the job went to John Death of Wivenhoe who was appointed for a period of three months and assumed all the powers of the Board of Guardians. John Death was to be paid ten shillings for every case he was asked to investigate and to take to court if necessary. No sooner had John been appointed than he submitted a report to the Guardians regarding Samuel Sargent of Stanway where he found 'no nuisance'. It looks as if his powers extended to paupers who were on out-relief as well as those in the workhouse. Later in the month the inspector dealt with a case that appeared to be unconnected with a workhouse owned property. One of the roles of the Guardians was to keep an eye on the health of the local population and in particular to deal with matters which were health problems and could cause disease. The case the inspector had to deal with which was unconnected with the workhouse was most likely a local resident who, for example, would not clear a ditch or was causing a health hazard by throwing refuse into a ditch.

Disparity in out-relief

A committee had been set up by the Guardians to look into various disparities in out-relief between the various districts as administered by the relieving officers. It appears that every case of out-relief was investigated over the three out-relief districts and the following recommendations were made:

Phebe Silby	a reduction of one shilling in her casual relief
Thomas Goody	to be offered two shillings a week and one loaf weekly or admittance to the House (workhouse)
Thomas Hibbs	to have four shillings a week as permanent allowance and nothing extra
Mary Aldridge	to have one shilling and six pence weekly and two loaves as permanent relief and nothing extra
Widow Aldridge	to have one shilling a week instead of meat
Ann Hills	to have two shillings a week and a loaf with no extra relief

Three of the cases investigated said specifically that there was to be no extra relief and maybe the relieving officer occasionally allowed these people extra cash. Thomas Goody was made an offer of relief and if he did not accept it then he would be admitted to the workhouse. The committee's report after mentioning the above specific cases generalised on what they had found throughout the Union area. They were critical of the relieving officer of the second district who, they felt, was too generous in his allowances and also carried on with the allowances too long. The reason the report gave was that the relieving officer had made insufficient enquiries into the family to gauge the relief required. The report was also critical of some of the medical officers who were also issuing medical certificates for relief 'without due consideration'. The recommendations of the committee included some criticism of the Guardians who were not vetting correctly some out-relief cases who the

Relieving Officer considered should be on permanent relief. It was also recommended that when the medical officer recommended an allowance of meat that this case should be brought to the Guardians for sanction. Finally some cases of relief were chargeable to the Common Fund of the workhouse accounts rather than to a specific parish and it was considered that these expenses should be vetted by the Guardians.

Health hazard

June 1862 was a busy month for the Guardians as following on from the inspector's work mentioned above they now received a letter from the vicar at Peldon reporting that there was 'an accumulation of filth in a ditch adjoining the dwelling houses situated near to the Plough in Peldon as to be a nuisance'. This type of nuisance has occurred in various minutes of Union workhouses and it seems that although the premises concerned had no connection with the workhouse the Guardians had a responsibility to the public to deal with cases where an infectious disease may break out. It was not until ten years later in 1872 that the Public Health Act was passed which officially passed health matters to the Union Guardians. The Guardians in this case handed the matter over to the Nuisance Inspector. A follow up report from Mr Death a month later said that the land agent responsible for the property had undertaken to clear the ditch and therefore no further action would be taken.

September 1862

Complaint from Widow Ellis of Wivenhoe

Widow Ellis had complained direct to the Poor Law Commissioners and they had passed the letter to the Guardians. It is most likely that she did not write the letter herself but this was done by someone else that knew the system who was most likely to have been her vicar. She complained that her out-relief had been stopped. The Guardians made enquiries into the case and found that it was possible for her to conduct her employment and make a living wage without the need for out-relief. She said in her letter that she was not able to walk backwards and forwards for her work and therefore was unable to carry out her employment. Although the minutes do not specify what work was being carried out at her home it was probably connected with the woollen industry and in the opinion of the Guardian this could be undertaken without walking 'backwards and forwards'. The Guardians reported back to the Commissioners that they were satisfied that the discontinuance of the relief was justified. They also added that they had offered Widow Ellis the House (workhouse) if she so wished but this had been declined.

December 1862

Out of the workhouse for Christmas

The Guardians considered the case of Joseph Tampin of Abberton who had left the workhouse and gone to live with his daughter somewhere within the Tendring Union area. They would have made sure first that he would be looked after and they now agreed a weekly allowance of two shillings and six pence to be paid by the Tendring Union which would be chargeable back to the Lexden Union as Joseph had Abberton as his settled parish.

February 1863

Complaint against medical officer

Mr Locke, one of the medical officers, replied to a complaint regarding his attendance on Mrs Webber. Apparently he had made out a prescription for Mrs Webber but had not actually attended her until the following day due to his own ill health. The Guardians considered there had been "some remissiveness" (incorrect spelling) on the part of Mr Lock and he was issued with a reprimand reminding him of his responsibilities. Although the details of the complaint are not recorded one can assume that the problem was that the doctor prescribed medicine without seeing the patient.

March 1863

Further complaint against Mr Locke the medical officer

The letter of complaint said that Mr Locke was sent for on the morning of 13 March as one of the Taylor nine children of Aldham was suffering from scalatina (scarlet fever). By 4pm the doctor had not attended and so Mr Taylor sent one of his other children to find him. He was located at the Queens Head in Aldham. He attended the child but all the parties that came in contact with him that afternoon concluded that he was intoxicated. The Guardians sent a copy of the letter to Mr Locke for his reply. Mr Locke replied but the Board considered his reply and his conduct in the matter unsatisfactory. No action was taken on the matter notwithstanding that this was the second complaint in two months. All the clerk was instructed to do was to keep the details to hand should there be a further complaint. I feel sure that at any other Union he would have been dismissed.

May 1863

Smallpox cases in Colchester

It had been brought to the attention of the Guardians that there were cases of smallpox in Colchester. The clerk was instructed to write to all the medical officers drawing their attention to the matter and to instruct them to take whatever measures they considered necessary to stop the disease spreading to the Lexden area.

Inmate statistics

It was noted above that the 1861 census saw the maximum number of inmates in the Lexden Workhouse and that numbers fell thereafter. Herewith the figures up to 1901.

Number of inmates	1841	94
	1861	238
	1871	193
	1891	136
	1901	124

The twentieth century
The 1901 census

Males	76	The total includes 6 staff and 18 children under 14. The
Females	54	percentage of children to the total number of inmates was 14%
Total	130	

Included in the census figures for 1901 were five tramps who recorded their places of birth as:

Nottingham, Stratford (London), Woodbridge Suffolk, Little Holland and the City of London

June 1926
Vagrants

By the twentieth century there were few 'paupers' in Union workhouses as they had taken on the role more of a hospital for the old and infirm rather than a home for the poor. It is surprising though that a clerk's minute in June 1926 referred to the number of vagrants being offered relief which numbered 205 for a two week period compared with a similar period in 1924 when only 67 obtained relief. For 1926 this means that on average 14 vagrants a day were being admitted overnight into the workhouse. The reason, said the report, was because 'neighbouring (vagrant) wards had been closed and the recent industrial conditions in the country'. The report was probably referring to the nearby Colchester Union Workhouse and the 'industrial conditions' were the General Strike which occurred in the same year as the June 1926 report.

1928

Smallpox

Smallpox was always a problem in many of the Essex Union Workhouses in the nineteenth century but this infectious disease reared its ugly head once more in the twentieth century when in 1928 the Guardians of Lexden sent a letter to all the other Essex Unions advising them that they had a suspected case of smallpox in their Casual Ward and that this ward was now temporarily closed.

26 March 1930

Last meeting of Guardians

The Guardians' minutes for all the Essex workhouses were of course written out by hand by the clerk from the 1830s up to the early part of the twentieth century. On the whole the minutes were very legible and apart from one or two Unions the minutes contained detailed information on the various incidents in the workhouse which have formed the basis of this book. By the 1920s and up to the time of the last Guardian's meeting the minutes were being typed and apart from financial matters and reports from various committees there was little or no information about individual workhouse cases. Children were no longer in workhouses and we have the Children's Act of 1908 to thank for that. There were Old Age Pensions and State Insurance Benefits to take care of the sick and unemployed and consequently the role of the workhouse Guardians was coming to an end and there were no more snippets of information about individual cases.

Chapter 10

MALDON AND ITS ENVIRONS

PARISH WORKHOUSES

The following 32 parishes in the above area were grouped together in 1834 following the Poor Law Amendment Act to form the Maldon Union. Before 1834 each parish have had its own poorhouse or workhouse.

Althorne, Asheldham, Bradwell, Burnham. Cold Norton, Creeksea, Dengie, Goldhanger, Hazeleigh, Heybridge, Langford, Latchingdon, Maldon All Saints, Maldon St Marys, Maldon St Peters, Mayland, Mundon, North Fambridge, Purleigh, St Lawrence, Southminster, Steeple, Stow Maries, Tillingham, Tollesbury, Tolleshunt D'Arcy, Tolleshunt Knights, Tolleshunt Major, Great Totham, Little Totham, Woodham Mortimer and WoodhamWalter.

Later additions were the parishes of:

Gt Braxted   Lt Braxted   Ulting   Wickham Bishops

The government undertook a survey of parish workhouses in 1777 and the following 14 parishes in this area had a workhouse open in that year.

Burnham	Goldhanger	Maldon
Purleigh	Southminster	Steeple
Stow Maries	Tillingham	Tolleshunt Major
Tolleshunt d'Arcy	Tollesbury	Gt Totham
Lt Totham	Woodham Ferres	

In 1777 the survey data shows that the Steeple and Tillingham workhouses could accommodate up to six persons whereas that for Stow Maries d'Arcy could take up to ten inmates. It is probable that in these three cases the respective parishes may not have appointed a workhouse master in view of their small size. The properties were probably a single cottage owned by the parish where the local overseer supervised the inmates and arranged for work to be carried out by the able-bodied. It is probable that the paupers did not live at these three 'workhouses' but just used them as a place to carry out work in return for financial relief from the overseer.

Maldon

Maldon Parish Workhouse which later became The Union Workhouse

Maldon parish workhouse was built in 1719 on Market Hill following the bequest of Thomas Plume who died in 1704. In his will he directed that a workhouse be built for the poor of Maldon. The workhouse took inmates that were resident in the three historic Maldon parishes of All Saints, St Peter's and St Mary's.

It was normal for each parish to look after its own sick residents whether they be admitted to the local parish workhouse due to being ill and out of work or they were in receipt of out-relief for the same reason. The Maldon parish workhouse was the only one built in the Maldon as early as the 1720s and there seems to have been a problem regarding who was being admitted. Possibly the workhouse was taking sick paupers from parishes outside Maldon which prompted the parish vestry of Maldon to issue a new instruction. The parish 'resolved that no person whatsoever, young or old, having the small pox come out on them or being reasonably judged to be in danger of the smallpox and also that no person whatsoever being sick of any distemper shall be admitted into the workhouse, other than the parish poor of the three parishes'. Presumably the workhouse was becoming overcrowded with sick paupers of other parishes which prompted the parish vestry to issue this new directive that only the sick paupers of the Maldon parishes of All Saints, St Mary and St Peters could be admitted.

In 1726 Widow Hurrell was appointed mistress of the workhouse at a salary of £6 per year. Probably at this time the workhouse could accommodate up to about 30 inmates which was probably as many as one person could cope with. The workhouse was enlarged in 1750 to include the workhouse master's and wife's accommodation and at the west end a new extension was built which included cellars and a kitchen. The government survey of 1777 indicated that the workhouse could cater for up to 40 inmates although by 1792 the number had dropped on average to only 23 inmates. The parish records give details of the number of inmates during the period 1811 to 1816 which show some interesting fluctuations. Basically the average number of inmates was increasing dramatically over the five year period with an increase in the numbers over the winter periods. The summer of 1813 averaged 26 inmates rising to 61 over the winter period and falling back to 35 in the following summer. With many residents classed as agricultural labourers there was little work in the winter months, especially as winters were a lot more severe than they are now, and consequently numbers in the workhouse were bound to increase for the winter period.

Summer	1811	average number of inmates	18
Winter	1811/12		23
Summer	1812		21
Winter	1812/13		25
Summer	1813		26
Winter	1813/14		61
Summer	1814		35
October	1815		49
March	1816		89

The town of Maldon was originally made up of three ecclesiastical parishes and there were three parish churches. Eventually the ecclesiastical parishes of All Saints' and St Peter combined at the higher end of the town with the parish and the church of St Mary being down by the river. It seems that in 1813 there were two governors appointed to administer the workhouse representing the two halves of the town but these arrangements did not prove to be a success in the early 1800s. The parish vestry of St Peter, in agreement with the parishes of All Saints and St Mary, decided to only have one governor/workhouse master to run the workhouse. Richard Arnold got the job at a salary of fifty guineas a year. The expenses of the workhouse would be charged out to the three parishes in proportion to the number of their inmates.

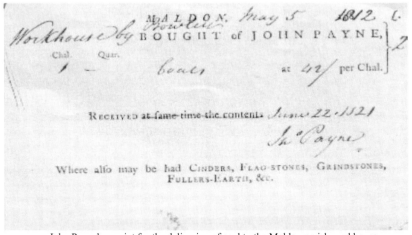

John Payne's receipt for the delivering of coal to the Maldon parish workhouse

Bradwell Juxta Mare

Bradwell does not feature in the government list of workhouse in 1777 as it was not built until some time after September 1787. The resolution said that 'it was unanimously agreed by the churchwardens, overseers and chief inhabitants...........to build a workhouse for the necessary reception of the poor of the parish'. As an afterthought, and in a different hand, the words 'with the consent of the neighbouring magistrate' were added. The workhouse was of an average size compared with other rural Essex workhouses and could accommodate probably up to a maximum of 20/30 inmates although in size it was the equivalent of a block of four up and four down cottages with an extra loft room.

The overseer's accounts contain the official agreement with the master of the workhouse in 1808. James Dobson signed the agreement which allowed him four shillings and six pence per head from which to feed the inmates with the parish providing clothing, coal and wood. The master agreed to provide three hot dinners a week and other meals at his discretion. The parish was to provide 'implements of all description for manufacturing' with any profit from the sales to be retained by the master. The inmates were to be brought to church every Sunday by the master.

The parish vestry took an inventory of the workhouse in 1812. The rooms are named and the layout seems to be that there were four rooms on the ground floor, four on the first floor and three garret rooms together with a cellar.

Ground floor	Great lower room, Keeping room, Brewing kitchen,
First floor	Masters sleeping room, four further bed chambers
Garrett	Two bed chambers and a lumber room
Cellar	

The bedrooms were small with no more than three beds in each and it is noted that in the lumber room there were six spinning wheels and three old chairs and an old kneading trough. Spinning had long since declined and the wheels had been relegated to the junk room. When the workhouse was sold off in 1844 the plan showed that the building was about 50 feet long and 26 feet deep (15.4 metres x 8 metres). The workhouse was converted into four cottages.

Burnham

In March 1730 the parish vestry agreed that the almshouses could be converted in a workhouse for the poor of the parish. By 1753 the parish vestry agreed to the expense of setting up the workhouse with spinning wheels with the income from the sale of any goods to be set off against the general running of the workhouse.

Most parish vestries took an inventory of their workhouse at some time or another and besides seeing what the workhouse contained the inventory also listed the rooms to give a good idea of the size of the property. The Burnham inventory of 1760 listed up to five rooms on the ground floor and four bedchambers upstairs. From the number of beds it did not seem that the workhouse could house more than 10 inmates but the government survey of 1777 recorded that the maximum capacity was 40 inmates.

Latchingdon

There are no available records to say when the workhouse was built but the parish workhouse was not open at the time of the government survey in 1777 but opened subsequently and was still operating when the new Maldon Union was formed in 1835. There are overseers' records in existence for the 1830s which show that between 1832 to 1836 the number in the workhouse fluctuated between seven and fourteen inmates. The new Maldon Union in 1836 did not select the Latchingdon workhouse to carry on operating pending enlargement of the Maldon parish workhouse and consequently the remaining 10 inmates in January 1836 were transferred to one of the other four workhouses in the area depending on their sex and age. The workhouse was probably the size of two cottages of the two up two down variety.

Purleigh

Purleigh parish workhouse is shown on a map of the parish dated 1815 as being at the north end of Howe Green Road near to the junction of Church Hill and The Glebe. The workhouse was built by at least 1777 as the government survey of that year quoted the workhouse as housing up to 20 inmates. Comparing this number with other workhouses the size would have been the equivalent of about two or three terraced cottages. Overseer's bills for the year 1786 refer to a property, on more than one occasion, as the 'old workhouse' although other references for work done at the workhouse in the same year just refer to the building as 'the workhouse'. There may have been a previous property owned by the parish that was referred to as the 'old'. but on one of the bills the overseer has referred to both 'the workhouse' and 'the old workhouse' Of the many items supplied to the workhouse and paid for by the parish one was a 'pint of gin for the workhouse' - for the master or the inmates? - and another was the fee for attending to Mary Brand who had the smallpox.

The overseer's records contain a list of all the inmates of the workhouse and their clothing requirements for the year 1815. There were a total of 18 persons made up of ten males, six females and two children belonging to Sarah Stebbing who was one of the female inmates.

The parish vestry made a new agreement with the workhouse master in 1825 based on the price of flour. The weekly rate per inmate was to be four shillings each when flour was sixty shillings per sack with the weekly rate rising or falling by three pence per inmate when the price of flour went up or down by five shillings per sack. In 1825 there were 16 inmates.

Southminster

The parish vestry passed a resolution on the 15th June 1721 to build a workhouse. The resolution referred to 'the multitude of poor in the parish' Although they use the words 'forthwith erected' the resolution goes on to instruct the churchwardens and the overseers to 'purchase some convenient house or houses'. The parish vestry completed their arrangements to either build or buy by September 1722 as the first workhouse master was appointed in that month. The wording used in the agreement was that Joseph Butcher was to be the 'sole master of the workhouse now erected'. The inference is that the parish had a purpose built workhouse erected. The minutes of 1729 show that Mr Butcher was still running the workhouse seven years later. Some years later the parish had been left some money and in addition to giving coal to the poor of the parish there was sufficient money to appoint a schoolmaster to teach the poor children of the parish in reading writing and arithmetic.

The government survey of parish workhouses in 1777 records that the Southminster workhouse was capable of taking a maximum of 30 inmates.

The parish entered into a new agreement in 1800 with John and Elizabeth Wash as workhouse master and mistress. Among the various arrangements was that the workhouse master and his wife should 'learn all the children and persons sent to them to spin'. It seems that, in addition to inmates having to work spinning, other paupers receiving out-relief had to work in the workhouse during the hours from 8am to 4pm with half an hour for breakfast and one hour for dinner during the winter months. During the summer the hours were from 6am to 6pm with the same meal breaks. Finally the agreement said that 'the old people and children should be sent to church every Sunday neat and clean and without any excuse sickness excepted'.

The overseer's account book includes an inventory of the workhouse taken in 1801. There were three rooms on the ground floor and three bedrooms above which only seemed to have ten beds in total. This was a lot less than the maximum capacity in 1777. Southminster workhouse does not get a mention when the new Maldon Guardians took over in 1835 and presumably it had either closed some time earlier or it did not feature in their plans for the future.

Tolleshunt d'Arcy

The overseer's account book mentions the parish workhouse in 1764 and it was probably built a few years earlier. A vestry minute of 1769 records that no 'out of workhouse' relief (out-relief) shall be allowed except as agreed by the parish vestry. Probably this special minute was prompted by the overseers giving relief without authority. The minute went on to record that the churchwardens and the overseers, and any parishioners who wished, should attend the workhouse every Monday at 5pm to consider workhouse expenditure and applications for out-relief. The workhouse inmates were referred to as 'the family'.

The government survey of parish workhouses in 1777 recorded that Tolleshunt d'Arcy workhouse could house up to 10 inmates with the same number recorded for Tolleshunt Major. The government survey included some mistakes and, as with other parishes in Essex with similar names, the listing probably refers to just the one workhouse at Tolleshunt d'Arcy which, for pauper purposes, incorporated Tolleshunt Major.

An inventory of 1778 showed that there were about five rooms on the ground floor with a similar number of bedrooms above. One ground floor room was designated a spinning room. This number of rooms seemed to be capable of housing more than the maximum of ten inmates recorded a year earlier.

An agreement with a new workhouse master in 1811 included an agreement whereby Jonas Thorn, the new workhouse master, was 'to keep the paupers in the said house constantly employed in the yarn manufactory'. Although the agreement does not specify the master probably kept any profit from the spinning operations.

THE MALDON UNION WORKHOUSE

Each of the original 32 parishes appointed one representative to the Board of Guardians but the larger parishes of Maldon St Marys, Maldon St Peters, Burnham and Southminster were all allowed two representatives each making a total of 36 elected Guardians. The parishes of Great Braxted, Little Braxted, Ulting and Wickham Bishops were added in 1880 on the dissolution of the Witham Union Workhouse. They were allocated one representative each.

The Maldon Union Guardians first met in December 1835 and took over the old Maldon parish workhouse which was situated on Market Hill, Maldon and all the other parish workhouses in their Union area. The Maldon parish workhouse building could only accommodate about 50 paupers although records show that over some winters numbers up to 80 inmates had been recorded. The instruction from the Poor Law Commissioners was that inmates should be classified by age, sex and physical ability and it was usual for the new Guardians to rearrange their existing parish workhouses pending the establishment of a new purpose workhouse. In Maldon's case the Guardians decided not to build a new workhouse but to enlarge the existing Maldon parish workhouse. It was decided initially to bring all the able bodied men from the three other parish workhouse into the Maldon workhouse and to use the other parish workhouses at Bradwell, Purleigh and Tolleshunt d'Arcy for the women, the aged and infirm and the children. Despite there being the poor from

32 parishes to be accommodated the Guardians decided they would make improvements to the existing parish workhouse at Maldon to house all the poor from the surrounding parishes and eventually close the other three parish workhouses. Consequently they rebuilt the upper floor of this two storey building and with further improvements the end result was that up to 350 men, women and children could be housed and the other three parish workhouses could be closed.. This situation existed until 1872 when a new workhouse that would house up to 450 inmates was built in Spital Road in a mock Tudor Gothic design.

Soon after the Guardians had had their first meeting in 1835 the they appointed a new master at the Maldon workhouse 'to farm such poor persons as shall be admitted'. Later in the nineteenth century some workhouse inmates were actually sent to farms to work under the control

Maldon Union workhouse built in 1872/73

of the farmer but in the context of the new appointment at Maldon the word 'farm' means to agree to the maintenance and care of the poor within the workhouse. In some instances in other counties, parish bodies in the pre-Union days 'farmed out' the care of their poor, usually within the workhouse, to a contractor but these arrangements were never very satisfactory.

The first national census after the Union workhouse came into being was in 1841 and the number of inmates was as follows:

The census of 1841

Males	80	The total includes 6 staff and 76 children under
Females	96	14. The percentage of children to the total number of inmates was 45%
Total	176	

The 1777 survey indicated that up to 242 inmates could be accommodated in the twelve parish workhouses that were open in that year although it was unlikely that they were all working to capacity. If the 'actual' number in 1777 was, say, 200 inmates then the numbers had fallen to under 200 when there were only four workhouses in 1835 with probably a further decrease by the time of the census of 1841.

The Guardian's minute books

Most of the snippets of workhouse life come from the Guardian's minute books and as you will note I have been looking at the 1840s and 1850s for the Union Workhouses in earlier chapters. I therefore picked the 1860s for Maldon but the clerk to the Guardians during this period chose not to record all those interesting bits and pieces that appear for the previous Union workhouses. Although all the weekly or fortnightly meetings were very comprehensively minuted as far administration matters were concerned there was nothing personal regarding any of the inmates. Every meeting was very much to do with income and expenditure with the Guardians agreeing to the payment of expenses in respect of the supply of food for the workhouse. You can imagine that to feed and clothe 2/300 inmates involved a mammoth exercise with 20 to 30 suppliers having to be paid on a regular basis. In addition to housekeeping expenses the Guardians were continually paying out money to officers responsible for out-relief for those paupers not living in the workhouse. There were also payments to lunatic asylums (usually Brentwood) where Maldon residents were housed together with payments to other workhouses where for some reason residents of the Maldon district were residing. All these administrative duties filled up many pages of minutes at each meeting and possibly the clerk in the 1860s felt he did not wish to record in detail all the incidents relating to the inmates. Clerks at other Union though seemed to find the time to record all the above administrative matters together with the interesting snippets concerning the inmates. Consequently I have jumped to the late1870s for interesting snippets.

The Union minutes from 1878 to 1881

A new clerk was now in office who in addition to recording all the financial comings and goings also noted in detail what was discussed concerning the inmates. It was important that these so called minor matters were logged in detail as they often concerned allowances to inmates for which a record was essential and they often resulted in a vote by the Guardians which was also necessary to record. By the late 1870s the body that governed the Union workhouses throughout the country had changed its name on two occasions. Initially the government set up the Poor Law Commissioners when the Poor Law Act of 1834 was passed. After 1847 the name changed to the Poor Law Board. This body survived until 1871 when the government changed the name once again to the Local Government Board. This new body had a wider brief than just the poor and was responsible for the health of the community as well. Many references by clerks in the minutes still referred to the governing body as the Poor Law Commissioners.

February 1878

Assault and battery

The clerk was directed to make enquiries into the facts of the case concerning the alleged assault and battery by John Davis of Purleigh on his son Charles William Davis. Charles was now an inmate in the workhouse. If sufficient evidence could be found then the case was to be placed before the Justices in order that proceedings could be taken against the father. Presumably the incident happened when Charles was at his home and he was subsequently taken into the workhouse for his own protection. Unfortunately there is no further record of this incident which indicates that the Guardians could not find sufficient evidence for a case. The only good thing is that if the alleged charges were true then Charles was better off in the safety of the workhouse, despite its deprivations, and away from his father.

November 1878

The Mason children

It is not often that one finds Guardians disagreeing on the course of action to be taken but on a number of occasions the chairman of Maldon Union Workhouse Governors would put a matter to the vote if there were differing opinions. The three Mason children had recently been removed from their home in Bradwell into the workhouse. No ages were given but probably two of them were under ten and one was about twelve. The previous week a relative had taken them out of the workhouse to look after them and presumably their parents or parent were not in a position to do this. The Guardians now received a letter from the Revd. Warner of Seddlescombe Rectory near Battle applying for non-resident relief for the three Mason children. Whoever was looking after the children probably could not write and it was usual for the local clergy to write letters for parishioners. The matter was discussed by the Guardians and it was proposed that out-relief of two shillings and six pence a week be granted to Fanny and Kate Mason but there was no mention of the other child Annie. An amendment to the proposition was proposed that each of the three children receive two shillings and six pence a week. There were sixteen Guardians present at the meeting in addition to the Chairman, who did not vote, with five voting for the amendment and seven voting for the original proposition. Presumably four Guardians abstained. So, the person looking after the children received nothing for Annie. Although the ages of the children are not known Annie was probably of an age when she could have go out into service, say about 12, and the Guardians took this into consideration. Two weeks later another letter was received from the Revd Warner pleading the case for relief for Annie. This time the Guardians agreed to give her the same weekly allowance as her sisters.

November 1878
Application for arrest
A reward of £2 was offered by the Guardians for the arrest of George Brown of Goldhanger who had absconded from the workhouse leaving his three children in the workhouse. No mention of a mother.

December 1878
Request for extra fee
Mr Tomlinson, one of the medical officers, had written to the Guardians applying for an extra fee in respect of the many attendances he had made to the Union Workhouse due to the recent outbreak of fever. It was proposed and seconded that a gratuity of £5 be awarded to Mr Tomlinson. The proposal was lost on a vote and so no gratuity was granted. The Guardians agreed though to write to Mr Tomlinson giving him their 'cordial thanks in acknowledgement of his services and his great care during the recent outbreak of fever in the workhouse'. The impression from reading the minutes of the various Unions is that some medical officers do not always give value for their annual fee as their attendance at the workhouse often clashed with their work for their private clients. Maybe the Maldon Guardians had suffered such experiences which prompted them to turn down the doctor's request.

January 1879

Supply of bread

Another example of the Maldon Guardians taking a tough line was in connection with the bread being supplied by Mr Henry Steven of Great Totham. A complaint had been made, probably by the workhouse master, and so a sample of the bread was produced to the Guardians. They agreed that the quality had fallen and so the clerk was instructed to write to Mr Steven advising him that unless the quality improved another baker would be appointed and that he would be charged with any expenses incurred in the changeover (advertising expenses). The supply of bread to 200 plus inmates was a valuable contract and consequently the Guardians could afford to come hard on this supplier.

July 1879

Petition to close public houses on a Sunday

A letter was received from the National Alliance Society seeking the Union's support for their petition to parliament to close public houses on a Sunday. The Chairman put the request to the vote which was four votes for and eight votes against. No further action taken.

December 1879

The Taylor family

The Guardians were in the process of taking into the workhouse the Taylor family which consisted of Mrs Elizabeth Taylor and her three children one of whom was illegitimate. A letter had been received from the medical officer for Burnham, Mr Coombe, requesting that the family not be moved into the workhouse for the time being as there were fever cases in the row of cottages in which they lived and the doctor did not want a contagious disease taken into the workhouse. It was agreed that the Taylor family would receive out-relief to the extent of two shillings a week and four loaves of bread for the time being.

December 1879

Man living in a shed

The Guardians received a letter from the assistant overseer of the poor for Tillingham bringing to their attention a man in his village called Herbert who lived in a shed 'in a miserable manner'. He was a case that the Guardians should consider for transfer to the workhouse. The clerk was instructed to write back saying that no official application had been made to enter the workhouse and that the man's mode of life appears to be from choice and not necessity. Consequently the Guardians said that they could not interfere. The Guardians did offer the opinion that they thought it doubtful that the owner of the shed could be prosecuted as the shed had not been offered as a place for human habitation.

January 1880

Burnham's drinking water

The medical officer responsible for the Burnham area wrote to the Guardians, probably for information only, that he had received a report from the Medical Officer for Health (either a county of government appointment) which said that the water from the town pump at Burnham was unsuitable for drinking. The report said that a large proportion of the Maldon population used the pump and it had been decided that officials from all parties should meet to discuss the matter. There was no follow up report in the minutes on the water quality and probably the reason for advising the Union Workhouse was to put them on notice in case an epidemic materialised in due course which could be put down to this situation. In 1872 the Public Health Act had been passed which recognised the Union as the official authority for maintaining health in its area if there was no urban sanitary authority.

Request for expenses

A letter was received from the (police) constable of Heybridge with a request for the reimbursement of expenses in the sum of ten shillings incurred by him for the hire of a horse and cart to search for George Boutman. A warrant had been issued for his arrest for deserting his wife and children. Presumably the family were now in the workhouse and Mr Boutman had absconded from his home and had made no financial offer for their keep in the workhouse. The Union had already posted a reward of £2 for his arrest. The Chairman put the request for expenses to the vote which was lost by 12 votes to 10 with 6 abstentions. At that meeting there were 28 present out of a maximum of 36 elected Guardians which was a very good turnout as usually those present numbered just over half.

May 1880

Dissolution of Witham Union

The Witham Union Workhouse was in the course of dissolution and the Maldon Union had been allocated responsibility for the parishes of Great and Little Braxted, Wickham Bishops and Ulting. Amongst other administrative matters relating to the taking on of these extra parishes was the appointment of a medical officer although the discussions did not include Ulting which was being offered to another doctor. The Guardians decided on Dr Gimson at a salary of £25 a year plus midwifery cases at fifteen shillings each plus two shillings and sixpence for each vaccination performed at the person's home or three shillings if performed at a Vaccination Station some distance from the villages. At the next meeting the Guardians were advised that Dr Gimson had decided not to take on the post and he proposed his partner, Mr C de Lisle Brock. Mr Brock was offered and accepted the position. Although the inmates of the Witham Union were transferred out in 1880 the Witham Guardians carried on with their various responsibilities with the Guardians finally closing their books in 1883.

December 1880
Complaint by William Barrie
The Local Government Board forwarded a copy of a letter of complaint to the Guardians made by William Barrie, an inmate, containing two specific complaints. In April last Mr Barrie complained that Mr Baldwin (position unknown) had been abusive to him and used intimidating language. The second complaint was that on his admittance to the workhouse, also in April, he was put in a filthy bed and had to sleep in a room which was also filthy. The Board of Guardians interviewed Mr Barrie, Mr Baldwin and also the workhouse master, Mr Timperley. The Board's conclusion was that the clerk was instructed to write back to the Local Government Board saying that with regard to complaint number two that it contained 'not a particle of truth'. Members of the Visiting Committee said that they had never seen a bed or a room at Maldon Workhouse as described by William Barrie and on the contrary all the wards were scrupulously clean. Regarding complaint number one the Guardians were of the opinion that of their knowledge of Mr Barrie over a number of years, during which he had been in and out of the workhouse, they tended to believe Mr Baldwin who said that he had not verbally abused Mr Barrie. The other factor in their conclusion was why Mr Barrie had not made this complaint when he first came into the workhouse again eight months ago.

January 1881
Request for out-relief from Tollesbury's dredgerman
The dredging of oysters off the Essex coast was a large industry in times gone by although probably in decline by the 1880s. Nine families from Tollesbury all employed in the dredging of oysters wrote to the Guardians applying for out-relief. They all said that they were all married with five or six children each and explained that their wages had all fallen to only nine or ten shillings a week. This sum was insufficient to feed and cloth their families and they had all got into debt as they had

to borrow money for this purpose. The recent bad weather (it was January) and storms had damaged their boats to the extent that they would be unable to continue their calling until they were repaired. The Guardians decided that a Labour Test Station be established at Tollesbury and that out-relief be given to the men subject to them picking oakum (unravelling old ropes) at the prescribed rate per day. The Guardians were obviously not going to hand out relief without something in return. A formal proposition was put forward to the Guardians present along the lines of the foregoing but an amendment was proposed that the men should earn their relief by picking oakum in the workhouse and not at home in Tollesbury. There were seven votes for the original proposition that the men should receive their relief at home in Tollesbury and seven votes for the relief to be earned in the Workhouse. The Chairman, who had not voted previously, had the casting vote which was for the dredgermen to receive their out-relief in their home village of Tollesbury. Common sense prevailed.

The twentieth century
The census of 1901

Males	84	The total includes 9 staff and 13 children
Females	58	under 14. The percentage of children to the
		total number of inmates was 10%
Total	142	

The most significant figure is the percentage of children in the workhouse which fell from 45% in 1841 to only 10% in 1901. There was no schoolmaster or schoolmistress on the staff which means that the 13 children in 1901 were all taught in Maldon's Infant and Primary schools. Education within the workhouse environment had now come to an end with all workhouse children being taught in normal schools.

1930
The life of the workhouse ended, like the others in Essex, in 1930 when Essex County Council took over its control. The workhouse buildings eventually became part of St Peter's Hospital, Maldon.

Chapter 11

ONGAR AND ITS ENVIRONS

PARISH WORKHOUSES

The following 26 parishes in the above area were grouped together in 1834 following the Poor Law Amendment Act to form the Ongar Union. Before 1834 each parish may have had its own poorhouse or workhouse.

Blackmore, Bobbingworth, Doddinghurst, Fyfield, Greensted, High Laver, Lamborne, Kelvedon Hatch, Little Laver, Moreton, Navestock, Chipping Ongar, High Ongar, Norton Mandeville, Abbots Roding, Berners Roding, Beauchamp Roding, Shelley, Shellow Bowells, Stanford Rivers, Stapleford Abbots, Stapleford Tawney, Stondon Massey, Theydon Mount, Willingale Doe, Willingale Spain.

The government undertook a survey of parish workhouses in 1777 and the following four parishes in this area had a workhouse open in that year.

Lamborne   Navestock   Stanford Rivers   Willingale Spain

The notable exception to this list is the absence of a parish workhouse at either Chipping Ongar or High Ongar which were the largest parishes in the area. Chipping Ongar workhouse was established in 1748 and rebuilt in 1795 on a different site. Possibly the old property was not being used as a workhouse in 1777. High Ongar did have a subsequent to 1777 although there are no records of the date of opening.

The number of parish workhouses in the area was small compared with the number of parishes but the whole area was sparsely populated. Chipping Ongar had a population of 800 in 1840 with High Ongar having the highest population of only 1200. All the other parishes only had a few hundred residents. The population of all the parishes prior to the 1840s would have been even smaller and consequently there was not the need for a parish workhouse in the small communities. Willingale Spain was a very small parish in 1777 with a capability of housing only

12 inmates in their workhouse and it probably acted as a centre for the poor in neighbouring parishes as well.

Chipping Ongar

The first indication that Chipping Ongar had a poorhouse was a record that one was erected in 1748 adjacent to the St Martins church rectory. In the late 1700s many parishes had poorhouses or workhouses and these often closed down for periods when they were not needed or for reasons of the expense of running them and some opened up again subsequently. Possibly the Ongar workhouse was not open at the time of the 1777 government survey as it does not feature in the list of Essex workhouses. In 1795 a decision was made to pull down the old workhouse and build a bigger one on the same site. Consequently the workhouse was still in existence but was probably not being used. The parish changed its mind after representation from the Rector who said that the present site was 'inconvenient'. As the existing location was on church land the parish vestry agreed to the new location, which was offered by the Rector, which was on part of the glebe land owned by the church provided that the building took up no more than the area of the old workhouse.

The cost of the new workhouse was £153 and the vestry agreed to borrow £100 over 10 years. The new workhouse was eventually completed in 1797 and the site was possibly on church land just to the north of St Martin's church. The £100 was lent by a local man, Mr John Crabb of Shelley Hall, but surprisingly this gentleman wished to have repayment in full later the same year. Consequently the vestry repaid £50 of the loan from the local poor rate and borrowed the balance elsewhere.

Some years earlier to the building of the new workhouse the government passed Gilbert's Act in 1782 which allowed parishes to combine into groups to build one large workhouse to accommodate all the poor of those parishes in the group. This arrangement was the forerunner of the government sponsored Union Workhouses in 1834. The Ongar vestry considered combining with other parishes but at the end of the day took the matter no further (see Stanford Rivers). Three years after the new workhouse was built (1800) the vestry talked about enlarging the workhouse but once again nothing was done. One can only presume that although Ongar's poor was on the increase, the vestry felt they could cope with the need for increased accommodation although in subsequent years extensions were built.

One of the inmates of the Chipping Ongar workhouse in 1807 was William Travell aged 49. The overseer's records contain correspondence between the parish and the Royal Hospital at Greenwich where Mr Travell was hospitalised before being transferred to his home parish. William Travell was a sail maker and had served on the HMS l'Aigle and HMS Hecla before becoming unwell and ending up in Greenwich Hospital. The records say that he was insane and dying and the parish was trying to recover outstanding monies owed to him by his last ship. The outcome was that two pounds fourteen shillings and nine pence was owed and would be paid to the parish forthwith.

A sub committee was formed in 1815 by Ongar vestry to look into the expense of running the workhouse. The report made various financial recommendations and one of the other recommendations was to appoint a new workhouse governor (master). The expense of running the workhouse was now to be controlled by Ongar vestry. This must have been the case before but possibly financial control was now lax and everything needed tightening up. At the time of the survey there were 11 inmates with the governor (workhouse master) being Mrs Cracknell who was to be replaced. Later in 1815 Mr Jessop of Epping was appointed and in 1820 Mr John Heard was the new governor. In 1820 the vestry drew up some new rules for the running of the workhouse with particular reference to the accountancy side of things. Despite this being one of the principal recommendations of the sub-committee in 1815 nothing seems to have been done at that time. Mr Heard held the governor's job for eight years until 1828 when Mr William Ward was appointed at a salary of £10 a year. The salary included the services of his wife which probably included their board and lodging.

In addition to the various financial improvements the vestry drew up a set of rules which had to be pinned up in every room of the workhouse. There were 13 rules which covered items like cleanliness and godliness together with rules concerning who could be admitted to the workhouse. The rules also allowed inmates to bring their personal possessions into the workhouse provided they had permission from the Ongar overseer (of the poor). To distinguish parish property from personal property the parish had all their effects marked with the letters 'COP'. The rule concerning when inmates should be back in the workhouse stated that during the summer months inmates must be back by 9pm and 7pm in the winter when the doors would be locked. Presumably some of the inmates went out to work on local farms or in domestic service which did not include accommodation.

In 1829 the vestry discussed the possibility once again of a grouping with neighbouring parishes with only one workhouse but again nothing was done. Stanford Rivers though took the initiative and combined with nine other local parishes and built a group workhouse in 1830-31 for about 100 inmates (see Stanford Rivers).

High Ongar

Chipping Ongar has always been the more important parish of the two Ongars and the main shopping centre today is situated there. Whereas today Chipping Ongar's population is far in excess of that at High Ongar, back in the eighteenth and nineteenth centuries they were similar. Chipping Ongar did have a parish workhouse in the 1700s but there is no record of one at High Ongar. The vestry records do though refer to the poor of the parish being housed in 1733 in an almshouse which seems to have been run by the parish rather than specific trustees. The same vestry record lists the names of the parishioners who were in receipt of weekly out-relief through the overseer. In March 1733 there were 30 names on the list and this low number indicates that the expenditure on out-relief was manageable for this parish and there was not the need for a workhouse to be built Later in 1776 there is reference to a 'parish house'. This was probably just a property owned by the parish in which they housed a poor family on a rent free basis which was not actually a workhouse with a master. This assumption is borne out by the government's survey of parish workhouses in 1777 where there is no record of a workhouse at High Ongar.

A workhouse was eventually built which survived up till the time that the new Ongar Union was established and it was initially used by the Guardians in 1836 to house inmates that were aged and infirm. Eventually all the inmates were transferred to the Union workhouse at Stanford Rivers and the workhouse was sold in the late 1830s.

Stanford Rivers

The Stanford Rivers parish workhouse was built some time prior to 1777 but unfortunately records have not survived as to the exact date. The government survey of that year stated that the workhouse could accommodate up to 30 inmates. An inventory of the workhouse dated 1809 gave an accurate description of the rooms and their contents. There were twelve rooms which seem to have been spread over two floors with back and front rooms on each floor. In addition there was a cellar and a woodhouse. At the end of the inventory is a note which says that the woodhouse contained a bed which belongs to 'Old Edwards'. Obviously he brought it with him when he was admitted but it is not clear whether he was still alive.

A further inventory in 1830 called one of the rooms the 'Women's Room' and this seemed not to be a bedroom but a women's workroom or sitting room. Another workroom contained ten spinning wheels and the one book on the inventory was the bible.

An Act was passed in 1782, Gilbert's Act, which had as its main objective the ability of a number of parishes to combine into a group and have just one large parish workhouse to serve all the parishes in the group the object being to reduce the Poor Rate for each parish in the group. The more far reaching government report and recommendations for the establishment of groups of parishes (Unions) throughout the country came in 1834 but Stanford Rivers and other neighbouring parishes did the very same thing five years earlier in 1829. This combining of parish workhouses in the 1834 Act was probably not the idea of the Stanford Rivers group but almost certainly emanated from Gilbert's Act which, with the consent of two thirds of ratepayers, authorised parishes to combine into a group. This 1782 Act was specifically written to accommodate the old, sick and infirm in a large workhouse but not the able-bodied men and women. Thomas Gilbert is the same man that organised the government survey in 1777. The one large difference between the 1782 and the 1834 Act was that the latter was drafted to accommodate all classes of the poor and not just the old and sick. The Stanford Rivers group drew up an Agreement on the 3rd May 1829 signed by ten parishes to build or purchase or rent a building in the parish of Stanford Rivers. The parishes in question were as follows:

Abbotts Roothing	Bobbingworth	Greensted
Shelley	Stanford Rivers	Stapleford Abbot
Stapleford Tawney	Stondon Massey	Little Laver
Great Warley		

The first nine parishes in the above list are all to be found around Stanford Rivers, with the notable absence of Ongar, but the odd one out is Great Warley near Brentwood which is many miles away. Maybe the two Ongar Vestries felt that they had sufficient financial resources to run their own workhouses without the need to group together with other parishes. The Agreement which was signed by three Guardians of the Poor (overseers) for each parish agreed as follows:

…two third parts in number and value according to the poor rates……..of the respective parishes………..the said parishes shall be united for the better maintaining and employing their poor and that a convenient house with proper buildings and accommodation thereto, and with lands fit for gardens, orchards and the keeping of cows for general cultivation, shall be built purchased or hired in the parish of Stanford Rivers. ....That the expense of running the said house shall..............be paid by the guardians of the parishes in their due proportions according to the amount of money raised by the poor rates by their several parishes.

Workhouse Incorporation for the Ongar Hundred.

Maintenance Account of *the Parish of Stanford Rivers* **during the Month ending on the** *21st* **day of** *Feby* **183*3***

1st. Class.——*Males and Females under the Age of* 10 *Years, Rated at* 2 *Parts.*
2nd. Class.——*Males between the Ages of* 10 *and* 15 *Years, and Females above the Age of* 10 *Years, Rated at* 3 *Parts.*
3rd. Class.——*Males above the Age of* 15 *Years, Rated at* 4 *Parts.*

Class.	Number of Paupers	Number of Weeks	Maintenance. Rate Per Week. (s. d.)	Maintenance. Amount. (£ s. d.)	Apparel. Rate Per Week. (s. d.)	Apparel. Amount. (£ s. d.)
3	3	1				
	4	3	3 .	2 5 .	4 3	5 . 2 10
2	4	1				
	5	3	2 3	2 2 9 .	3	4 9 . 2 7 6
1	3	4	1 6	18 .	2	2 . 1 .
				5 5 9		11 9 . 5 17 6

Quarterly rate on the Medium, at 6 in the £   6 7 . or
Additional charge for extra keep 2/- 1/6   2 Weeks   1 4   1 4

£ 12 5 10

Guardians expenses   12 2 10

This Maintenance Account was in respect of the residents of Stanford Rivers parish who were being looked after in the joint Stanford Rivers workhouse established in 1829

The method of splitting up the expense of the proposed workhouse is exactly what the government suggested later in 1834. The workhouse was built in 1830 and the design appears also to have been adopted by the government in 1834. The recommended size for the government's Union workhouses was to accommodate about 300 inmates whereas Stanford Rivers was built for only 100 inmates. The design of the building at Stanford Rivers was very similar to the model design as produced by the government. In fact the new Ongar Workhouse Guardians just took over the Stanford Rivers parish workhouse as it was in 1837, although it was enlarged over the next three years. Although the workhouse was situated in Stanford Rivers the title changed in 1834 and was then known as the Ongar Union Workhouse.

The design was quite revolutionary as it was no longer a large building that looked like a house but a three storey brick structure that looked more like a Victorian factory. A similar workhouse had been built in Southwell, Nottingham also some years before the government's recommended design and it is quite likely that both the design of Southwell and Stanford Rivers formed the basis of all future Union workhouses. The Stanford Rivers workhouse had a central hub which contained a committee room on the ground floor above which was the accommodation for the master and his wife. From the windows of the master's office he could see into the various exercise yards and keep an eye on what was going on. At the front of the hub two wings extended on either side for the accommodation for the various classes of inmate. The design for workhouses after 1834, when the government drew up a recommended design style, was also based on a central hub with wings extending in all directions like the wheel of a bicycle. Whoever designed the workhouse at Stanford Rivers, which eventually became the Ongar Union Workhouse, had great foresight as his revolutionary design was very close to what became the norm subsequently.

Despite the group parish workhouse being built in 1829 to accommodate up to 100 inmates the actual number was much less than this. The accounts exist for the workhouse for the period 1832 to 1834 which shows that the number of inmates increased slowly from 23 to 31 over these two years. Although the workhouse covered ten parishes they were all very small which is why the total number is low but of course Chipping Ongar and High Ongar did not join the group. These two workhouses also had about 20/30 inmates each which made a total of about 80 paupers in workhouses in the Ongar area.

Greensted

Greensted parish was one of the parishes that formed the Stanford Rivers group in 1829 to build a joint workhouse. Previously they had established their own parish workhouse on waste land belonging to the Lord of the Manor of Greensted. The parish were granted in 1810 a piece of waste land 'abutting the King's Highway leading from Greensted Green to Toot Hill......containing in length ten rods and in breadth five rods......to erect a commodious brick messuage with suitable outbuildings ....for use as a workhouse'.

Lambourne

Lambourne had a parish workhouse by at least 1777 as the parish was listed in the government survey of that year which said that the workhouse could accommodate up to 40 inmates. This was a very high number for such a small parish but in view of the fact that all the surrounding parishes were small the Lambourne workhouse may have taken the poor of other parishes.

In 1810 the parish vestry agreed to make a part payment to Thomas Johnson, a carpenter of Lambourne, to repair the Old Church House and build a new house for the poor of the parish. This seems to be a new workhouse to replace the existing one.

An agreement was made in 1822 with Thomas Wilson 'to inhabit the workhouse at Lambourne End to farm the poor' and that he shall 'teach all those who are able to knit and spin'. The word 'farm' in this context means 'to look after' and the expression was common in the nineteenth century in connection with workhouse inmates.

One of the surviving records for the workhouse is the labour accounts for the period 1832/36. This ledger shows the names of the inmates who were hired out to local farms and how much the parish charged the farmer. The basic charge was two old pence per day up to five old pence for farm labourers although one or two inmates were charged out at one shilling and six pence a day which probably meant that they had a skill. Fourteen men were being hired out which would put the total number in the workhouse at about 30/40 allowing for women, children and the infirm.

The workhouse was being used as a parish workhouse right up the time that the new Ongar Union was formed in 1836 but the premises did not feature in the plans that the new Ongar Guardians had for the future. The vestry usually held their parish meetings in the workhouse with the last one being held there on the 10th May 1836 and thereafter meetings were held in the parish church. By this date any inmates would have been transferred to one of the other local workhouses and the workhouse would then have been sold.

Navestock

The first mention of a workhouse in the parish was in 1741 when a lease was drawn up for renting the premises known as the White House to be used as a workhouse for the parish. The government survey of 1777 stated that Navestock workhouse was capable of housing up to 25 inmates. A parish map of 1768 shows the workhouse marked as such on Navestock Heath with very few properties in the immediate area. It is not clear whether this property is the White House of 1741. The Tithe Award Map of 1836 shows the workhouse as the site of the present Plough public house although earlier references in records quote the workhouse as being 'a little to the south of the vicarage' or 'a little to the south of the Plough'. The records only give fleeting mentions of the location of the workhouse and as they seem to vary so much it is possible that more than one property has been used over its one hundred year life By the time that the last workhouse was taken over by the Ongar Union in the 1830s the number of inmates had risen to about 30.

THE ONGAR UNION WORKHOUSE

The total population of the 26 parishes in 1834 was just under 11,000 and consequently they were all very small. High Ongar and Chipping Ongar had about 1000 residents each and they were awarded an extra representative on the Board. Stanford Rivers was the next largest parish who also contributed a further person making a total Board of Guardians of 29.

The meetings of the Board of Guardians were held at the Town Hall, Chipping Ongar every two weeks whereas most other Essex Boards held their meetings at the Union Workhouse. Stanford Rivers parish had combined with nine other parishes prior to the establishment of Union Workhouses and built a combined workhouse in 1830 to accommodate 100 inmates. The construction and style of this building is described in the section on Stanford Rivers' parish workhouse and as it conformed to the style suggested by the Poor Law Commissioners in 1834, the Guardians decided to adopt the Stanford Rivers workhouse as the Union Workhouse to serve the 26 parishes.

Initially in 1836 the Guardians were using three of the existing five parish workhouses in the 26 parishes. The largest at Stanford Rivers, which eventually became the Union workhouse, could accommodate 100 persons and was used for able bodied males and females whereas the smaller houses at Chipping Ongar were used to accommodate children of paupers and that at High Ongar for the aged and infirm. The parish workhouses at Lambourne and Navestock were closed. By May 1836 the

Ongar Union workhouse built in 1829 by a group of ten parishes in Stanford Rivers
parish which was adopted as the Union workhouse in 1837

The school block built to the left of the main building

Guardians had transferred the pauper children to the female section of
the Stanford Rivers workhouse which left Chipping Ongar empty. This
property would be retained and used at the discretion of the Guardians.
Later the aged and infirm at High Ongar were also transferred to
Stanford Rivers and the parish workhouses at Chipping and High Ongar
were sold off.

In 1837 the Ongar Union formally purchased the Stanford Rivers workhouse from the ten parishes and over later years built further wings that increased the maximum of inmates from 100 to 200.

The census of 1841

Males	46	The total includes 5 staff and 31 children under 14. The percentage of children to the total number of inmates was 44%
Females	30	
Total	76	

This small Union workhouse could initially only accommodate up to 100 inmates in 1841 which is why the figures above are small compared with the other Essex workhouses.

Guardian's minutes 1865 -1871

I was roughly progressing through the nineteenth century for the Union workhouses in alphabetical order but as there were no interesting personal stories for Maldon for the 1860s I took a later period for that Union and have reverted to the 1860s for the Ongar Union.

Construction of new drain

The Guardian's minutes for the 1860s highlight an extension of the responsibility of the Guardians. It was not until 1872 with the passing of the Public Health Act that Union workhouses were formally responsible for the health of the community. Prior to this date there seems to have been an informal arrangement whereby the Guardians of Union workhouses got involved in health matters. The minutes record that they paid for the construction of a drain at the back of the Two Brewers public house and several of the houses adjacent. The cost was £15 and they agreed with Mr Corrigan, the publican, that he would repay the Union at the rate of £1 per quarter.

October 1865

Proposed new parish workhouse for Shelley

This discussion was on the Union's agenda in October 1865 which was quite extraordinary considering Union Workhouses had been in existence throughout Essex for 30 years and old parish workhouses had long since been sold off. Presumably the suggestion had come from the Shelley Parish vestry who wanted to build a new parish workhouse on a two and a half acre site. The request was proposed and seconded but there was an amendment to the proposition that the new workhouse should NOT be built. The amendment was carried by 17 votes to 9. It is also surprising that nine Guardian representatives were in favour of the new workhouse which was contrary to the whole concept of Union Workhouses.

Remedying the evils of the workhouse
October 1865 also saw a proposition which was in connection with 'remedying the evils of the workhouse'. This and subsequent resolutions were all in connection with the drainage problem in the workhouse and a sub committee was formed to look into the matter and supervise the improvements.

February 1866
Expenses claim turned down
Mr Potter who was the medical officer covering Chipping Ongar attended a pauper, James Parker, at his home in connection with a fractured leg. The doctor saw James on numerous occasions until he was fit enough to be transferred to the Union Workhouse although his leg was still bandaged and in splints. Mr Potter received an expense of £3 for attending to James Parker. When in the workhouse James came under the control of Mr Shiletto who was the medical officer at Stanford Rivers. The Guardians now received a further expenses claim of £3 from Mr Shiletto for attending to James Parker. The Guardians looked into the claim, which they turned aside, as they argued that Mr Shiletto provided no special medical attention to James as this had all been done by Mr Potter who had also used his own bandages and splints and these had not been changed whilst he was at the workhouse.

Application for out relief
The Board considered at their meeting on the 20 February an application for out relief for the Barker family. John Barker had two children both having been ill recently and requiring nursing. The mother had died the previous October. The family had previously had financial assistance (out relief) but this had been discontinued about a month ago when an elderly pauper lady was presumably being paid to nurse the children. The elderly lady was now saying that due to her age and infirmity she had to give up nursing the children. The Barker cottage was in a very isolated area and the nearest neighbours were an aged couple who were unable to give any help to the family. Although the minutes do not say, presumably John Barker now had to give up work for the time being to nurse his children himself. The Guardians sensibly agreed to meet the cost of out relief.

September 1866
Proposals to build new workhouse.

As mentioned earlier the Ongar Union Workhouse at Stanford Rivers was not purpose built but an extended version of the Stanford Rivers Parish Workhouse which was built for ten parishes just before the change over to Union Workhouses. The minutes had made mention on various occasions for the need to build a completely new workhouse and this matter cropped up again in September 1866. Earlier resolutions had been defeated but an amendment had been passed in 1865 to look into the possibility of further improvements to the existing workhouse. The matter was now moving forward and plans were drawn up for the improvements which included upgrading the drainage system. Three tenders had been received for £350, £265 and £260 and the Guardians were recommending to the Poor Law Commissioners that the tender of £260 from Mr John Hammond be accepted.

November 1866
Sale of parish property

When parish workhouses closed in the 1830s they were sold off by the parishes and the proceeds sent to the Union Workhouse. Parishes also owned houses that were inhabited by paupers (poorhouses) but were not actually workhouses with a workhouse master. Over the years the minutes record various parishes advising the Guardians that they were in the process of selling this type of property and in November Shellow Bowells parish were in the course of selling a property for £50.

January 1867
The case of Eleanor Sampson

Eleanor Sampson was in the Essex County Lunatic Asylum at Brentwood which had opened in 1853. Ongar Union was responsible for the cost of her keep at the Brentwood institution. Apparently the brother, Robert Sampson, advised the Guardians that their father, who had died recently, originally lived and worked with his family in Cobham, Surrey where he rented a mill in 1805. The tenancy only lasted one year before he moved to Great Waltham. Paupers were allocated settlement rights depending on where they originally came from but there was no documentation in the case of Eleanor. The Guardians wrote to the Epsom Union, which covered Cobham, saying that Eleanor was their responsibility despite there being no settlement documentation. It probably came as no surprise to the Ongar Guardians that the Epsom Union declined to be responsible for Eleanor as they could not produce settlement documentation. Notwithstanding there being no documentation the whole case appeared thin as the father had only lived in Cobham for a year. From Ongar's point of view they were trying to get Epsom to pay for Eleanor, the expense of which would be quite considerable over her lifetime. There was no further comment on this case over the next month and one assumed that the Ongar Guardians dropped their claim to Epsom and continued to pay for Eleanor's keep at the Brentwood asylum.

February 1867

The story though did not end there as Ongar now obtained a Court Order ordering the Guardians at Epsom to pay the Ongar Union the sum of £26 incurred by Ongar for the board and lodging and medicines for Eleanor for her time at the asylum. Apparently the case was proved that Eleanor belonged to a parish within the Epsom Union. Presumably they were able to prove she was born there. The next we hear is that Epsom appealed against the Court Order but later the appeal was withdrawn and they agreed to pay the associated costs. Eleanor would probably have stayed at Brentwood with, in future, the Epsom Union paying for her keep together with the £26. I am sure the Ongar Guardians were very pleased at the outcome.

December 1867

Sacking of nurse

The master reported to the Guardians that the nurse, Ann Turner, in his opinion could no longer carry out her duties 'due to her age and illness'. The Guardians agreed and advertised for a new nurse at £15 a year. They told Ann that she was being replaced but could continue in her position until a new nurse was appointed. To their credit the Guardians ascertained that Ann did not live in and consequently she did not rely on the workhouse for her accommodation.

February 1868

An illegitimate child in Hastings Workhouse

The clerk advised the Guardians that he had received an order for the removal of Thomas Booth, an illegitimate child of Martha Booth, from Hastings Union Workhouse to Ongar workhouse. Evidence had been produced that the father was Thomas Woolmer of Stanford River parish who had recently died. Apparently the case had been brought about because the mother, Martha, had deserted the child, presumably at Hastings, and he was now alone and in need of care and attention. The Hastings Guardians wished him to be sent to the workhouse of his home parish. The clerk also read out a letter from an Emily Booth, obviously a relation of the deserted mother, offering to take charge of Thomas if the Board paid her two shillings and six pence a week to care for the child who would otherwise now spend his early life in the workhouse. The Guardians, surprisingly in this case, were not prepared to pay the allowance but agreed to accept Thomas into Ongar workhouse.

August 1869
Land for schoolhouse and dormitories
The Board of Guardians approached Mr Capel Cure the owner of the adjacent land with a view to purchasing half an acre abutting the workhouse for the purpose of erecting a schoolhouse and dormitories. Mr Capel Cure first of all said that he did not have the power to sell the land and possibly this was because the land was held in trust. Subsequently Mr Capel Cure agreed to sell another plot at a price of £50 over which he had control also adjacent to the workhouse.

December 1869
Thomas Harrington's transfer request
The clerk had been asked to look into the circumstances surrounding Thomas Harrington's request to be transferred from the Romford Union Workhouse to Ongar which they contended was his home parish. The investigation revealed that Thomas had been in the Romford Workhouse for the past eleven years and before admittance had lived at Chadwell Heath. He only came to Beauchamp Roding for a period of three weeks when living at Chadwell Heath to bind hay for a Mr Speller. This visit for work did not justify that Beauchamp Roding was his home parish and consequently the clerk was asked to apply to Romford for a copy of the Examination papers on which Romford based their Order of Removal. The case did not crop up in the minutes for some time until a letter was received from Romford Union saying that they had withdrawn the Order as they had been given the wrong facts of the case. Obviously Thomas Harrington had not been truthful when he was interviewed in connection with the transfer request. I would have thought that as he was only asking to be transferred from one workhouse to another there would have been little difference in the two regimes.

March 1870
John Driver taken into apprenticeship
Thomas Stubbing of Stapleford Tawney was a cordwainer who worked in leather whose job was to mainly make horse saddles and harness gear. He had agreed to take John Driver aged 20, an inmate of the workhouse, as an apprentice cordwainer for a period of three years. The Board

agreed and it was resolved that Thomas Stubbing would receive the sum of £5 as a one off payment for John's board and lodging. An indenture was signed by all parties. Mr Stubbing agreed to take John notwithstanding that the medical officer produced a certificate saying that John was a cripple. It was the policy of the Poor Law Commissioners that Union Workhouses would wherever possible get boys and young men out of the workhouse into apprenticeships and in the case of young females into domestic service.

July 1870
Complaints against Dr Gilmour
The Guardians had heard several complaints against Doctor Gilmour, one of the medical officers, and on this occasion the complainant and the doctor were summoned to a Guardians meeting. All the evidence was heard but unfortunately the details were not recorded by the clerk, whereas clerks at other Unions seemed to write a comprehensive minute. Nevertheless the Guardians felt that Doctor Gilmour was guilty of neglect and that 'a severe reprimand' be administered.

November 1870
New schoolhouse and infections infirmary
In August 1869 we saw the Guardians negotiating with Mr Capel Cure for extra land to build a schoolhouse. It looks as if their plans were now to include an infirmary as the plans for both buildings had been sent to the Poor Law Commissioners for approval. The plans had now been received back and the minutes indicated that many objections and suggestions had been made. The proposed schoolhouse was being designed to hold 30 children. One of the objections was that the play sheds should be covered rather than left open to the elements as in the Ongar plans. The Guardians did not wish to go to the additional expense of roofing in the play sheds and consequently they decided to dispense with this aspect of the plan.

The clerk's job was fairly onerous and many of his minutes were fairly sketchy when dealing with complaints, for example, from inmates. A certain amount of interpretation has to be added to what appeared in the minutes. Contrary to this style of minuting, which incidentally was common to most Unions, the clerk on the matter of the proposed new buildings wrote copious minutes on the debate regarding the various objections to the plans. It is clear that both the clerk and the chairman of the Guardians felt very strongly about the whole matter and the minutes reflect how they felt about the Poor Law Commissioners which was not complimentary. At the end of the discussion the chairman considered three course of action in connection with the dispute and the Guardians decided that the favoured course of action 'was not to enter into any more correspondence but to accept what the Poor Law Commissioners wanted'.

Consequently a resolution was proposed and seconded that the Guardians would go along with the objections and suggestions and re-submit the plans accordingly. The chairman, who obviously felt strongly about the matter, proposed an amendment which read:

Considering that the many and various complaints made, and defects pointed out to the improvements suggested in respect of the Union House by the several Poor Law Inspectors for the last six years. And considering the endeavours that have been made by the Guardians to remove those complaints and namely those defects, and considering the failure of those endeavours from the difficult and changeful views of the Poor Law Inspectors and the seemingly impossibility to satisfy those requirements, considering also the divided opinion of the Board as to the desirability of expending any considerable sum in the repair and alteration of the old House, taking these things into consideration the Board does not see its way to a permanent settlement of the long vexed question. And therefore desires to abandon any further action on this matter and desires the Poor Law Commissioners to take such steps as it is empowered to adopt and which it may consider most advantageous to the interest of all classes in the Union.

Whilst not grammatically correct, the above is as it appeared in the minute book and due credit must go to the clerk for getting all the points down on paper. This amendment was similar to the first resolution but included reference to an on-going battle with the inspectors over six years. There is also reference to the fact that some of the other Guardians were not happy with spending money on improving the workhouse. The chairman brought all his frustrations together in this very long winded amendment to the original resolution which in effect was very similar in its conclusion that the Guardians would have to comply with the inspector's recommendations. As well the plans being sent to London for the Commissioners to approve they would have sent their Inspectors to Ongar to inspect the proposals on the ground.

The outcome was that the chairman's long amendment was lost and the original proposal was passed. In April 1871 the amended plans were passed by the Poor Law Commissioners.

October 1871
Complaint against Doctor Gilmour
Doctor Gilmour was once again the subject of a complaint on the charge of neglect following the previous complaints in July 1870. This time the clerk records the details which referred to a pauper child at Fyfield named Rose Madle. The Guardians authorised a visit by the doctor for

the 8th September, which he did not undertake, and the child died the next morning. The doctor explained that he did attend at 7am on the morning of the 9th but the child died a few hours later. The reason why he did not make the visit on the 8th was because he was ill and his substitute had left the area and could not make the visit in his place. He had not at that stage found a replacement stand-in doctor. The Guardians found that he could not be excused for not having a substitute and they recommended that the matter be placed before the Local Government Board. This was a newly formed government body which succeeded the Poor Law Commissioners and the Poor Law Board. A subsequent minute recorded that the Local Government Board found Doctor Gilmour guilty of neglect for not ensuring that a substitute was available to attend to Rose on the 8th.

1871
Enlargements to the workhouse
By 1871 the workhouse had been enlarged to take up to 200 inmates and in this year the workhouse school and infirmary were built. Both the new buildings had two stories with the school having a boys entrance and a girls entrance. Despite the workhouse being capable of accommodating more inmates the total number of inmates was only between 100 and 150.

1881
The census for this year showed that the workhouse had six staff and their families together with 129 inmates. Twenty years later in 1901 the number of inmates had dropped to 113.

The twentieth century
The census of 1901

Males	84	The total includes 7 staff and 11 children under 14. The
Females	36	percentage of children to the total number of inmates was 10%
Total	120	

Like Dunmow, Halstead and Witham the Ongar workhouse did not last until 1930 when other Unions came under the control of Essex County Council. Ongar Union closed in 1920 and the inmates, who by this time were just the old and infirm, were transferred to St Mary's Infirmary, Epping. The building stood empty for six years until it was taken over by Piggott Brothers the tent and flag makers in 1926. The building is presently undergoing redevelopment.

Chapter 12

ORSETT AND ITS ENVIRONS

PARISH WORKHOUSES

The following 18 parishes in the above area were grouped together in 1834 following the Poor Law Amendment Act to form the Orsett Union. Before 1834 each parish may have had its own poorhouse or workhouse.

Aveley, Bulphan, Chadwell St Mary, Corringham, Fobbing, Horndon-on-the-Hill, Langdon Hills, Mucking, North Ockendon, South Ockendon, Orsett, Stanford-le-Hope, Stifford, Grays Thurrock, Little Thurrock, West Thurrock, East Tilbury, West Tilbury.

The government undertook a survey of parish workhouses in 1777 and the following five parishes in this area had a workhouse open in that year.

Aveley   Corringham   Stifford   Grays Thurrock   Stanford-le-Hope

Surprisingly Orsett does not feature in this list as it was one of the largest parishes in the area. The following section on Orsett parish shows that the parish workhouse was not built until about 1800.

Orsett

James Bloomfield of Orsett Rectory produced a booklet in 1864 in connection with Orsett's charitable trusts. He refers to a piece of land called Slades Hold near Orsett Fen on which there was a parish workhouse which was subsequently converted into five cottages. Unfortunately there is no date for when the workhouse was built. This property is probably the parish workhouse which is referred to in the vestry records below and the conversion into cottages would have taken place when the Orsett Union took over this parish workhouse in 1835.

The map shows the old parish workhouse on the road out of Orsett towards Baker Street

A very old Orsett vestry memorandum book mentions an agreement in 1799 to build a workhouse. The memorandum book records an undated memorandum which the agreement, probably for the year 1800, is appointing Mr John Parsons as master of the workhouse. He was required to:

maintain with good and wholesome food and small (weak) beer any number of paupers that may be sent into the workhouse at the rate of three shillings and nine pence per week. Should any of the number fall sick with smallpox to nurse and provide from the falling to their getting up at the rate of seven shillings and six pence per week. To nurse and provide with necessaries every woman that may be in labour in the house at the rate of ten shillings per week for four weeks..............To provide firing (wood) for the use of the house and to provide at least three hot meals a week. To keep the poor in decent apparel. To bring as many as are able to church once at least every Sunday and to attend with them himself. Not to be absent from the family (the name often used to describe the inmates) for more than three days at any one time....... (The vestry agree to) pay for all furniture for use of the family and to pay for all expenses for funerals. To allow Mr Parsons (to keep) every emolument arising from the labour of the paupers......

At the end of another old vestry minute book there is a record which was kept for a few years of the names of the inmates of the parish workhouse. Following the agreement to build the workhouse in 1799 one can assume that it was built in the early part of 1800 for the first list of paupers is dated 4th August 1800. The first list of names is as follows:

Mrs James and her 3 children
John Sewell and his wife
Thomas Sash and his wife
John Cadman
Molly Maylin and Molly the younger

Mrs Jennings and her 3 children
John Garrod
James Hills
John Gardner

The total is 18 but against the names of James Hills and John Cadman is the note that they are 'due to go out'. By 1802 the number had risen to 21. Mrs James and her children were still there but the Jennings family had gone and in their place was Mrs Siggins and her four children. Over the next six years until 1808 the numbers in the workhouse gradually reduced to 13 although John Sewell was still there with his wife as was Mrs Maylin and her daughter although in 1808 she was recorded as Mary not Molly. A Mrs Jennings was in the workhouse in 1808 and if she was the same one as previously in 1800 there was no mention of her three children. Possibly after eight years they had all grown up and left the workhouse to go out to work leaving their mother there! With the number reducing to only 13 in 1808 it looks as if the parish were thinking of closing the workhouse as notice was given in March of that year to Horndon on the Hill parish to withdraw their paupers by midsummer's day. Presumably Orsett had a number of Horndon's poor in their workhouse. By 1810 though the numbers had risen again and there were 28 inmates. Also at this there were about a dozen more residents of the parish in receipt of out-relief.

In 1807 the vestry employed Samuel Shuttleworth, Surgeon, to administer to the poor of the parish at a salary of sixteen pounds sixteen shillings a year. This arrangement would have probably included those paupers in the parish workhouse and also those on out-relief in other accommodation. Six years later in 1813 the vestry appointed another doctor, Mr John Robinson to take over the job at an increased salary of £25 a year. This time the Agreement specifically mentions attending to the poor of the parish and also the casual poor in the specific areas of medicine, surgery and midwifery.

The vestry memorandum book mentions on many occasions agreeing to provide those pauper families who were living outside the workhouse and presumably on out-relief with clothing. A typical entry for 1811 reads:

The following things were granted to the following persons:

Mrs Purkis   Cloth for two boys , shirts and a pair of shoes
Mr Wright   8 yards of cloth and a waistcoat for his boy
John Kempster   4 pairs of shoes and a hat
Widow Grout   2 pairs of shoes, 2 shifts

Samuel Dorrington's children   1 suit for the boy. A change for the girl and shoes.
Widow Seamer   2 shifts and a pair of stockings, pair of shoes, handkerchief and a gown.

The parish vestry did all they could to find employment for young paupers when they came of age to go out to work. An agreement was drawn up in 1820 relating to a boy and a girl for a period of one year each. The boy, William Dye, would be taken by Robert Barnes with an allowance of three shillings and sixpence per week to 'board, lodge and cloth' for a period of one year. Mr Joseph Pye agreed to take Sarah Read with an allowance of three shillings per week for the year for a similar arrangement. There is no mention what the youngsters would be doing but usually the boy would go to work on a farm and the girl would go into domestic service.

The parish workhouse closed in 1837 when the inmates were transferred to the new Orsett Union Workhouse. The property was then leased out for fourteen years to Mr Joseph Spurgeon at a rent of £20 a year from Michaelmas 1844. Unfortunately the lease does not give the exact location of the parish workhouse apart from saying that the building had a garden and a shed thereon but it is probably the same workhouse referred to by James Bloomfield in his booklet of 1864. Although the old parish workhouse was originally owned by the parish of Orsett it was usual when the inmates were transferred to the new Union workhouse that the property would be sold with the proceeds going to the Union to offset somewhat the cost of the new building. If the property was still in the ownership of Orsett parish in 1844 then it was unusual for the property to be leased out for fourteen years.

Aveley

The parish workhouse is mentioned in the overseer's expense ledger of 1759 and it was probably established some years earlier. One of the responsibilities of workhouse masters was, in addition to organising work for the adult inmates, to teach the children the basics of reading and writing. This condition was invariably written into the standard master's contract but those that I have seen have very often been signed by the new master with a cross indicating that he could not write. This was probably the case at Aveley as the accounts show that a schoolmaster was employed in the 1760s to school the poor children which may well have included children of those families on out-relief.

The parish vestry entered into a new agreement in 1773 with Richard Wright to let Mashfoot House to the parish 'for a house of industry to house the distressed poor'. It is not clear whether this fourteen year lease was a renewal of an existing arrangement or whether the parish were changing workhouses. It seems likely though that Mashfoot House was a new and larger establishment as a year later in July 1774 the Aveley vestry made an agreement with the parish of Stifford allowing the poor of Stifford to be taken into the Aveley workhouse. The arrangement was that all the expenses of running the workhouse would be divided proportionate to the rates collected by the two parishes as would any income derived by work done by the inmates.

In 1777 the government's survey of parish workhouses showed that the Aveley workhouse could accommodate up to 40 inmates but the survey also indicated that there was a workhouse at Stifford which could take up to 20 inmates. There are a number of inaccuracies in the government survey and maybe when Stifford parish made their return they were referring to the joint workhouse at Aveley where they made up half of the accommodation. The overseer's accounts for 1787 show that the joint arrangement with Stifford continued but the Aveley vestry were paying Warley parish workhouse for housing ten of Aveley's poor. Maybe the joint workhouse was now becoming overcrowded as we see that in the following year the accounts only feature the expenses for Aveley and it seems as if the arrangement was discontinued. Payments to Warley no longer featured in the accounts and possibly Aveley's poor were brought back to Aveley. In the same year Aveley parish sold off by public auction 59 items which appeared to be all the contents of the workhouse as the inventory contained various beds, bedding, kitchen items and six spinning wheels.

It looks as if the workhouse closed in 1787 but the records are not clear as to what the local arrangements were for the poor of the parish thereafter as it was not until 1796 that an arrangement was made with West Thurrock parish for the Aveley poor to be housed in a joint workhouse in the West Thurrock parish.

By 1810 a new arrangement had been made and this time Aveley's poor were being housed in Wennington parish in a joint workhouse being run by West Thurrock, Aveley and Rainham. This arrangement ran through to the 1830s.

Bulphan

Bulphan workhouse had not been built when the government survey of parish workhouses took place in 1777 and Bulphan parish records do not record an opening date. The workhouse was small compared with other Essex parishes as the vestry took an inventory in May 1812 which indicated that the property consisted of six rooms and probably was the size of two cottages. The three bedrooms list seven beds although the summary only quotes there being six beds. The inventory was probably taken as the workhouse was closing for six days later the parish entered into an agreement with South Ockendon parish that this parish would take Bulphan's poor into their workhouse at the rate of one shilling per week. The arrangement was that Bulphan would pay for a minimum of six inmates at all times even if the number fell below this level. The only other condition imposed by South Ockendon was that they would take no single woman who was pregnant.

Langdon Hills

The parish vestry agreed in April 1763 to rebuild the poorhouse. It appears that the property was not at this stage a large structure in the form of a proper workhouse with resident workhouse master but just a cottage capable of housing two poor families. The minute specifies that the new poorhouse would consist of two large rooms with separate butteries (kitchens) with ovens. Whether the two halves were independent or not is not clear. The parish did have a proper workhouse at some later date although there are no records as to when it was built. Possibly the house for the poor mentioned above was enlarged and a workhouse master employed.

In 1784 the vestry passed a resolution to discontinue the allowances to Elizabeth Beckham, a widow, for the maintenance of her children unless she goes and resides in the parish poorhouse and also that she wear the badge of the parish to designate that she is on poor relief. It is confusing when vestry minutes refer to a 'poorhouse' as they could be just be referring to a house for the poor of the parish or a proper workhouse with a master. In the case of Elizabeth Beckham it does seem as if the parish are referring to a proper parish workhouse. A year later in 1785 an agreement was made with Jeffery Crick of Billericay for the 'farming out of the poor of the parish of Langdon Hills into his care'. 'Farming' in this context just means that he would take over the running of the workhouse and take care of the inmates. He was to be paid the sum of two shillings per person to provide all the necessary food and accommodation with the exception of clothing. The parish would have provided new shoes and clothing when needed. Jeffery Crick of Billericay also gets a mention in the section on East Horndon parish (Billericay Union) when he undertook a similar function for the poor of that parish.

North Ockendon

North Ockendon workhouse was probably built some time after 1777 as it does not feature in the government survey of that year. In 1791 the parish papers contain an estimate for building a wing on to 'the old workhouse' inferring that it had been in existence for some years. The estimate was for £96 with the parish to pay for carting the materials to the site. Further work was done at the workhouse in 1792 by John Mathew costing £20. The records contain a list of the residents who were in receipt of out-relief in 1791. There were 22 families living in North Ockendon and the overseer also paid out for 10 other families who now lived in adjoining parishes but were officially recorded as the responsibility of North Ockendon parish. The majority of the 32 families had up to five children each with one family on relief with six children and one with seven. In addition to those on out-relief the workhouse was looking after up to 10 people at any one time. The workhouse master in 1802 was Thomas Sullings. The workhouse probably closed some time between 1810 and 1820 as paupers were being looked after at South Ockendon workhouse in 1823.

South Ockendon

Like Bulphan above, South Ockendon workhouse had not been built by 1777 and unfortunately no records have survived which charts the history of this institution. The workhouse was probably built though in the 1780s as we see in the Essex Quarter Session papers for 1788 a complaint by John Whitley the governor of South Ockendon workhouse. He stated under oath that Sarah Jilson, one of the pauper inmates, had 'at divers times refused to employ herself according to the direction of him the said John Whitley and that some time since the said Sarah Jilson struck the said John Whitley a violent blow at the said workhouse and hath several times abused several divers other paupers in the said workhouse and struck Sarah Measy one of the paupers several violent blows'. Unfortunately there is no record of what happened to Sarah Jilson. If found guilty she would almost definitely have received a custodial sentence.

It seems that there were always vacancies at the South Ockendon workhouse as it is noted that South Ockendon took Bulpan's poor in 1812 and in the North Ockendon records it is noted that they sent their poor to the South Ockendon workhouse. One particular case in 1823 was about three mothers with one child each from North Ockendon being admitted to South Ockendon workhouse. North Ockendon records what clothing they took with them to the South Ockendon workhouse. This record was necessary because when they came out of the workhouse there would be no confusion as to which their personal clothes were and which had been supplied by the workhouse. South Ockendon workhouse continued to grow in numbers and by the time that the Orsett Union Guardians took over the running of the workhouse in 1835 the workhouse was capable of housing up to 60 inmates.

Stanford-le-Hope and Corringham

Both Stanford-le-Hope and Corringham are recorded as having workhouses in 1777 when they both had a maximum capacity of 20 inmates. As can be seen in the above notes on parish workhouses in the Orsett area the other large parishes in the area either had their own or shared a workhouse but none of these schemes included either Stanford-le-Hope or Corringham. It is possible that the workhouse was a joint workhouse covering both parishes and both parish clerks completed the government's return giving the impression that there were two workhouse each with a capacity for 20 inmates. Records have not survived for the 1800s for both parishes and as these two parishes only had a few hundred residents in the early nineteenth century it is probable that both closed well before the Orsett Union was formed in 1835.

Stifford

The history of Stifford's parish workhouse is very much tied in with Aveley parish. The above section on Aveley shows that in 1774 the joint agreement with Aveley allowed Stifford's poor to be accommodated in the workhouse at Aveley. This arrangement continued until about 1787 when Aveley workhouse closed. As the section on West Thurrock below shows the Stifford poor were then transferred to a new workhouse opened by West Thurrock parish. In 1796 there was a further arrangement whereby Aveley joined the West Thurrock group and although Stifford was not specifically mentioned in the agreement the poor of Stifford probably continued to be housed in the West Thurrock workhouse. Later in about 1810 West Thurrock opened a new workhouse in Wennington but this time the specific arrangements did not include Stifford. South Ockendon opened a workhouse in the early 1800s and possibly Stifford's poor were accommodated there.

West Thurrock

West Thurrock parish opened a joint workhouse with Stifford in 1787 at the same time that the joint workhouse between Aveley and Stifford closed. The property was called Stonehouse and situated in West Thurrock parish. A lease was taken for a period of fourteen years. In 1791 an inventory was taken of the West Thurrock joint workhouse which indicated that there were eleven rooms over three floors together with a cellar. On the top floor there were four garret rooms built into the roof. The person in charge would appear to be Mrs Drabble as she had her own bedroom with her own teapot and tea canister. There were five spinning wheels in one of the back garret rooms.

The lease of the Stonehouse property expired in 1801 and as the repairs to the house were becoming so expensive the workhouse closed. From 1804 to 1806 the paupers were sent to the workhouse at Mile End. From 1806 we see a new agreement without Stifford parish being included (see Stifford above). The new workhouse was to be situated at Noke House in the parish of Wennington and the three parishes in the agreement were West Thurrock, Aveley and Rainham. Rainham, although an adjacent parish, is mentioned in the chapter on the Romford Union.

An inventory of the workhouse at Wennington listed six rooms on the ground floor - dining room, kitchen, pantry, shop (brew house), parlour, pantry - together with a cellar. Upstairs there were four bedrooms, one each for men and women together with a nursery and a further bedroom.

This arrangement ran through to 1831 when notice was given to the parishes of Rainham and Aveley that West Thurrock no longer wished to continue the joint arrangement. West Thurrock said they would withdraw all of their own poor and re-house them without any joint arrangement with other parishes. Subsequently West Thurrock decided not to establish their own workhouse but to house their poor in the Grays Thurrock workhouse.

When the new Orsett Union Guardians took over the parish workhouses in 1835 the workhouse at Grays Thurrock which was capable of housing 45 inmates.

West Thurrock - Aveley - Rainham

Annual Expenses
The overseer's records for Rainham parish include the annual

expense for the joint workhouse at Wennington. Amounts have been rounded to the nearest pound.

	West Thurrock	Rainham	Aveley
1816	£16	£16	£13
1818	£20	£20	£16
1822	£15	£15	£11
1824	£21	£21	£17
1831	£11	£11	£9

It would appear that the cost to each parish was not proportionate to the number of inmates from each parish but proportionate to the total rateable value of each parish. West Thurrock and Rainham both paid nine twenty-fifths each and Aveley seven twenty-fifths of the total cost for the year. Inmates came and went and it would have been difficult to calculate the total number of weeks that all of West Thurrock's, for example, poor were resident in the workhouse. For the period 1816 to 1824 the costs were reasonably static but the cost fell by almost 50% by 1831. This was the year that West Thurrock broke the agreement and made their own arrangements for their poor. The expenses calculations do not mention the number of paupers, as this was not a consideration, but probably by 1831 the numbers had fallen to the extent that Rainham and Aveley could easily provide alternative accommodation for their poor.

THE ORSETT UNION WORKHOUSE

Of the initial 18 parishes that made up the Union Orsett was the largest parish in the 1830s with a population of about 1,300. Consequently Orsett had an extra two representatives and Grays Thurrock one extra making a total Board of 21 Guardians. For those that know this part of south Essex they are aware that the population structure has altered dramatically since those early days of the Guardians in the 1830s. Those parishes near to the Thames, like the Thurrocks and Tilbury now far outstrip the population of Orsett which is not much different from that when the Union workhouse was built.

The first meeting of the Guardians was on the 14th October 1835. One of their first tasks was to appoint a Workhouse Committee to inspect the existing parish workhouses which now came under the control of the Guardians. Their first report identified parish workhouses at Orsett, Grays (Thurrock) and South Ockendon. The South Ockendon workhouse was capable of housing 60 inmates, Grays 45 and Orsett 40. Consequently the three workhouses had the potential of housing up to

145 inmates although at the time of the first national survey in 1841 after the new workhouse opened the actual number was only 103 including staff. The new rules prescribed that the various classes of poor be separated and consequently the three parish workhouses needed work done on them to accommodate separately the men, the women, the children and the sick.

The Union workhouse built in 1837 is shown in the centre of Orsett on the site of the present Orsett Hospital

The new Union workhouse was built in 1837 with the architect being Sampson Kempthorne. Initially the design was the cruciform shape and built to accommodate up to 200 paupers. Like the other Union workhouses in Essex there were many extra buildings constructed over the next ten or so years which included a fever ward, a ward for vagrants and workshops. The initial cost of building was £3115 and by 1860 the total spent on building works was £6500. The location of the workhouse was in Rowley Road and the whole of the buildings were demolished in the 1960s when the new Orsett Hospital was built on the site with a new entrance in School Road. All that remains of the Victorian era buildings is a row of cottages in Rowley Road opposite the entrance to the old workhouse.

The first national census after the workhouse opened in 1837 was in 1841 and the figures show that it was only being used to about 50% of its capacity. In 1777 the four parish workhouses in the area could accommodate up to 90 inmates and consequently over the next 60 years the number of in-house poor in the area had increased very slowly. There is no information on how many residents were on out-relief in the respective periods but data from other Unions indicates that the numbers for those on out-relief grew at a faster pace than those actually in the workhouse.

The census of 1841

Males	43	The total includes 3 staff and 48 children under 14. The percentage of children to the total number of inmates was 48%
Females	59	
Total	103	

For the Orsett Union Workhouse I have looked at the minute books for the late 1870s. Since the workhouse was built in 1837 the following 40 years had seen great advances being made in the administration of the country in general and workhouse life in particular. Two examples were the improvements seen in the way the workhouse was run by the establishing of additional committees with special responsibilities and also the establishment of new external bodies. In addition to the ruling body, the Guardians, and the external officers like the medical officers and the local relieving officers, there were now the Finance Committee, the Assessment Committee, the Boarding Out Committee and the School Attendance Committee. The new outside body that governed the running of Union Workhouses was the Local government Board, which took over from the Poor Law Commissioners, the Rural Sanitary Board and the local School Board. I will not go into detail to explain the function of these government bodies apart from saying that compulsory education came into being with the Education Act of 1870 which brought the workhouse school within the system.

April 1877
The workhouse master's wine
The master reported to the Guardians that his stock of wine was nearly exhausted. He was authorised to purchase a hogshead (fifty two and a half gallons) of similar wine. This does not appear to be just the tipple of the current master as even after the change of master in October 1878 we see the new master ordering wine. The master and his wife enjoyed free board and lodging and probably ate very well.

James Croxan absconds

The April minutes reported that the master advised the Guardians that he had recently taken into the workhouse Eleanor Croxan and her two children as the father, James Croxan, had absconded from their accommodation. The family were now chargeable to the Common Fund of the Union which meant that their costs were not chargeable to the parish from which they came. The expense of keeping an inmate in the workhouse was always charged out to parish responsible but possibly in the case of the Croxan family the authorities were not able to establish at this stage to what parish they belonged. The clerk was instructed to put the wheels in motion for an arrest warrant to be issued for running away and deserting his wife and children. A reward of £2 was offered for information leading to an arrest and conviction.

May 1877

Smallpox in the workhouse

The initial design of all the Essex workhouses provided for an infirmary but none had any special arrangements for cases of infectious diseases. An inspector of the Local Government Board attended the Guardians' meeting to investigate the causes of smallpox in the workhouse. Some cases had developed in the workhouse and some cases had been brought in on the authority of the Rural Sanitary Authority. The inspector named 18 cases where in his opinion hospitalisation should be arranged outside the Union workhouse. In the meantime the Guardians were to arrange for extra nurses to be employed and the Witham Institute for Nurses would be written to for this purpose. The medical officer, Doctor Corbett, who had been attending to the cases, and there were many more than 18, asked how he should go about charging for all the extra work involved. His salary just covered the day to day medical problems and it had always been the case in institutions to recompense for extra work. He was told to submit an account at the end of the quarter for his extra expense incurred and thereafter until the epidemic subsided.

July 1877

Colorado beetles

The clerk had received a number of posters from the Privy Council Office concerning the recent plague of Colorado beetles. The clerk was asked to send them to the parishes for display. I wonder what proportion of the rural parishioners could read?

Smallpox epidemic
The inspector who visited the workhouse in May made various recommendations one of which was that the workhouse should have a separate infection diseases ward to isolate those cases. The Guardians took this on board and in July were considering alterations to the workhouse to establish a separate infectious diseases ward.

Depth of pauper graves
The Guardians considered at their July meeting a proposition that the depth of pauper graves should be regulated. It was proposed that there should be four feet (1.2 metres) of earth above the top of the coffin. The reason for this new rule was almost certainly linked to the smallpox epidemic when the death rate increased at the workhouse. It is possible that, in their haste to bury the many that died, the gravediggers were not digging graves deep enough.

October 1877
Smallpox epidemic
It looks as if the epidemic had come to an end as the Guardians agreed extra payments to those involved in the crisis:

Dr Corbett	£40		The chaplain	£10
Mr Watts	£15		The master	£10
The nurse	£2.10s		The matron	£2.10s

The chaplain's annual salary was £50 and so he received two and a half month's extra salary with the nurse also earning £50 a year but her £2.50 was only two and a half weeks extra. The matron earned £30 a year and so her bonus was one month's salary.

Extra land to be purchased
Mr Wingfield Baker who owned the adjacent land to the workhouse agreed to sell a small strip for £13. This piece of land was probably for the erection of a separate infirmary as a result of the smallpox epidemic.

November 1877
Schooling arrangements.
The Education Act of 1870 had been passed which introduced compulsory education for all children up to the age of 13. School Boards were established covering every community and Orsett parish now had its village school. The chaplain of the workhouse complained to the Guardians that the number of children being educated in the Union school was too great and the schoolmaster could not cope. In view of the

establishment of the new village school it was recommended that arrangements be made for some of the children be sent to this school. One can image the reception that workhouse children would have received if they turned up wearing their standard workhouse uniform apart from the stigma of being a pauper in the workhouse.

December 1877
The School Board also anticipated the problems that workhouse children would encounter and so they wrote to the Guardians agreeing that selected boys, no mention of girls, could attend but suggested that they do not appear wearing the standard workhouse smock. The Guardians agreed and suggested that the selected boys be supplied with a jacket and a waistcoat.

The same month saw the Education Act catching up with the workhouse school and they had a visit from the school inspectors. The Guardians received a Certificate of Efficiency together with a copy of their report and one gets the impression that the 'efficiency' was very borderline as the report gave a warning to the Guardians that they must keep up standards or else they may not get a certificate next time. This would mean of course that the workhouse school would have to close.

Claim by coffin contractor
Mr Payne had the contract to supply coffins to the workhouse. He had applied recently for compensation for his business as he had been ill, incurred medical expenses and also loss of trade. Apparently due to the smallpox epidemic his stock of coffins and the tools of his trade had become infected and were destroyed to prevent infection spreading and probably he had been ill himself with the disease. The Guardians voted to recompense Mr Payne but sanction for this unusual payment had not been ratified by the Local Government Board. The Local government Board said that Mr Payne should apply to the Rural Sanitary Authority who presumably were involved in destroying his stock and tools.

February 1878
Allowance for Alice
Alice Nicholls was 13 and a pauper who was boarded out with a family. She was now of an age when she could go out to work and an application was made for the sum of £1 to purchase an outfit in order that she could go into domestic service. The request was sanctioned. The Union Workhouse had a Boarding Out Committee who looked after children like Alice to check that they were being looked after properly and that there were sufficient funds available for their keep.

Clothes for Eliza Brown and daughter

In the same month the Guardians approved a similar request when Eliza Brown applied to leave the workhouse with her daughter. The Guardians would have investigated the reasons for her request to leave and made sure that she would be adequately looked after and, if necessary, out relief would have been approved.

Ann Dunstan's request to leave

At the same meeting the Guardians also considered the request of Ann Dunstan to leave the Union. As she had a daughter in the workhouse and was not offering to take her with her the application was refused.

March 1878
New fever ward

Reference is made to the 'new fever ward' in connection with some repairs and it looks as if the recommendation for a separate ward to be organised in the summer of 1877 had been implemented.

May 1878
Apprehension of William Dunstan

We had seen three months ago that Ann Dunstan wanted to leave the workhouse which, quite rightly, was refused. A minute of May 1879 records that a William Dunstan had been apprehended and convicted of deserting his wife and family. This William must be Ann's husband and she would have been taken into the workhouse when he absconded the family home. There are various cases in the minutes when warrants are issued for arrest after desertion but seldom do you see the outcome. William Dunstan was sentenced to three months imprisonment with hard labour. One can understand why Ann wanted to get out of the workhouse as it was not her fault she ended up there but of course it was not right she leave her daughter there.

Bread contract

The local traders who acquired contracts to supply food and goods to the workhouse and to the recipients of out relief did very well out of this extra business. As often happens corners get cut or traders get greedy and as a result a complaint had been made against Mr F Biggs of Fobbing in connection with his supply of bread. One of the rural relieving officers reported to the Guardians that the bread supplied by Mr Biggs over the past three weeks had been insufficiently baked and also over the last week eighteen loaves were all nearly two ounces light. The clerk was instructed to write to Mr Bigg reminding him that bread must be delivered in accordance with his contract. Mr Bigg at the same meeting had requested that he be allowed to change his delivery date for one of his rounds at Horndon on the Hill and Langdon Hills from a Saturday to a Friday. This would have been to those on out relief. The Guardians declined to agree to this change possibly as a result of the under weight problem.

August 1878

Charges for Mr Harvey senior

Robert Harvey a tea dealer of Grays was summoned before the Guardians to discuss what financial support he could afford in connection with his father who was an inmate in the workhouse. For some reason Mr Harvey chose not to look after his father in his own home but to let him reside in the workhouse. Obviously the father had no income which is why he was in the workhouse but if there were relations that could have looked after him then they had to pay for his keep. The Board of Guardians demanded a contribution of four shillings and six pence a week for board and lodging but Mr Harvey pleaded his inability to pay this sum. He offered two shillings and six pence but after discussion both parties accepted a sum of three shillings.

Oakum for sale

The master reported to the Guardians that he now had 12cwt of oakum for sale. The inmates were supplied with old ropes (oakum), some of which would be tarred, to unravel. The resulting piles of oakum would be sold for remaking into new ropes. The Guardians delegated the matter to the House Committee for attention. They would probably ask the master to get the best price he could.

October 1878

Advertisement for new master

Like any large institution, whether it be a commercial firm or the workhouse, there are always staff changes. The minutes record changes to almost every salaried position at the workhouse over the years and there are always a handful of applicants for the job. The master's position is obviously very sort after and changes less often and the application for a new master resulted in 34 applications. The Guardians formed a sub committee for the purpose of vetting the applications and from this number chose six for interview. They were asked to attend for an interview and told that their expenses would be paid. After the interviews were finished the sub committee narrowed the short list to three. The thirteen members present were told that they had one vote each and asked to name their choice. The voting went as follows:

Mr Robinson   8 votes   Mr Brownjohn 4 votes   Mr Pomeroy 1 vote

Mr Robinson was offered the position at a salary of £45 a year together with his keep which seems rather low as in the minute for October 1877 we see both the nurse and the chaplain earning £50 a year. Possibly a probationary starting salary!!

November 1878
Pigs to be bought
The master applied to the Guardians for permission to purchase two pigs for the purpose of consuming the waste food products. Permission was granted. Throughout the minutes it was noted that pigs were bought, fattened up using food waste and killed for use in the kitchens.

The twentieth century
The census of 1901

Males	92	The total includes 9 staff and 19 children under
Females	69	14. The percentage of children to the total number of inmates was 12%
Total	161	

The twentieth century saw more additions to the workhouse than had been seen in the previous sixty years with extra buildings being constructed in 1907, 1910, a women's infirmary in 1911 and other additions in 1913 and 1929. By the time that the workhouse was handed over to Essex County Council in 1930 the workhouse could accommodate 416 inmates.

There were few 'poor' in Orsett Workhouse in the twentieth century and like the other Essex workhouse at this time the only inmates were the aged and infirm. The Essex Vagrancy Committee in 1917, which cannot have existed long after this date, ordered that the Orsett Workhouse was in future only to accept the aged and infirm. The name 'workhouse' was dropped after 1930 and the building became known as the Orsett Institution before becoming the Orsett Lodge Hospital. In 1960 the workhouse was pulled down and replaced with modern buildings which became the Orsett Hospital.

Chapter 13

ROCHFORD AND ITS ENVIRONS

PARISH WORKHOUSES

The following 25 parishes in the above area were grouped together in 1834 following the Poor Law Amendment Act to form the Rochford Union. Before 1834 each parish may have had its own poorhouse or workhouse.

Ashingdon, Barling, Canewdon, Eastwood, Fambridge South, Foulness, Hadleigh, Havengore, Hawkwell, Hockley, Leigh, Paglesham, Prittlewell, Rawreth, Rayleigh, Rochford, Shoebury North, Shoebury South, Shopland, Southchurch, Stambridge Great, Stambridge Little, Sutton, Wakering Great, Wakering Little.

Canvey Island Parish was added to the Union in 1881 when it was transferred from Billericay Union. Previously Canvey Island was split between parishes in the Benfleet area before being incorporated into a parish of its own.

The government undertook a survey of parish workhouses in 1777 and the following parishes in this area had a workhouse open in that year.

Foulness/Shoebury   Hockley   Rayleigh   Rochford

Although the parish of Prittlewell had a larger population than Rayleigh and Rochford in 1777 its workhouse does not feature in the government's list. There appears to have been a workhouse in Prittlewell prior to the government survey but it is possible that it had closed by 1777 as a new workhouse was not built until 1786.

Rochford

Rochford parish in the eighteenth century had almost the largest population in the Rochford area equalling that at Prittlewell as both had populations in excess of 1000 people. No date is available for the establishment of a parish workhouse in Rochford but it would possibly have been as early as the period 1730/1750 as other smaller parishes had established workhouses by this time. Surprisingly the overseer's accounts make no mention of any expense for the workhouse and any detailed workhouse records do not start until the 1770s. Possibly then the workhouse was not built until this decade and the poor may have been housed in the joint workhouse set up by Prittlewell and Eastwood parish.

Rochford parish appointed Thomas Gepp and his wife from Colchester as workhouse master and mistress in 1774. The formal agreement refers to the workhouse as 'the House of Industry'. The salary for the couple was £15 a year to include accommodation and firing (wood for the fire). There was to be no weekly allowance per head of inmates but the Gepps were to feed the inmates out of their salary. The parish would probably supply clothing when needed. Their duties, in addition to looking after the inmates, was to teach the inmates to spin and card wool and also teach any others that may be sent by the parish to work in the workhouse.

A year later in 1775 the parish agreed to 'farm' the workhouse to Thomas Wakeling of Thaxted, wool comber, at the rate of three shillings and six pence per inmate per week with Mr Wakeling on this occasion to provide meat, drink, clothing, linen and bedding, candles, soap and earthenware. This 'farming out' of the workhouse is where the whole running expenses are incurred by the person taking on the role with the parish only looking after the property and providing doctor and midwifery services. The arrangement with Mr Wakeling was that if the number in the workhouse rose above 14 persons then his weekly allowance would rise. A similar 'farming' agreement three years later in 1778 with a different person gave a weekly allowance of up to twelve persons with a higher weekly rate thereafter. Notwithstanding that there only seems to have been up to 12 or 14 inmates in the 1770s the parish returned a survey form to the government which stated that in 1777 there was accommodation for up to 24 inmates.

An inventory of the workhouse was taken in 1776 which shows that there were five rooms downstairs and four bedrooms upstairs. There was also a garret room which contained old items. In the kitchen there were 12 wooden dishes and 12 mugs giving an indication of how many persons were living in the workhouse. This figure ties in with the 'farming' agreements above but it is difficult to see that the workhouse could house up to 24 inmates according to the survey a year later. Records do exist though for the numbers in the workhouse for various years as follows:

| 1774 - 13 | 1804 - 19 | 1809 - 20 | 1829 - 19 |

The above figures do seem to indicate that the workhouse could reasonably accommodate up to, say 15 persons, and it looks as if numbers started to increase above this figure in the early nineteenth century. The parish consequently entered into an agreement with Mr John Allen, carpenter of Rochford, to build a new workhouse in 1808 at a cost of two hundred guineas. Unfortunately there are no records of the size of the building but the location was on the corner of Queen Elizabeth's Chase. Unlike most parish workhouses the property was not just one building where everyone lived including the master but four buildings clustered together one of which was for the master and his family.

When Union Workhouses were set up throughout the country and Essex in 1834 it was as a result of the work done by the Poor Law Commission previously and their subsequent report to parliament. A survey was conducted throughout the country just prior to the publishing of the Commission's report asking parishes whether they had a workhouse and what were the ages of the inmates. Rochford parish was included in the survey and their return read as follows:

> Yes, we do have a workhouse and its inmates are chiefly old infirm
> men and women, the children of convicts and orphans. There are
> six men between the ages of 60 and 82; six boys between 4 and
> fourteen, two women aged 23 and 43; five girls between 1 and 17.

There were 19 inmates in 1833 and the number would have fluctuated little until 1837 when the new Union Workhouse opened also in Rochford.

Canewdon

At a vestry meeting on the third of May 1781 it was unanimously agreed 'that it would greatly help the poor rates of the parish of Canewdon if a workhouse was erected in the said parish.......and that some house proper for the poor should be converted into a workhouse for the use of the poor'.

The overseer's accounts for 1792 contain a record of the inventory of personal goods taken into the workhouse by inmates. All of these personal items would not have been used by the prospective inmate but a record had to be kept for when the person left so that there would be no misunderstanding. Isaac Casons brought with him two beds, four chairs, one boiler, a frying pan, 'a bad one', a pail and some kitchen utensils. Isaac's possessions were valued at three pounds fifty pence but other inmates had more possessions with John Suckling's being worth nearly twelve pounds which included an oak table, a tea table and a small table. There were also two feather beds worth £8 and 'a clock pawned to Mr Clay' worth £2.

In 1811 the parish advertised in the Chelmsford papers for a new workhouse master to look after the inmates and to employ them in manufacturing. The overseer's records include various letters from applicants for the job but one applicant followed up with a further letter after he had seen the workhouse. He said that there were:

1.　　　　No windows for any business (meaning a shop window)
2.　　　　No room for myself or my children
3.　　　　The house was shabby in appearance.
4.　　　　There was no larder
5.　　　　A great of trouble and expense (would be incurred) in making a place to do anything besides my own business.

This applicant obviously did not know what a parish workhouse was like and probably thought that he would be taking some retail premises with a built in workforce where he could carry out his own business.

The inmates were transferred to Rochford parish workhouse when the new Rochford Union Guardians took over control of the parish workhouses from 1835 until the new Union workhouse was built in 1837.

Eastwood

At a parish meeting in 1728 it was resolved to erect a workhouse to be used jointly with two or more adjacent parishes. Although the other parishes are not named it can be seen that Prittlewell parish passed a similar resolution in 1728 and consequently Eastwood and Prittlewell were almost certainly two out of the number that agreed to establish a joint workhouse. It is not certain whether the joint workhouse was established or not but Prittlewell workhouse was definitely in existence in 1759 but there was no mention of an Eastwood/Prittlewood workhouse in the government's survey of 1777. Nevertheless Eastwood did eventually open their own workhouse, probably in the early 1800s, although records of this early period have not survived. The overseer's accounts from 1827 mention the Eastwood workhouse which was being run by Mrs Harvey who only had eight men and children in her charge. She was being paid at the rate of three shillings per inmate per week. The workhouse continued in operation until the new Rochford Union workhouse was built in 1837.

Foulness/North Shoebury/South Shoebury

Foulness, North Shoebury and South Shoebury have always been separate parishes and although they all had separate overseers and churchwardens their overseer's records all appear in the same ledger. The parishes were all adjacent and possibly they were economising by not having to purchase separate ledgers for their accounting. This closeness probably prompted them, when there was a need, to combine forces and open one workhouse to serve all three parishes. A resolution was passed in 1763 to erect a workhouse for the three parishes. The poor rates in 1765 for the parishes were as follows:

Foulness - £2560   South Shoebury - £553   North Shoebury - £550

Foulness's population was much higher than that of the two Shoeburys which is reflected in their income from the poor rate. The cost of running the workhouse would have probably been split proportionate to their poor rate. Entries in the overseer's accounts from 1759 mention 'workhouse expenses' for all three parishes and probably the overseer was referring to parish poorhouses rather than a formal workhouse with a master. As an example children from the workhouse! (poorhouse) were given two shillings 'to go to the Wakering fair'. This entry appeared in the accounts for Foulness. In the accounts for South Shoebury Mr Baker in 1762 carted coal and beef to the workhouse. The North Shoebury accounts also mention workhouse expenses. As all the entries were in the same hand the reference to 'workhouse' probably refers to the respective parish poorhouses. In view of the small populations of these three villages it is unlikely that each had its own workhouse with a workhouse master and probably each parish had its own poor house where individuals or families were housed prior to the one large workhouse being built in 1763.

The joint workhouse building must have been large as at the government survey in 1777 it could accommodate up to 30 inmates. It is not clear as to the location of the workhouse but an entry in the North Shoebury overseer's accounts for 1813 mentions paying the Rev. Sumner for a half year's rent for the workhouse in the sum of ten pounds ten shillings.

When the new Rochford Union workhouse was built in 1837 the workhouse was no longer used for this purpose and the building probably suffered during a terrific gale a year earlier when it narrowly escaped being blown down. The property was unfortunately burnt down in 1877.

Hadleigh

Hadleigh parish maintained its own workhouse but records have not survived to trace its establishment and location. It was not included in the government's list of workhouses in 1777 and consequently was established at a later date. When the property was sold off in 1839 the parish vestry described it as a 'copyhold mesuage or tenement lately used as the workhouse of the parish of Hadleigh with a large garden adjoining'. The sale price was £72. At the same time the parish authorised the selling off of another property owned by the parish and called Pound House which was a freehold cottage which was let to a Mr Dalby. This second property must have been used at some time as a house for the poor of the parish, without a workhouse master, as the proceeds were also to go to the new Rochford Union Guardians on sale. The sale price was £50.

Hockley and Hawkwell

Hockley parish's first workhouse was located at the junction of Spa Road and Southend Road. There were also almshouses on Drovers Hill. In 1777 the parish workhouse could accommodate up to 20 inmates. In 1811 both the workhouse and the almshouses were sold and the proceeds were used to build a new workhouse next to the parish church of Saint Peter and St. Paul. When Union Guardians first met in the period post 1834 they closed the parish workhouse and transferred the inmates to the Rochford parish workhouse pending the building of the new Union workhouse. The workhouse was eventually sold in 1843 for £202 with the proceeds being sent to the Rochford Guardians. *(History of Rochford - Cryer)*

Surprisingly Hawkwell, which is adjacent to Hockley, had its own parish workhouse and this was situated in Ironwell Lane. The population of Hawkwell in 1801 was only 220 compared with the population at Hockley which was 612. There was no rule of thumb as to what population could support a parish workhouse as it was the case of firstly there being a need and secondly could the parish afford to maintain it. Usually though parishes with a population of less than 250 people did not have a workhouse and it is surprising that Hawkwell had one especially being so close to the one at Hockley.

Leigh

The Strand Wharf and Strand Quay area of Leigh was the main landing point for vessels and in this area the overseers of the poor rented in 1773 a property for the use as a workhouse. Four years later in 1777 the government survey of parish workhouses did not list this property as a workhouse and maybe it was only a parish poorhouse without a workhouse master and just used for the employment of paupers who did not live in the property. The property though was quite substantial and over three floors and would have accommodated about 15/20 paupers had they been living in the house. By the size of the property it would appear to have been a full workhouse with master and maybe the Leigh overseer did not make his return to the government. By 1790 though it had closed and been converted back into three cottages. Shortly afterwards the parish were using a cottage in Billet Lane which at that time was a steep road going down to quay and exiting by the Crooked Billet public house. This road has now gone as the railway line now passes through it.

Paglesham

The Paglesham workhouse does not feature in the government's survey of 1777 but there is reference in the parish accounts to expenditure on workhouse clothing in 1812. The workhouse was probably established around 1800. The workhouse property was known as 'Pound House' from the adjacent parish pound and leased by the parish.

In 1820 the parish agreed that William Sexton and his wife should take over the management of the workhouse at the rate of three shillings and six pence per inmate and also run the Sunday School for a fee of five guineas a year with the children meeting at the workhouse. Presumably the Sunday School was for parish children in addition to those in the workhouse. According to the times of the parish church services the children would go 'thence to the church in order' presumably after their own Sunday School.

Entries from the overseer's minute book record that in May 1826 the workhouse mistress, Mrs Sexton, 'agreed to take the boy Fletcher into the (work) house on the usual terms'. There was no longer any mention of her husband William Sexton. In October 1827 the young Fletcher features again when the parish vestry agree 'to send the boy Fletcher to sea'. Later in the year Mrs Sextons was allowed two pounds to cloth the four Stag children. The Fletcher family crops up again in

1828 when 'the girl Fletcher went this day into service'. She was given an allowance of one shilling and six pence together with any clothes that may be required.

A vestry minute of 1829 resolved to abolish the Sunday School which was established in 1809. In 1830 though the vestry appointed William Golden to keep Sunday School at the workhouse at the rate of two shillings per week. Mrs Sexton got into trouble with the vestry as she was putting up hers sons in the workhouse. She was told that they were not to lodge in the workhouse and must reside elsewhere. Possibly the Sexton family had their own cottage elsewhere and Mrs Sexton was breaking the rules by allowing the sons to sleep in the workhouse. In 1830 the Fletcher family feature again when Ann Fletcher was taken into service by Mrs Winterbon for a year. This could be the third Fletcher child that was in the workhouse unless the Fletcher girl that went into service two years earlier came back to the workhouse. Mrs Sexton left the workhouse in 1834 and although a successor was appointed he only had the job for three years before the workhouse was closed and the inmates were transferred to the new Union workhouse at Rochford.

Prittlewell

It is recorded that Prittlewell was renting a property as a parish workhouse in 1759 although discussion on the matter started as early as the 1720s and there may have been a parish workhouse as early as 1728 as a resolution was passed to erect a workhouse in conjunction with adjacent parishes. Eastwood was one of the other parishes that passed this resolution at the same time. Unfortunately there are no records available to confirm the existence prior to 1759 although on the evidence from Eastwood parish it does seem as if this project went ahead.. If a workhouse had opened in 1759, or even earlier, one would have thought that it would have appeared in the list of Essex parish workhouses which was drawn up after a government survey in 1777. There is no record though of a workhouse at Prittlewell in 1777 and possibly it was not open in that year but resumed subsequently.

In 1786 a new parish workhouse was built in East Street, Prittlewell at the junction of Suttons Road. It looks as if an extension was to be built at the workhouse in about 1820 as the overseer's records contain a specification of work to be carried out. Under the heading of 'Bricklaying' the specification was to 'dig out foundations as low as it may require' for a solid brick wall up to the level of the plate (where we would have the damp course today). The walls were to be of wood construction and the ceilings to be lathe and plaster. The roof was to be plain tiles. The specification also called for the breaking through from the 'old house' and making new doorways to link the old part to the new part. Unfortunately no measurements are mentioned for the extension but it appears to be at least one room on each floor.

Many workhouse inmates throughout Essex were forced to wear a standard uniform as cloth was bought in bulk for this purpose. In 1813 the parish vestry agreed that for the workhouse inmates they would all wear clothes made of a coarse grey cloth and on the collar of any outer garment they would have a large letter 'P' sewn on to the collar. Both males and females would be supplied with brown worsted stockings.

The workhouse was in use until 1837 when the new Rochford Union Workhouse was built. Thereafter the property was converted into cottages which were called Mill Hill Cottages. The cottages were pulled down in 1960 and a block of flats now stands on the site.

Rayleigh

Rayleigh's parish workhouse was situated between Back Lane, which is now Bellingham Lane, and the High Street. The workhouse consisted of two houses with an accommodation of up to 20 inmates. The workhouse was built at some time prior to 1777. The parish entered into an Agreement in 1796 with John Pearson to care for the inmates of the workhouse. The arrangement was that the parish would pay for them to be 'decently clothed into the (work) House' and thereafter John Pearson was responsible for providing food, drink and clothing. Mr Pearson would receive three shillings per week per inmate and his extra responsibilities were to keep the inmates employed at work all the furniture, utensils and spinning wheels would be provided by the parish.

In 1809 the workhouse was running at its capacity as during that year the number of inmates totalled 19 or 20. An invoice submitted by the master or governor, William Spurge, for the month of January was for just over £17. He had 19 inmates in his care for four weeks at four shillings per head which accounted for just over £15 with the balance being made up one family who were there for one week and four days and another family who just had three meals. Two additional items were charged for and these were for looking after three lunatics and paying for the burial of Mary Ray. It is not clear whether the lunatics are included in the 19 inmates and he received an extra allowance for their care or they were lodged at the workhouse prior to be transferred to an asylum.

When the parish entered into an Agreement with a new governor in 1820 there were a number of arrangements which are not seen in other parishes. Besides all the usual conditions for looking after the inmates there was an arrangement whereby the governor received six pence for any inmate dying in the workhouse for 'putting the said person in the coffin'. The governor was specifically charged with ensuring that any linen provided by the parish 'be kept in decent order'. Agreements with workhouse masters are made up by the parish vestry and although they follow a fairly standard format there are always inserted clauses which differ from one parish to another. As we have seen above extra clauses are always added and as time goes on these agreements get longer and longer. A different condition in a new agreement for 1831 referred to inmates of the workhouse going out to work away from the workhouse. The arrangement was that any earnings by the inmate would be wholly taken by the parish to offset their board and lodging.

The parish vestry passed a resolution in April 1836 to sell the parish workhouse with the proceeds to be sent to the new Rochford Union Guardians. The sale would not have taken place though until the new Union workhouse was opened in 1837 when the inmates would have been transferred to their new home in the town.

Great Wakering/Little Wakering/Southchurch

At Great Wake ring's parish meeting on the 3rd April 1727 it was agreed that the officers of the parish could in conjunction 'with officers of neighbouring parishes' build a workhouse in some convenient place. It is not clear whether a workhouse was built or nor as the overseer's accounts do not show any workhouse expenditure in the subsequent period. From 1740 though the accounts do show a half yearly payment to Rochford parish workhouse. It looks as if Great Wakering did not have a workhouse, with or without other parishes, in the period from 1727 onwards but placed their poor in Rochford workhouse and paid for their keep in that institution.

None of the above three parishes had a workhouse in 1777 according to the government's survey of parish workhouses of that year but by 1792 the parishes of Great and Little Wakering with Southchurch had established a joint workhouse in Great Wakering. The overseer for the poor for Great Wakering records in 1792 'the state of the (work) House' with the names of inmates from each parish. The number from each parish was as follows:

Great Wakering - 9   Little Wakering - 6   Southchurch - 9   Total- 24

The numbers fluctuated over the subsequent year but usually Great Wakering had more paupers in the workhouse than the other parishes. In 1794 the parish passed a resolution that as there was little for the inmates to do that 'a spinning business be introduced'.

On the 2nd November 1803 Great Wakering parish passed a resolution requesting that the parishes of Little Wakering and Southchurch withdraw their poor from the Great Wakering workhouse. No reason was given but looking at the overseer's accounts it does look as if the poor rate income from these two parishes compared with what was collected from Great Wakering's rate payers was disproportionate to what Great Wakering was paying out to these parishes on out-relief expenses. So although apportioning the cost of running the workhouse was not a problem Great Wakering probably decided that each parish should bear the cost of their own poor. The next list of workhouse inmates in 1803 names only had sixteen Great Wakering parishioners though rose to 23 by 1808.

The site of the last workhouse in Great Wakering was on The Street in a property which subsequently became the George public house. The workhouse existed until it was taken over by the Rochford Union in the 1830s and sold in 1838.

THE ROCHFORD UNION WORKHOUSE

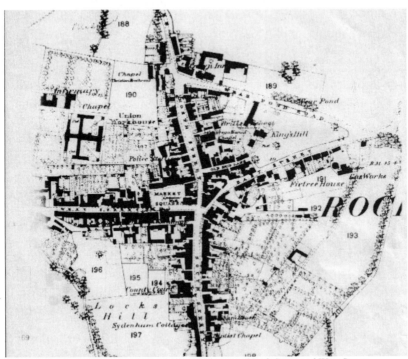

Rochford Union workhouse built 1837 between North Street and West Street

Many of the parishes listed at the start of this chapter were very small with Havengore, which is an island between Foulness Island and Southend, being the smallest parish with a population of only 18 persons in the 1830s. One hundred years later in 1931 when the parish workhouses closed Havengore's population had fallen to 12. The new Union workhouse of the 1830s covered what we know today as Southend and one may wonder why the town does not feature in the list of parishes above. Southend had not been so named in the time of parish workhouses and there was nothing there apart from a few fisherman's cottages. The largest centre of population in the census of 1841, only four years after the workhouse was built, was Prittlewell with 2380 persons, with Rochford and Rayleigh coming next with 1722 and 1651 respectively. Although Havengore Island was the smallest parish the population of Little Potton Island within the parish of Little Wakering was only 12 with Rusley Island within the parish of Great Wakering having a population of just 13.

The Union workhouse was built in 1837 for 300 inmates. The workhouse was located in Rochford between North Street and West Street behind the shops and houses in these two roads in the centre of Rochford. The entrance was off West Street.

The seashore at what we now know as Southend was separated from the parish of Prittlewell, where the centre was around the St Mary the Virgin church, by fields. The only habitation in the area of the present Southend Kursal was the oyster fishermen who had established their wooden housing and fishing huts along this section of seashore. It was not until the Fenchurch Street line of the railway came to Southend in 1856 that Prittlewell expanded to the seashore and along the front in both directions encompassing the old fishing community. Consequently, at the time that the Rochford Union Workhouse was built in 1837 Rochford parish, along with Rayleigh and Prittlewell were the largest centres of population in the area.

The census of 1841

The resident population of the Rochford Workhouse on census night in 1841 was as follows:

Males	105	The total includes 7 staff and 100 children under 14. The percentage of children to the total number of inmates was 56%
Females	80	
Total	185	

The workhouse infirmary block which still stands today

Guardians' minutes

We will look at the Guardians' minute books for the early 1880s and see if the nearness to the Thames and the other surrounding rivers affected the business put before the Guardians. The very first item I came across concerned some shipwrecked seamen.

February 1881

Shipwrecked seamen

Two shipwrecked seamen had come from the *Portia* and were now in the workhouse. They wished to leave but did not have any personal possessions apart from their workhouse clothes. The clerk was asked to write to the Mariners Society to see if they would assist. The outcome was that only one left the workhouse and the Society paid for clothing and a rail ticket to London. For the other, who stayed in the workhouse, the Society agreed to pay one shilling a week towards his keep. Maybe this seaman felt that he was safer in the workhouse where he was fed and clothed rather than facing the perils of the sea again.

March 1881

Inquest on James Truss

The clerk reported on the inquest on James Truss which was conducted at the workhouse. Apparently he cut his own throat whilst in the infirmary but the evidence on the case showed that his wound was insufficient to cause death and that he died from natural causes.

Canvey Island paupers

It had come to the attention of the Guardians that the Billericay Union had stopped the out-relief to certain paupers on Canvey Island. No reason at this stage was given but Rochford took it upon them to write to the Local Government Board for permission to pay the paupers out of their own funds. It later transpired that Canvey Island's poor; both in the Billericay workhouse and those on out-relief were being transferred to Rochford and due to an administration mix up those on out-relief were not getting paid. At the next meeting of the Guardians everything was formalised and a medical officer was appointed for Canvey Island as was a vaccination officer and also, and most importantly, a relieving officer.

July 1881
Thundersley property

The parish of Thundersley was included in the Billericay Union when the parishes were divided up in 1834 and references to the Thundersley parish workhouse are included in the chapter on Billericay. It seems strange that the parish should ask the Rochford Guardians for permission to let two very dilapidated cottages and four acres of land owned by the parish. Possibly Thundersley was transferred to the Rochford Union by the 1880s. It is most likely that this property was the old parish workhouse or an old parish poorhouse as otherwise the parish would not have had to ask the Guardians if they could let the property. All property previously used as a parish workhouse or poorhouse was usually sold off and the proceeds passed to the Union. Probably when the Union workhouse was built the parish poorhouse could not be sold as it was let and that had been the case up till 1881. It looks as if the property was let again until May of 1882 when the plan was to sell the property at auction. Later in September 1882 we see the Guardians giving permission for the property to be let once again and presumably the cottages did not sell at auction maybe because of their poor state of repair. It has been seen before that it was not the policy of Union Guardians to spend any further funds on parish properties.

September 1881
Inquest on William Gibbon

An inquest was held in the workhouse on William Gibbon who had died in the workhouse following injuries received caused by a loaded wagon passing over his body. Evidence was produced which concluded that death was 'accidental'.

October 1881
Boarding out of paupers
It was mentioned in the first chapter that Oliver Twist was advertised to be taken out of the workhouse with an incentive of a cash sum being offered. The implication in the Charles Dickens book was that Oliver was advertised by name but this was not the norm in Essex's workhouses. The October 1881 minutes record that the clerk had advertised for the boarding out of pauper children with expenses to be paid by the Union Workhouse. Three applications were received and the Guardians were offering to pay at the rate of three shillings a week for board and lodging plus one shilling a week for clothing, school fees and medical expenses. Of the three applicants one was Mrs Thorogood who was of the religious sect called the Peculiar People. It was proposed and seconded that the religious persuasion of the applicant should not be a bar to a pauper being boarded out. An amendment to that proposition was that she should not be allowed to take pauper children. The amendment was carried by eight votes to two and so Mrs Thorogood did not get a pauper child.

Subsequently a further application was made by Mrs Thorogood. The Guardians ascertained that there were four children in the workhouse whose parents were from the Peculiar People sect. It was now agreed that Mrs Thorogood could have two of them at the rates mentioned above. The connection with the Peculiar People relates to the chapel in North Street which was sited to the north east of the workhouse.

November 1881
Cess pools
Mains drainage was coming to that part of Rochford where the workhouse was located and the House Committee were asked to inspect the cess pool drainage system at the workhouse with a view to a connection being made to the mains drainage. The clerk read out the report from the House Committee which said that there was only one cess pool which operated quite efficiently and only needed to be emptied every four years. The conclusion was that there was no nuisance being caused by the present system and no need for a connection to the mains to be made.

December 1881
Inspector's report
Workhouse inspections often took place more than once a year and whilst the inspector was aware that the standard of accommodation and

food in a workhouse was on the whole poor, which of course was the intention as it was not an hotel; they were keen to comment on hygiene and matters of this nature. The inspector's report commented that there was ringworm in the girls' school but there was no entry of such in the medical book. The lavatory arrangements for the children also came in for adverse comment. It was left to the matron to look into these matters and she reported to the Guardians that each child had now been issued with their own brush, comb, towel, flannel and soap. These items would be considered a luxury for the average child of the 1880s let alone a workhouse pauper. The House Committee said that they would report later on the state of the lavatories for the girls.

March 1882
Boys for the navy
The Guardians were advised that some of the boys in the workhouse were keen to join the Navy. The clerk was asked to write to the coast guard at Sheerness for information. It transpired that the entry requirements were stringent and only one boy qualified. When approached the boy said he had changed his mind. It would have been his opportunity to get out of the workhouse, be fed and clothed and also paid for his service to Queen Victoria.

June 1882
John Jarvis's pension
It was usual that if a pauper in the workhouse was in receipt of a pension from some prior employment then the Guardians could claim it to offset the cost of his board and lodging. This was happening in the case of John Jarvis whose mercantile marine pension was being paid whilst he was in the workhouse to a Mr Williams. Mr Williams objected and a ruling came from the Board of Trade that in the case of this type of pension the workhouse had no right to claim it. The minutes were silent on the background to the Board's decision.

June 1882
Industrial trainer
There were very few salaried appointments of people that were based in a workhouse and in addition to the workhouse master and matron, usually husband and wife, the other officers were usually the porter, the nurse and occasionally the chaplain. The other salaried appointments were people who mainly worked outside the workhouse apart from the medical officer, who was responsible for the inmates, who would come in when required. A new appointment at Rochford was that of an

industrial trainer and the job was being advertised for a female at a salary of £25 a year.

The Rochford Union Workhouse Ancillary Buildings erected
In the early 1900s.

The job was to teach the girls and young women the basics of needlework and domestic chores with a view to them eventually being admitted into domestic service.

Like today, there are grants for employing people in specific jobs and the Guardians wrote to the Local Government Board to see if they could apply for a grant for their industrial trainer. The reply was that the government only viewed this office as a 'caretaker' and not an industrial trainer. They went on to say that the training given was only to make the children fit for agricultural pursuits, in the case of boys, and for domestic service in the case of girls. Consequently this training did not qualify for a government grant.

Salaried appointments

The quarterly salaries paid by the Rochford Union in June 1882 were as follows:

	£	s	d
Master and Matron combined	25	0	0
Porter	5	0	0
Nurse	6	10	0
Industrial Trainer (male)	6	10	0
Industrial Trainer (female)	5	0	0
Medical Officer (for workhouse and Rochford local area)	28	10	0
Medical Officers for rural areas	16	15	0
Medical Officers for rural areas	14	10	0
Medical Officers for rural areas	27	10	0
Relieving Officers	27	15	0
Relieving Officers	23	15	0
Assistant Relieving Officers	2	10	0
Assistant Relieving Officers	1	10	0
Rate Collectors	6	10	0
Rate Collectors	2	10	0
Rate Collectors	5	0	0
Rate Collectors3	3	15	0
Rate Collectors	2	10	0
Rate Collector for Prittlewell	27	10	0

Only the first six in the above list lived in with the medical officers and the other appointments living and carrying out their duties in Rochford and the outlying parishes. It looks as if the new industrial trainer for the females was to be paid the same as that for the males. The previous incumbent, who is the one in the list above, received £20 a year.

September 1882

Pauper inquest

The master reported to the Guardians that he had taken into the workhouse the body of a man who had fallen from his horse. The man was not a pauper and presumably the incident had happened in the proximity of the workhouse. The inquest was held in the workhouse. The Guardians made a new rule that deceased people who were not previously resident of the workhouse should generally not be brought into the workhouse but it was left to the workhouse master to use his discretion in these matters.

March 1883
Workhouse water
Over the last year or so there had been various comments in the minutes concerning the state of the pump that brought the water up from the well and it was clear that major repairs were needed. It looks as if either the pump had completely broken down or the Guardians planned to effect repairs as a contract was now arranged with Mr J Penton to cart water to the workhouse whilst repairs were going on.

May 1883
Abraham Ford deceased
It was usual for the Guardians to approach the relations of persons in the workhouse for a contribution towards their board and lodging. A figure was agreed upon relative to the means. Abraham Ford had died in the workhouse and the Guardians were making enquiries as to his assets. The report back was that he owned three very old boats valued at £1. The cost of the funeral with expenses came to just over £3 and the clerk had approached his sons for payment. It is unclear if the sons paid up but the Guardians were advised that at the funeral it was reported that the undertaker's men were seen smoking on the hearse. The Guardians reprimanded the funeral contractor for 'such indecent behaviour'.

June 1883
Emigration to Australia
No-one wanted to stay in the workhouse longer than necessary as conditions were deliberately so bad and one of the ways of getting out and starting a new life was to emigrate. Mary Ann Burrell and her four children applied to leave the workhouse to emigrate to Queensland, Australia and asked for expenses. The Guardians were always keen to reduce the numbers as there would in this case have five less mouths to feed and clothe which could go on for many years. In principle the request was granted but the Guardians wanted to know why Queensland was chosen as this was not the area to which most emigrants went. They also were obliged to ensure that satisfactory arrangements would be in place for the children on their arrival. Mr Burrell said that she already

had a sister and two sons in that state who would assist the family when they arrived. She also confirmed that she had documentary evidence that the Government of Queensland would give the family an assisted passage. Consequently the Guardians agreed an allowance of £30 which, compared to the annual salary of £25 for the nurse, appears generous.

September 1883
Industrial trainer
The Local Government Board now advises the Guardians that a parliamentary grant will be received in respect of the male industrial trainer. It looks as if the government had changed its mind on a grant for this position as a grant was declined in June 1882. No mention though of a grant for the female industrial trainer.

June 1884
Mrs Kendall the female industrial trainer
The Guardians were advised that 'Mrs Kendall the female industrial trainer had become mad and removed from the workhouse'. The Guardians subsequently learned that at some time prior to her appointment at Rochford she had been in a lunatic asylum for some months. The Guardians asked to see her references to see if they were aware that she had previously been institutionalised. Presumably this fact was not disclosed at her interview and one wonders how this oncoming insanity, whilst at the workhouse, affected the girls in her charge.

August 1884
Ann Seymour
Mrs Ann Seymour was a widow and was an inmate with five children in the workhouse. She requested that she leave the (work) House with one child and leave four there. The workhouse was usually referred by inmates as the "House". Requests of this type are usually turned aside as the rule is usually all go or all stay but in this case the Guardians agreed that she could leave with three children. Possibly the two left behind were the eldest and coming up to the age where they could be sent out to work. Mrs Seymour was granted out-relief to the extent of five shillings a week plus.

October 1884
Mr Pilgrim the porter
The minutes recorded that the master reported to the Guardians that the porter had abused him and charged him with being drunk. The porter, Mr Pilgrim, was interviewed and whilst not commenting on the abuse did

say that he considered the master to be drunk. The Guardians investigated the matter and it was decided that the charges against the master had no foundation. The Board consequently cautioned the porter as to his future conduct. There are various instances in Essex workhouses where the master and the porter did not get on although the blame was usually spread between the two.

November 1884

Pauper funerals

Previously in May 1883 we saw the funeral contractor reprimanded for his staff smoking at a pauper funeral and this time the accusation was that 'the proper (coffin) bearers were not employed'. I suppose that with no relatives attending a pauper funeral whether inside or outside the workhouse standards had fallen.

December 1884

Christmas dinner

Every year in December the Guardians approved the expense of a Christmas dinner for the inmates. It is a pity that the details of the dinner are not recorded but on this occasion the resolution for the expense was not passed automatically. A resolution was put forward that those inmates admitted in November and December should not receive the Christmas dinner except those admitted who were sick. An amendment was then proposed that everyone should get the Christmas dinner. A further amendment was that a list of all the inmates be produced and that the Guardians decide who should not receive the dinner irrespective of when they were admitted. Presumably if some were to be excluded then the Guardians would pick out the troublesome inmates. This last amendment was carried and the Guardians selected eight inmates who would not receive the dinner.

January 1885

Fraudulent cheques

The clerk reported that two cheques had been presented to their bankers for payment of a type that had not been in use for three years. The authorised signatures had been forged and consequently they were not paid and so there was no loss to the Union. The loser though was a Mr Downes who had obviously received the cheques for payment for goods and had tried to pay them into his bank account. The police were informed and it transpired that the cheques had been taken out of an old unused cheque book. The minutes for November 1885 record that an arrest had been made.

February 1885

Herbert Smith's apprenticeship

Mr Cork of Rayleigh attended the Guardians' meeting and said that he was willing to take Herbert Smith as an apprenticed shoemaker. He asked for a premium of £10 for board and lodging to take the boy. The Guardians offered seven pounds ten shillings together with a set of clothes. The agreement was that Mr Cork was to feed and clothe the boy for two years and pay him six pence a week for the first year and one shilling a week for the second year. For the third year his pay would be four shillings a week and the boy would provide his own clothes. Mr Cork initially objected to the terms but subsequently agreed at a later meeting. Mr Cork refused though to enter into a contract to provide medical attention for Herbert when necessary.

November 1885

The master's accounts

At every meeting, which was usually every fortnight, the master would present his account book for provisions bought and the general expenses for running the workhouse for approval. The auditors reported that there were discrepancies relating to the food account. The master was interviewed and admitted he had altered the books to make things balance as there had been a deficiency in the bread account for which he could not account. Probably inmates were stealing bread and he had to doctor the account to make it balance. The master received a 'severe reprimand' and was advised to keep better control over food supplies in the future.

In addition to agreeing the master's books the Guardians once a quarter confirmed the amounts chargeable out to the parishes for their contribution to the running of the workhouse. The parishes in their turn would levy a poor rate and the collectors would have the responsibility of collecting these monies. There are now 28 parishes that contribute towards the running of Rochford workhouse and their contributions for a typical quarter were as follows:

Prittlewell	£1862	Rawreth	£152
Foulness	£430	Lt. Wakering	£140
Gt Wakering	£320	S Benfleet	£140
Canewdon	£308	Thundersley	£120
Rochford	£276	Barling	£120
Rayleigh	£270	N. Shoebury	£110
Eastwood	£250	Hadleig	£108
Hockley	£240	Hawkswell	£90
S. Shoebury	£238	Shopland	£80
Canvey Island	£200	Lt Stambridge	£72
Leigh	£194	Sutton	£68
Southchurch	£184	S. Fambridge	£60
Paglesham	£170	Ashingdon	£60
Gt Stambridge	£156	Havengore	£16

As to be expected Prittlewell paid the most having by far the largest population of just under 8000 in 1881 but it is surprising that Foulness, Great Wakering and Canewdon paid more than Rochford and Rayleigh who had larger populations. The assessment by the Guardians do not strictly relate to the size of a parish population but although each parish bore a part of the actual running costs of the workhouse the parish also paid an amount relative to the number of paupers in that parish who were either accommodated in the workhouse or on out-relief. It follows, therefore, that there was more hardship for the residents of Foulness, Gt Wakering and Canewdon and consequently more reliance by these parishes on out-relief or actual residence in the workhouse. All these three parishes were in highly rural areas where farm improving mechanisation meant that fewer labourers were being employed on the land which led to many agricultural workers being out of work and having to rely on out-relief or being taken into the workhouse.

1886

Mention is made in the chapter on Chelmsford Union Workhouse that there was a fire at this workhouse in 1886 which destroyed most of the workhouse buildings. The minutes for Rochford record that the Guardians were agreeable to accommodate temporarily 33 of Chelmsford's inmates.

March 1886
Geoffrey Nunn
Doctor Grigg of Prittlewell had written to the Local Government Board complaining that Rochford Union had stopped the out-relief for Geoffrey Nunn of Canewdon on political grounds. The correspondence had been

passed on to the Guardians who replied to the Local Government Board and said that this decision was unknown to them and had been made by the local relieving officer. The reply went on to say that they (the Rochford Union) would never refuse relief on political grounds. The Guardians felt that in view of the serious implications of the case they should publish all the correspondence in the local newspaper in case the public thought they were discriminating politically. Although further correspondence passed between the Guardians and the Local Government Board there was no further comment on what happened to the relieving officer or what the 'political grounds' were.

The enlargement of the workhouse

Like all of the Essex workhouses Rochford grew considerably over the one hundred years as a Union workhouse. In 1858 an infirmary was built away from the main residential blocks and this would have been deliberate policy to have it separate in view of the many infectious diseases that were prevalent in the 1800s. A separate chapel was built in 1865.

The twentieth century
The census of 1901

Males	138	The total includes 12 staff and 31 children
Females	70	under 14. The percentage of children to the total number of inmates was 16%
Total	208	

The total number of inmates was well below the capacity of 300 in 1901 with the very high percentage of children in 1841 (56%) down to only 16%. There were many smaller additions to the workhouse in the early part of the twentieth century. During the 1914-18 War the block used by the aged and infirm was taken over to accommodate German prisoners of war. Like other workhouses in Essex the infirmary in the 1920s was now being used for sick non pauper patients and became known as Rochford Hospital before being handed over in 1930 to the Southend-on- Sea Public Health Committee.

Chapter 14

ROMFORD AND ITS ENVIRONS

PARISH WORKHOUSES

The following 10 parishes in the above area were grouped together in 1834 following the Poor Law Amendment Act to form the Romford Union. Before 1834 each parish may have had its own poorhouse or workhouse.

Barking   **Cranham**   **Romford**   **Rainham**
Hornchurch   **Upminster**   **Dagenham**   **Gt.Warley**
Havering-atte-Bower **Wennington**

The government undertook a survey of parish workhouses in 1777 and the following three parishes in this area had a workhouse open in that year.

Barking   Dagenham   Upminster

The Romford parish workhouse does not get a mention as it was not built until after the date of the government survey.

Romford

There is reference in a deed dated 1702 to an inn called the Three Coneys abutting a workhouse near the Market Place. This 'workhouse' was probably just a property owned or rented by the parish for the poor or it may have been a workshop.

On the 16 September 1786 three of the 'Directors and Guardians of the Poor of the parish of Romford in the Liberty of Havering' entered into an agreement with Abraham Godden and Richard Moore to build a workhouse for the parish. The location was in a field called Joy's Mead on the west side of what is now North Street, Romford. The field built on was part of land owned by the Roger Reede Charity who had almshouses built on this west side of North Street. The agreement was very specific including instructions on the brickwork with the joints of the brickwork not to exceed three-eights of an inch. The foundations including the cellars were to be constructed by the 11th September 1787 with walls and stairs to the first floor by the 9th October. The second floor was to be ready by the 13th November ready to complete the roof. The contractors were to supply all the scaffolding at their expense and to leave the same for one month after completion of the shell for the other tradespersons to carry out their work to complete the roof and internal carpentry work. The building work was to include the provision by the contractors of all building materials with the exception of the roof tiles. The agreement also set out the conditions for part payments as the work progressed. The workhouse was duly built on time by 1787 at a cost of £3500/£4000 and the Guardians of the poor drew up rules for the master and mistress of the workhouse. There were ten main rules which are summarised as follows:

1. That the master shall register all the names and ages of the poor on admission and discharge or on death.
2. That a roll call be taken at 6am in summer, at 7am in winter and at 1pm all the year.
3. Daily accounts shall be kept of all provisions used, materials and tools supplied, and of all work done by the inmates.
4. That a record be kept of all tradesmen's bills.
5. An inventory shall be kept of all clothing and goods brought into the (work) House by the inmates.
6. That prayers be read every morning and evening and grace before each meal.
7. That the master do keep the outward door locked and that no alcohol shall be brought into the House.
8. That the master make sure that beds are made and rooms swept daily and rooms washed once a week in winter and twice a week in summer.
9. That the children are washed combed and cleaned before breakfast and taught to read.
10. That the master do take them that are sick to the apothecary.

Romford's parish workhouse was one of the largest in Essex and could accommodate up to 250 inmates. It was initially used by the new Romford Union Guardians for a few years until the new Union workhouse was built in Oldchurch Road. The old parish workhouse was sold in 1840 and pulled down.

Barking

The first Barking workhouse was discussed by the vestry in 1721 and opened in that year. The vestry decided to lease a block of four tenements in North Street at the rent of £10 a year. They were to be converted into a workhouse which probably meant the pulling down of some of the internal walls to make a large day room or workroom. Upstairs similar work may have been carried out to make dormitory bedrooms. There is no indication as to how many inmates the property could accommodate but probably initially about 20/30 persons. There are records that wool was purchased and this means that like other workhouses at this time the inmates were employed in some aspects of the wool and cloth industry.

There is recorded that one of the first workhouse masters was Thomas Pittman who had the job from 1734 to 1741. He probably died in this year as when the position was advertised one of the applicants was Mrs Amy Pittman who was probably his wife. There were four applications and Mrs Pittman secured the position on votes cast. Her salary was £21 a year. Amy held the job for twelve years.

The original lease had been renewed in 1753 and when it was due for review again in 1774 the parish vestry considered the building of a new workhouse. At about this time the vestry were concerned that there was a lack of work for the inmates and also a suitable place in which to work. A wooden shed was therefore built in the yard and the inmates were employed in picking oakum which was the unthreading of old ropes for re-use. The government survey of workhouses in 1777 showed that the Barking workhouse could now accommodate up to 70 inmates.

The new Barking parish workhouse was built in 1788 in North Street near to the Bull Inn at a cost of £4000. It was a substantial brick built building two storeys high with two wings and a basement. The frontage was 140 feet and on the ground floor there were the master and matron's apartment. There was a committee room for the governing body and also a store room and cellar. The long wings provided large workrooms for the looms as the wool industry was in full flow at this time. Upstairs were the bedchambers and there was a further wing that made up the square with a central courtyard. There was a Latin inscription on the front of the building which said:

'This house of industry at the sole expense of the inhabitants of Barking is to provide for and protect the industrious and to punish the idle and wicked'.

Those in charge of the administration of the workhouse were called 'Governors' and the original body were:

Rev. Peter Rushleigh, Vicar	Mr George Spurrell
Mr Bamber Gascoyne, Senior	Mr Edward Hulse, Lord of the Manor
Mr Bamber Gascoyne, Junior	Mr Thomas Pittman

In 1796 there were 112 inmates and one can well see why a large parish like Barking with a large parish workhouse felt aggrieved when it was decided to build in the 1830s the new Union workhouse at Romford incorporating Barking's poor. The parish workhouse was still in operation in the late 1830s but it is not clear when the inmates were transferred to the Romford Union. Notes for a *History of Barking* record that a Barking resident paid for 'a substantial dinner' for the inmates on the occasion of the wedding of Queen Victoria in 1837. The vestry minutes record that the workhouse was surveyed in 1836 following the establishment of the Romford Union and in 1839 the vestry were talking about selling or letting the property which indicates that the inmates had gone. The property was finally let in 1841 with the income to go to the Romford Union. The tenant converted the frontage into six shops and built cottages on the land at the rear. Part of the old workhouse was used as the National School.

Barking parish workhouse built in 1788

Cranham

The first mention of a poorhouse or workhouse was in 1782 when the vestry paid eight shillings for providing a loom for the poor. The property was probably the size of at least two cottages by today's standards and owned by the parish of Cranham. It is surprising that for a small parish there was a workhouse master who ran the building with his wife. Records show that the husband and wife came from South Ockendon to take up the position. There are various references in the vestry minutes to Cranham's poor being sent to other villages to be looked after in other poorhouses or workhouses and Cranham would be charged for their board and lodging. Between 1786 and 1788 three of the poor were sent to the parish workhouse at Great Warley. From 1797 the overflow from Cranham were sent to Upminster's workhouse and there are ten cases recorded between 1797 and 1816 when Cranham's poor were sent to the Upminster workhouse. The indication is that the workhouse was quite small and probably could not accommodate more than ten persons. After this date the arrangement was not continued as there were no further places available at Upminster for the poor of other parishes.

It looks as if what with Upminster taking no more of Cranham's poor, and maybe the cost of boarding them out at other parishes, the vestry decided in 1828 that the parish needed a larger workhouse. Consequently a petition was sent to the Lord of the Manor, Sir Thomas Apreece, for a grant of land on which to build a new workhouse. The cost to the parish of the land was £20 and the site was where the Jobbers Rest public house is today. The piece of land in St. Mary's lane was 36 feet deep with a frontage to the road of 174 feet. The actual building was 51 feet long and 20 feet deep with a spring water well outside. The garden area, therefore, would have been large and very suitable for the cultivation of fruit and vegetables. The number of inmates during the workhouse's short life of eight years was between 12 and 18 with a high proportion of children. In 1833, for example, there were three men, seven women and eight children. The inmates were transferred to the Romford Union Workhouse in 1836 and the property was sold for £205 to Mr George Rowe who incidentally bought the Upminster workhouse which closed at the same time. The old workhouse was converted into four cottages and later the Jobbers Rest public house was built on the site.

Dagenham

Dagenham parish established a workhouse during the period 1730/40 using a house called 'Wrights' which was owned by the John Comyns charity and previously used as almshouses. Attached to the workhouse was a large garden and 20 acres of land. The location was Church Elm Lane.

The person in charge of providing food for the workhouse in 1816 was Mrs Collier who was allowed an increase in the daily allowance per inmate from five shillings and six pence to six shillings and six pence in view of the high price of bread. Mr Vial from Gravesend had the contract to cloth the inmates for the sum of £20 a year. Mr Thomas Price was the master of the workhouse at this time and when his Agreement said that he would 'farm' the poor this meant that he was responsible for the general well being of the inmates.

Dagenham parish workhouse continued to exist until 1835 when the new Romford Union was formed and the 25 or so inmates were transferred to either Romford or Barking parish workhouses pending the building of the new Union workhouse in Oldchurch Road, Romford. The old workhouse was later converted back into almshouses.

Havering-atte-Bower

On the 22nd March 1792 the parish vestry entered into a lease with Thomas Neave for 21 years for a piece of land on the south east side of the road from Havering atte Bower to Broadgates. A subsequent lease describes the location as Havering Green. Although the original deed does not specifically refer to the property on the land as a workhouse the front of the document refers to it as 'Lease of the Workhouse'. It is also not clear whether the building had been used as a workhouse prior to 1792. Havering atte Bower does not feature in the government survey of parish workhouses in 1777 and consequently the workhouse was established at some time after this date.

An inventory that was taken in 1816 indicated that the workhouse was small and only had three rooms on the ground floor and three rooms upstairs. It looks as if one or more of the downstairs rooms was used as a bedroom. In 1816 another member of the Neave family signed an agreement to continue the lease on the cottage as a poorhouse (workhouse) for seven years which was renewable.

Hornchurch

The parish workhouse came into being in 1721 when a row of four cottages on the corner of High Street and Billet Lane were converted for this purpose. Previously the cottages were part of the Pennants almshouses which were set up in 1598. The site is now the Sainsburys supermarket. In 1727 the parish drew up an agreement with Thomas Langley to run the workhouse for a fee of £100 a year with Mr Langley providing all the food and other necessary provisions together with clothing for the inmates. Any profit for work done by the inmates could be kept by the workhouse master.

The workhouse does not get a mention in government's 1777 survey and it may have been closed in that year and reopened subsequently. As the property being used as the workhouse was previously almshouses there may have some confusion as to whether it qualified to be included in the survey.

By the early 1800s there were up to 40 inmates and an interesting minute by the vestry in 1829 relates to complaints by the workhouse master concerning the improper conduct of the inmates. The master reported that the 'improper conduct' related to the one staircase being used by the males and females when retiring to their beds. The parish vestry agreed to construct a separate staircase for each sex. A further alteration took place in 1831 when the back bedroom was petitioned off to accommodate any insane person and deceased corpses. Placing the insane in a separate room was probably only a temporary measure as there are various references to Hornchurch's insane being transferred to the 'Bethnal Green Madhouse'. Hornchurch vestry would be charged for the expense of keeping insane residents in the asylum.

A meeting of the vestry was convened in the workhouse in November 1831 in response to the government's request that parishes establish Boards of Health in the light of the cholera epidemic which was prevalent in 1831-32. The vestry decided to order the parish surveyors to have any ditches, drains and water courses thoroughly cleaned and privies to be emptied. The surveyors were instructed to apply to the magistrate for a summons if owners did not comply with their request. As far as parish property was concerned the vestry decided that the workhouse should be limed and white washed from top to bottom and the building thoroughly cleaned and kept ventilated. The overseer was instructed to inspect all the properties where families were in receipt of out-relief to ensure that they were clean and to employ someone to lime wash, clean drains and gutters if they could not afford or were not capable of doing this work. Those on out-relief would probably have been in rented property and should the landlord not undertake the appropriate work then the expense of getting it done would have been charged out to him.

In June 1836 there were six men and eight women in the workhouse. The new Romford Union had now been formed and the Romford Guardians decided that all parish workhouses would close with the exception of that at Barking and Romford. Eleven of Hornchurch's inmates were transferred to the Barking parish workhouse and three to Romford parish workhouse. The Hornchurch workhouse closed and was converted back into almshouses in 1837.

Rainham and Wennington

Rainham parish housed their poor in a workhouse in Wennington which was established in 1810 as a joint venture with Aveley and West Thurrock parishes (see above in Orsett Union area).

This arrangement continued until 1831 when West Thurrock broke away from the group and formed their own separate workhouse. It is not clear from the vestry minutes whether the Wennington workhouse closed in 1831 and Rainham parish established their own workhouse or the workhouse at Wennington continued to take Rainham's poor until it was taken over by the Romford Union and then closed in 1836. There are references in the Rainham vestry accounts from 1833 of insurance being paid on a workhouse but it is not clear whether they are referring to a new one established in Rainham or the old one in Wennington. Once again in 1840 the workhouse gets a mention and this time the parish were distributing goods from the workhouse to widows who were probably in need of the items. This distribution is obviously in connection with the closure but it is still not clear where the workhouse was located.

Upminster

Upminster Parish Workhouse built 1750

Prior to the building of the workhouse the poor of the parish were lodged in houses in the village and the family in residence was given out-relief for their keep. In Upminster's case there was also a poor box in the church which was common in many Essex villages. Up to the time of the building of the workhouse in 1750 there were 18 people lodged in the parish and talk about a parish workhouses started with a vestry meeting in 1749 when it was resolved:

'It is this day ordered and agreed that a house shall forthwith be built for the use of the poor and that £110, now in South Sea Annuities at 4%, be employed for the building the same and that the parishioners do continue to pay annually the interest of the same to the poor as has been done, and that those whose names are underwritten do take care to carry on the said building'.

The location of the workhouse was at the western end of St Mary's Lane at the bottom of Upminster hill opposite Bridge Avenue. The vestry contributed part of the money needed to build the workhouse but even when finished the building could not accommodate everyone. The excess would have been sent to an adjacent village's workhouse if there was room. In 1762 the inmates totalled 10 of which six were widows and the rest probably orphans. By 1783 the number of poor in Upminster had increased to the extent that there was never enough room for their own poor and it is recorded that some were housed in the Great Warley workhouse which does not feature in the 1777 list and must have been built subsequently. Consequently the vestry and the overseers of the poor decided to apply to the Lord of the Manor for permission to enclose part of his adjacent land to the workhouse to build an extension. The Manor Rolls record a grant of land to the vestry for the purpose required at a rent of twelve and a half pence a year by 1786 the extension was complete and those housed at Great Warley were transferred back to the enlarged Upminster workhouse. The government list of parish workhouses states that Upminster could accommodate 20 in 1777, which was prior to the extension, and it is recorded that the maximum number was 37 in 1803 when this figure is seen in the workhouse master's allowances claim. When Union workhouses came into being in 1834 the Upminster workhouse was sold off in 1836 and turned into six cottages.

Great Warley

Great Warley parish established a workhouse in 1783 on Headley Common which could accommodate up to 20 paupers. The records show that the workhouse took any overflow from the parishes of Upminster and Cranham. An inventory of the workhouse was taken in 1821 which showed that there were fourteen beds, fifteen sheets and twelve blankets. This gives some idea as to how many inmates there were in 1821.

The workhouse was sold in 1830 when Great Warley parish joined nine other parishes to establish a joint workhouse at Stanford Rivers (see Stanford Rivers in Ongar Union) It was surprising that Great Warley chose to join the Stanford Rivers group of parishes as the other nine parishes were all situated around Stanford Rivers whereas Great Warley was many miles away.

THE ROMFORD UNION WORKHOUSE

When the Poor Law Commissioners had decided to combine the ten parishes to form the Romford Union and build one new workhouse centred at Romford the Commissioners met opposition from the existing parishes of Romford and Barking who each had their own large parish workhouse. As each of these parishes had about 150/200 inmates in each of their parish workhouses they both felt that there was a need for a new Union Workhouse at both of these centres. The Commissioners disagreed and only wanted there to be one workhouse centred on Romford. This in itself was odd as all the other workhouses in Essex had been centred on the town with the largest population in the designated area. Barking's population was just over 9,000 and double the population of Romford which was about 4,400 in the 1830s. This unusual situation is demonstrated in the allocation of the Guardians which was 22 initially rising to 24 by the 1880s. The number of Guardians was relative to the population. With two very large parishes being joined together into one Union Workhouse the number of separate parishes involved was only ten compared with double this number in most of the other Unions.

Number of Guardians:	Barking	8	Cranham	1
	Romford	5	Rainham	1
	Hornchurch	3	Upminster	1
	Dagenham	2	Gt Warley	1
	Havering-atte-Bower	1	Wennington	1

The site selected for the new workhouse was very close to the centre of Romford but actually at the time in open countryside to the west of the town centre. In the 1830s there were fields surrounding the proposed site but in the year following the building of the workhouse in 1839 the railway arrived at Romford from Liverpool Street. The workhouse was built in the Oldchurch Road with its northern boundary being the new railway line. The Guardians selected three architects to produce plans, Messrs Savage, Kempthorne and Edwards. Mr Sampson Kempthorne was the architect chosen by the Poor Law Commissioners to draw up the plans for a typical workhouse which were included as a model for new workhouses. Mr Savage dropped out of the running and it was left to the Guardians to choose one of the remaining two. Of the twenty four Guardians there were nine on the Building Committee and they decided on which design to accept. The voting was five to four on favour of Mr Francis Edwards.

Mr Edwards had been asked to design a workhouse for up to 450 inmates which was the largest in Essex. Obviously the Guardians had taken into account the existing Romford and Barking parish workhouses where there were up to 400 inmates together with a sprinkling of small rural parish workhouses. The standard design suggested by Kempthorne, and followed by most of the architects, was for a central hub with wings extending from it in a cruciform design. Although Mr Edwards adopted the central hub his wings extended diagonally from the centre in the shape of an 'X'. There are few workhouses in the country with this 'X' shape design and none other designed by Francis Edwards.

The workhouse was built between 1838-39 with yellow stock bricks under a slate roof. The inmates of the other parish workhouses had already been transferred to either the Barking or Romford parish workhouses. Starting with the Barking parish workhouse 250 inmates were transferred in the second week of December 1839 and the inmates at the Romford parish workhouse were transferred shortly afterwards.

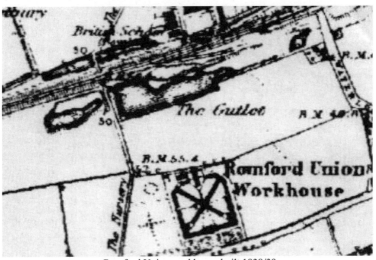

Romford Union workhouse built 1838/39

Christmas 1840

The Essex Standard was critical of the fare supplied to the paupers on Christmas Day. The paupers on that day shared 240 plum puddings. 'What is the world coming to?' asked the newspaper. I am not sure of the size of the plum puddings but there were less than 300 inmates at the time.

The census of 1841

Males	138	The total includes 7 staff and 93 children under
Females	145	14. The percentage of children to the total number
		of inmates was 34 %
Total	283	

If Barking parish transferred 250 inmates when the new Union workhouse opened and the Romford records show that they transferred their paupers to the new Union workhouse at roughly the same time the total of 283 a few years later in 1841 seems rather low. One would expect the total to be nearer 400 inmates and the explanation could have been that when the able paupers knew that they were being transferred to this new institution block they got themselves jobs and out of the workhouse. The Barking paupers especially would not have been too happy about moving away from their own area although many would not have had the ability to leave the workhouse for one reason or another.

The Guardians held weekly meeting whereas some of the other Essex Union Workhouses only held meetings every two weeks. I suppose that with the Romford Union being so large there were more matters to discuss. I have selected the Guardians minutes for the period 1882-83 for interesting snippets about life in the Romford workhouse

June 1882
New master and matron
The Guardians approved the application of Mr & Mrs Seymour Clarke as the new master and matron. Mr Clarke's salary was to be £70 per year and his wife as matron £40 a year. Few women worked in the 1880s, apart from low paid domestic servants, and to have a combined income of over £100 a year would have put them in the top bracket of Romford's earners. The Guardians agreed that their child aged seven could reside with them on the payment of two shillings and sixpence a week in respect of board and lodging.

Smallpox
In June 1882 the Local Government Board, the successor to the Poor Law Commissioners, brought to the Guardians' attention that in some workhouses where there were cases of smallpox that some of the staff that were involved in the nursing had not been vaccinated themselves. This had resulted in the spread of the disease both inside and outside the workhouse. The Local Government Board wished to impress upon all

Romford Union workhouse entrance block which still stands

Romford Union workhouse porter's lodge

Guardians that smallpox cases must be isolated in fever wards and that there must be no contact with these cases by staff or inmates who were not inoculated. Readers will note that smallpox was rife in workhouses throughout all the 1800s and the main problem in the design of the buildings was that there were no isolation wards for cases of infectious diseases.

July 1882
Request for fisherman apprentices
An interesting letter arrived at the Guardians' meeting from a Mr Christopher Fry of Grimsby who owned a fishing boat who was looking for two or three apprentices for sea service. The Guardians selected William Dobson and John Flack to be allowed to go for a one month trial. It is strange that he wrote to the Romford Union when there were many closer workhouses to Grimsby from which to recruit staff.

August 1882
Complaint regarding lunatics
A complaint had been received that lunatics were occasionally being lodged in the Receiving Ward. As the name suggests this was the ward that new entrants were admitted to until assessment was complete. The officer responsible explained that this does not occur very often and when it does it is usually only for a day or so whilst a lunatic is being transferred from a parish to the asylum at Brentwood. The officer confirmed that in future if a person is to be transferred to Brentwood from a parish then it would be direct and not via the workhouse. The Guardians also accepted that occasionally if a person had to come to the Union first then he or she would be accommodated in a different place.

Commissioners in Lunacy report
By coincidence the Commissioner in Lunacy visited the Romford Union in August and presented his report. He found that of the inmates three men and six women had been classified to be 'of unsound mind'. In addition, in the Reception Ward was a man named William Palmer recently brought in suffering from religious mania who was also refusing food. Regarding Mr Palmer, the Commissioner recommended that he be immediately transferred to the asylum at Brentwood. In addition to the list of nine cases the Commissioners identified two further inmates who they considered should be added to the 'unsound mind' list. Presumably the Commissioner's brief was to check on the conditions in which the nine plus the extra two lived to see that their living conditions and food was of no less a standard than the ordinary inmate. The report went on to comment on the wards and dining room which they found to be 'bare and cheerless'. They also commented that the baths are 'bad' and they could not see that anything had been done to alleviate an accident from scalding. Maybe those of unsound mind were being allowed to take a bath unsupervised. The visitor attended the inmates at dinner and whilst finding the food adequate commented that the knives and forks were very worn and useless. The tables were bare, he said, and a big spoon

served as a salt cellar. It was suggested that a few cheap prints would improve the appearance of the rooms. The inmates had no complaints and said that they were treated kindly and were cared for. One can only presume that all the above comments referred to the conditions in which those of unsound lived and not the other inmates.

October 1882

Workhouse expenses

The minutes published in full the income and expenses of the Union Workhouse for the half year to Michaelmas 1882 which included those on out-relief.

Workhouse Expenditure	£	**Income from parishes (Poor Rate)**	£
Running costs	1452	Barking	2309
Out relief	1783	Cranham	67
Non resident poor	65	Dagenham	434
School fees (out door)	44	Hornchurch	426
Assessment C'ttee exp	84	Havering-atte-B	96
Poor removal exp.	1	Romford	904
Cost of lunatics at B'wood	846	Rainham	197
Election exp	12	Upminster	188
Salaries	602	Gt Warley	138
Staff rations	102	Wennington	67
Extra medical fees	61		
Cost of vaccinations	87	Other income	1075
Registrations	66		
Legal exp.	6		
School fees (in door)	3		
Furniture & property	151		
Building repairs	206		
Other charges	330		
Total	£5901	Total	£5901

The out relief figure of £1783 represents the cost of providing for the poor who were not residents in the workhouse. The charge from the Brentwood County Lunatic Asylum for looking after their inmates who came from the parishes within the Union area was £846 and represents 14% of the total. The population of Barking had been increasing at a faster rate than Romford since the workhouse was built as reflected in the amount they have to pay to the Union which is charged out to the residents by way of the Poor rate relative to the respective populations.

November 1882
The fishing apprentices
Two pauper boys went to Grimsby in July and the Guardians had now received a letter from the fishing boat owner, Christopher Fry, stating that the boys, John Flack an orphan aged 14 and William Nicholls also 14 were both agreeable to becoming apprentices for sea service. The earlier minute said that the second boy was to be William Dobson but obviously things got changed. John was an orphan and so there was no one else to consult but as William Nicholls's parent were still in the workhouse permission had to be sought for their son to be allowed to stay at Grimsby which they readily gave. Although life on a fishing boat was undoubtedly hard in the 1880s it was a chance for a new life for William Nicholls which would have been better than staying in the workhouse.

Christmas 1882
I looked closely at the minutes of the weekly meeting on the run up to Christmas but there was no mention of any Christmas cheer for the inmates. In fact the weekly meeting fell on Boxing Day and it was held with a full agenda although only five Guardians were present. The previous week saw a turn out of 13 Guardians which was about the norm out of a maximum of 24. As a general rule the workhouse Guardians in Essex did approve extra rations on Christmas day but maybe as this was now the norm in this latter part of the century it did not worthy any specific comment in the minutes.

January 1883
The Inspector of Nuisances
The Guardians received a report from the Inspector of Nuisances on behalf of the Local Board of Health. The report quoted a law which stated that an occupant of premises shall not keep swine within 100 feet (31 metres) of any dwelling-house. The workhouse was breaking this law and notice had been given that the pigs should be removed within 42 days. Most workhouses kept a couple of pigs to get rid of the waste from the kitchens. The pigs eventually supplemented the pork rations.

County Lunatic Asylum
January saw a letter from the asylum at Brentwood regarding the overcrowding at the asylum. The Guardians had received a letter the year before complaining in general terms that Union Workhouses were committing inmates to the asylum where their condition was not serious. The correspondence now said that the asylum was overcrowded with

minor cases and that they were sending back to Romford two inmates who had been categorised by the asylum as 'harmless'. These two would now probably be added to the 'of unsound mind' category at Romford as was mentioned in a previous minute.

The Inspector of Schools
With the country getting more and more sophisticated there seemed to be an inspector for everything as far as workhouses were concerned and January also saw another report being received and this time it was from the Inspector of Schools. The clerk did not describe the report in full apart from minuting that the workhouse school had 'passed very fairly'.

March 1883
Accusation of seduction
The chairman drew the Guardians' attention to a newspaper report in the *South East Advertiser* regarding Mr Charles Culling the relieving officer for one of the divisions of the Union who had been accused of seduction and of being the father of an illegitimate child. Apparently the young lady, Flora Race aged 19, was in Mr Culling's service at the time of the alleged offence. The court heard that there was no corroboration of her statements and the case was dismissed. The chairman and the Guardians discussed the matter and whilst they thought that the case had brought the Union into a poor light they decided to take the matter no further.

Staff salaries
The quarterly salaries were listed in full in the March 1883 minutes and these have been grossed up the show the annual figure.

		£
Mr N Smith	Clerk to the Guardians	165
Rev. Goodlay	Chaplain	100
Mr H Clark	Master	70
Mrs Clark	Matron	40
Workhouse Medical Officer		75
Miss E Staler	Schoolmistress	35
L Faulkner	Nurse	30
Mr T Martin	Porter	30
Mr A Mead	Labour Master	20
Mr A Capron	Shoemaker	30
Mr C Culling	Relieving Officers	42
Mr C Enabling		55

In addition there were seven further medical officers serving the rural areas and also two Inquiry Officers.

April 1883
The Case against Mr Culling
Following Flora Race's dismissed case against Mr Culling the chairman reported that the case had been brought to the court again. Miss Race did not pursue the charge of seduction but presumably she provided evidence that Charles Culling was the father of her child. The outcome was that Mr Culling was ordered to pay Flora Race five shillings per week for the support of the child. Mr Culling subsequently tendered his resignation as a relieving officer. He asked for and received a testimonial confirming that he had worked for the Union for eight years and that his work had been satisfactory during this period. No mention was made of the court case.

Payment of commission to collectors of poor rates
Mr C Harvey was the collector of poor rates for the parish of Romford. He had applied to Romford vestry for agreement to change the rate of commission he was paid. Previously Mr Harvey was paid eight old pence in the pound for rates he collected of up to £4 and four old pence in the pound thereafter. He proposed that he receive a flat rate of seven old pence in the pound. This would mean that his overall commission would increase. The Guardians gave their approval subject to the agreement of the Local Government Board.

June 1883
Tea party for the aged and sick women
The master reported to the Guardians that Mrs Helme of Hornchurch had provided a tea party for the aged and infirm women in the infirmary. Mrs Helme had been assisted by the two Misses Fry and the three Misses Davey. The minute records that 'the old folk greatly appreciated the generosity of the visiting ladies'. The clerk was directed to write to Mrs Helme accordingly. The two Misses Fry are almost certainly the daughters of Elizabeth Fry the Quaker philanthropist and prison reformer who lived in Hornchurch at this time.

Beer for staff
The master and nurse, who were obviously not beer drinkers, asked last year if they could receive a monetary contribution in lieu of their beer ration. In 1882 this request was refused but a similar request in June 1883 received a more favourable response. The Guardians agreed that salaried staff could receive an increase in their salary at the rate of £5 per

annum for men and £4 per annum for women in lieu of their beer allowance.

Claim by the shoemaker

Mr Capron the resident shoemaker wrote a letter to the Guardians in June stating that his room had been broken into and various articles stolen. He enclosed a list which included two overcoats, two coats (jackets), two vests (waistcoats), one silk hat and a pair of boots. He was asking for recompense. He quoted in a postscript to the letter that a similar incident had happened in the workhouse in 1869 when his writing desk had been stolen and the workhouse miller had his clothes stolen. He said that the Guardians on that occasion made good the losses to the two men. The Guardians discussed the matter and decided to inform Mr Capron that whilst not accepting any responsibility for the stolen items that they would make an ex gratia payment of £2 towards the cost of replacement. Whilst the culprit could well have been an inmate this is unlikely as a pauper in the workhouse would have no use for the stolen items and would have been immediately noticed if any attempt was made to wear the clothes. If the culprit was not an inmate he or she though could have sold the items outside the workhouse.

The census of 1901
number of inmates

Males	243	The total includes 22 staff and 90 children under
Females	182	14. The percentage of children to the total
		number of inmates was 22%
Total	425	

The Romford workhouse was one of the few that were operating near to its capacity of 450 at the time of the 1901 census. The 22 staff was three times what it was in 1841 and the positions in 1901 were as follows:

Master	Caretaker (boys)
Matron	Caretaker (girls)
Assistant Master	Caretaker (general)
Assistant Matron	Stoker
Porter	Cook
Supt. Of Casuals	Laundress
Nurses (10)	

The list of staff salaries for 1883, earlier in this section, only lists seven staff that actually lived in but by twenty years later this had increased to 22. By 1901 the workhouse was already becoming less of a workhouse and more of a hospital as evidenced by the ten nurses on the staff. The 90 children mentioned in the census data would by 1901 all have been educated in the normal Romford schools with schooling within the workhouse having been phased out during the 1880s.

March 1930
The last meeting
The last meeting of the Guardians was held on the 25 March 1930. From the 1st April Essex County Council assumed responsibility. At the final meeting there were 758 inmates. Almost all this number was the old and infirm and not paupers, who were all accommodated in the various extra hospital wards which had been built since the 1901 census.

Chapter 15

SAFFRON WALDEN AND ITS ENVIRONS

PARISH WORKHOUSES

The following 24 parishes in the above area were grouped together in 1834 following the Poor Law Amendment Act to form the Saffron Walden Union. Before 1834 each parish may have had its own poorhouse or workhouse.

Arkesden, Ashdon, Chrishall, Clavering, Debden, Elmdon, Great Chesterford, Great Sampford, Hempstead, Langley, Little Chesterford, Little Sampford, Littlebury, Newport, Quendon, Radwinter, Rickling, Saffron Walden, Strethall, Wendens Ambo, Wendens Lofts, Wicken Bonhunt, Widdington and Wimbish.

The government undertook a survey of parish workhouses in 1777 and the only parish in this area that had a workhouse open in that year was Ashdon. Both the parish workhouses at Saffron Walden and Clavering had opened prior to 1777 but neither were mentioned in the survey. It is possible that if a workhouse was not mentioned in the government survey that, either the parish failed to make its return, or the workhouse, although opens prior to 1777, was not functioning at the time of the survey. In the case though of these two workhouses it does seem that they were both functioning in the year 1777.

SaffronWalden

The Saffron Walden workhouse was originally the White Hart public house at the top of the High Street opposite the present war memorial although at the time of purchase in 1734 the road was called Cuckingstool End. In 1798 the parish vestry was able to purchase the cottage next door and extended the workhouse into the cottage. The extension gave sufficient room for the parish to build a bridewell or prison. The workhouse was an extensive property by parish standards but strangely does not appear in the government list of 1777 although it was definitely in operation at that time.

The site of the Saffron Walden parish workhouse at the top of the High Street

In the next section on the new Saffron Walden Union Workhouse it can be seen that the formation of the new workhouse Guardians took place in April 1835 at which time the old parish workhouse was still in operation. In December 1835 there was a serious fire at the parish workhouse in the High Street which was in danger of spreading to the adjacent town goal. A report of the time said that many respectable local residents assisted in quelling the fire in about one and a half hours although the outcome was that the old workhouse was completely destroyed. Many other residents who were watching the conflagration and were in fear that they may one day have to be placed in the workhouse for one reason or another made comments to the effect that the fire was the best thing that could have happened to the workhouse. Little did these people know that the new Union workhouse in the Radwinter Road, which would be completed within the next year, would have a prison like regime decidedly worse than any parish workhouse. There was a suspicion that the fire was arson and the insurance company offered a £100 reward for information leading to a conviction. Although there was an opinion that the cause of the fire was arson, the Guardians for the new Union, who controlled the existing parish workhouses, drew up a new regulation that the parish workhouses would be no smoking areas.

Prior to the fire the Saffron Walden parish workhouse had a mill attached to the premises for the grinding of corn manually and the Guardians issued instruction regarding working hours over the 1835 Christmas period. The men were allowed to finish work on the Thursday evening and did not have to return to work until after the Christmas period on the Monday morning. In addition the Guardians decided that a full week's pay would be given despite the missed Friday and Saturday. As far as Christmas fare was concerned all inmates would be allowed one pint of beer on Christmas day and some plums would be put in their pudding. It is not clear where the paupers were accommodated at this Christmas period as the reports of the fire said that the workhouse was destroyed.

Cornelius Flack was a pauper living in the Saffron Walden parish workhouse in 1835 and he lucky enough to be allowed to go and work during the day for John Marshall, shoemaker in the town. It was arranged with Mr Marshall that Cornelius would be paid a wage of two shillings a week but this money was to be paid to the overseer of Saffron Walden parish.

The new Union workhouse in Radwinter Road was completed by October 1836 and the Saffron Walden paupers were transferred there in this month.

Ashdon

All Saints church, Ashdon and the village centre today are about half a mile apart the church being on a hill and the village in the valley below. Clustered to one side of the church and hidden from the road are a few properties which, the historians believe, are the remnants of the original village centre which moved from the hill to the valley at the time of the Black Death in the mid fourteenth century. Amongst this small group is the old guildhall which was built about 1500. One would have thought that if the village moved to the valley in the mid fourteenth century the guildhall would not have been built behind the church in 1500 but down in the village. The property though may have also been a church house but today it is referred to as the old guildhall. After the local guilds had ceased to exist, or for whatever use it was subsequently put, this property would have come under the control of the parish and in 1775 the house was converted into the parish workhouse.

The first master of the new workhouse was John Atherton and he had 25 inmates under his control. The national survey of parish workhouses states that the property could accommodate up to 30 inmates. As in most workhouses in this part of Essex the inmates were employed in spinning yarn and in 1777 two carding stocks were purchased. Although the return by the parish in 1777 stated that the workhouse could accommodate up to 30 inmates this figure does not

The old guildhall converted into Ashdon parish workhouse in 1775

seem to be borne out by an inventory of the workhouse in 1788. The downstairs rooms comprised 'The Ward' which appears to be the dining room together with the kitchen, bakehouse and a cellar. Outside was a barn. Upstairs there were three bedrooms and the inventory indicates that there were 21 beds some of which were proper bedsteads and some were just straw beds. It is possible that the maximum capacity was 30 but the workhouse was not full in 1788. There are records of further inventories in the early nineteenth century and the one for 1808 still lists about 20 beds but the number of plates and drinking vessels indicates that the number of inmates may have dropped to about twelve.

The workhouse lasted until at least 1831 but when the new Guardians were appointed in 1835, to establish their new Union workhouse at Saffron Walden, the Ashdon parish workhouse is no longer mentioned. Possibly the workhouse closed in 1834/35 and the inmates were transferred to the two remaining parish workhouses at Saffron Walden or Clavering. The old guildhall building had served its purpose as a home for the poor of Ashdon and was then sold off in 1837 and converted into three dwellings.

Clavering

Similar to Ashdon above, the old guildhall adjacent to the church gate at Clavering was converted into the parish workhouse in 1760. No mention was made of this workhouse in the national survey of 1777 which meant that it could have closed by this date. A resolution in the parish records in 1782 stated that if any of the poor of the parish were dissatisfied with their allowances (out-relief) then they would be sent to

The old guildhall in Clavering converted into the parish workhouse in 1760

the parish workhouse at Thaxted with Clavering paying for their keep. This resolution seems to indicate that the Clavering workhouse was not operating at this time or that the workhouse could not take any more paupers. Whichever was the case the workhouse was definitely open in the 1800s as there was a change of workhouse master in 1835 when John Willett and his wife took over the Clavering workhouse. The minutes record that 'for attention to the mill and the care of the Clavering workhouse (the salary) shall be twenty shillings per week from the time they removed from the workhouse at Saffron Walden'. It would seem that they occupied a similar role at the Saffron Walden workhouse. The minutes record a month later that John Willett died but it was decided that his wife could continue to manage the Clavering workhouse. This would not normally have been the case but as the new Union workhouse was nearing completion and Clavering workhouse would soon close then the Union Guardians made a sensible decision in this case. Mrs Willett's salary was reduced to fourteen shillings a week.

A list of some of the supplies delivered to the workhouse in 1835 included flour at twenty six shillings a sack, pork, good dutch cheese, country cheese, yellow soap and candles. The Poor Law

Commissioners who were the controlling body for the new Unions issued recommended diet sheets for use when the new workhouse was built. The new Saffron Walden Guardians reviewed the diets at their parish workhouses and decided that at Clavering on the days when rice pudding was on the menu that rice should be substituted for suet according to the recommended diet tables.

The parish workhouse at Clavering was one of only two in operation up to the time that the new Union workhouse was built in 1836. The other was the Saffron Walden parish workhouse. The Clavering paupers were transferred to the new Union workhouse in October 1836. The furniture in the Clavering workhouse was then sold by public auction in November 1836.

Newport

Newport Parish Workhouse built 1799

The first workhouse built in Newport was constructed in 1709 which could have been located on the south side of the High Street and Wicken Road junction. It appears that this building was a formal workhouse with a master and not just a house where the poor of the parish were lodged. If so, then the Newport parish workhouse was one of the earliest in the county. The entries in the vestry book refer to the increasing incidence of 'idleness and debauchery' in the town arising from 'a want of a good education in Christian principles and constant exercise in industry and labour'. The observations go on for some time in this vein culminating in the inhabitants of Newport wishing to 'correct this spreading contagion for the better education and maintenance of the poor and youth of our parish'. The inhabitants agreed to rent a house on two floors at a rent not exceeding £5 a year with the upstairs for beds and downstairs as a work room. The parish agreed to employ a workhouse master to oversee the spinning of woollen goods and any resulting sales would go towards the purchasing of food for the inmates. The master was paid a salary out of which he was to keep his charges. Rules were drawn for the running of the workhouse which were very strict and included a working day of 6am to 7pm in the summer with an earlier finish in other seasons. The agreed diet was bread and cheese with milk or broth in the morning and evening with meat at midday. On Sundays meat with a pudding would be served. Records show that the number of inmates fluctuated up to about twelve including children. It is unsure for how long this workhouse existed but it does not get a mention in the national survey of 1777. Possibly the workhouse closed prior to 1777 which is probably one of the reasons that another was built in a different location in 1799.

In 1799 the Hon. Percy Charles Wyndham, Lord of the Manor of Newport Pond, built a property 63 feet by 16 feet together with an outbuilding 12 feet by 7 feet as a 'common working room for the poor of Newport'. The address of this property is now 1 and 2 Bury Water Lane. When built the land was referred to as Bury Water Green. The workhouse in Bury Water Lane continued to cater for the poor of the parish up until the 1830s when the poor would have been transferred possibly to the parish workhouse at Saffron Walden prior to the new Union workhouse at Saffron Walden being built. The minutes of the Guardians of the new Union make no mention of Newport's parish workhouse from their inception in 1835 and therefore it looks as if the workhouse closed just prior to this date. There is though reference by the Guardians of the new Union to an agreement with Newport parish in October 1836 for the sale of six parish properties with the proceeds going to the Saffron Walden Union to offset the cost somewhat of the new Union workhouse. One of these six would almost certainly have been the old parish workhouse.

Great Sampford

Great Sampford parish vestry passed a resolution in September 1777 to build a workhouse and levied a special rate on the parishioners for this purpose. The workhouse was built within the year and an inventory of 1778 lists all the clothes that the fourteen paupers brought into the workhouse. This record was necessary in case they left and the workhouse master knew which clothes belonged to the paupers and which to the parish. The inventory then listed the contents of the workhouse which would appear to be the initial purchases which included fifteen pairs of sheets. A later inventory of 1786 recorded that there was one table with forms for seating and also twelve chairs.

A parish return of 1834 to the Poor Law Commissioners stated that the parish workhouse could accommodate up to 18 paupers. The return also stated that there were two rooms upstairs each containing three beds and the outbuildings had sufficient space for twelve persons as occasional sleeping apartments. There was also reference in the return to the 'Poor House', in addition to the workhouse, which could accommodate up to 40 persons. In the expenses section of the return there is no mention of any expense on clothes or food for those in the 'Poor House' and it is a puzzle to what the parish are referring. Possibly this was a property owned by the parish without a workhouse master where those on out-relief were sent to undertake craft work or spinning. Finally, the government return states that a total of 73 persons in the parish benefited from 'parochial relief'.

Great Samford parish workhouse does not seem to have been open in 1835 when the new Union Guardians took over the parish workhouses and presumably the inmates were transferred to the two remaining parish workhouses at Saffron Walden or Clavering some time at the end of 1834 or the beginning of 1835.

THE SAFFRON WALDEN UNION WORKHOUSE

Each of the 24 parishes had one representative on the Board of Guardians with Saffron Walden having four representatives. Clavering, Debden, Newport and Wimbish had two representatives each making a total of 31 Guardians. The 24 parishes only had a total population of about 18,000 with Saffron Walden being the largest with just under 5.000 people.

The 31 Guardians first met at the Rose and Crown public house in Saffron Walden on the 13 April 1835 with their first job being to take over the running of existing parish workhouses. It seems that at that time only the parish workhouses at Saffron Walden and Clavering were operating although the Guardian's minutes do make a passing reference to workhouses at Debden and Wimbish but it does not look as if they were open in 1835. It also looks as if Ashdon parish workhouse closed by the time the new Guardians were appointed but it is unclear what happened to the inmates of these three parishes if the workhouses closed in the 1830s as the new Union workhouse was not ready for occupancy

The entrance block (top) and accommodation wings of Saffron Walden Union workhouse looking attractive after recent conversion into apartments.

until October 1836. Possibly the inmates were transferred to either the Saffron Walden or Clavering parish workhouses. The next large task for the Guardians was to acquire a site for the new workhouse. Their first choice proved unsuitable and they eventually leased some land from the chairman of the Guardians', Lord Braybrooke, on the north side of Sewards End Road which subsequently changed its name to Radwinter Road by which it is known today. The workhouse was built in 1836 to accommodate just over 300 inmates with the architect being James Clephan of Silso who designed a number of other workhouses.

Clephan's design was the popular cruciform shape of three storeys with single storey buildings around the outside to form exercise yards for the various classes of inmate. The bricks used were white stock bricks which gave the building a more pleasing look compared to the darker bricks used in other workhouses. The Guardians held their first meeting in the new workhouse on the 14 October 1836 and during the same month the inmates of the parish workhouses at Saffron Walden and Clavering were transferred to the new Union workhouse in Radwinter Road.

The first national census after the workhouse opened in 1836 was in 1841 when the institution was working well below its capacity of 300+ inmates. The number of inmates and staff was as follows:

Males	49	The total includes 4 staff and 58 children
Females	49	under 14. The percentage of children to the
		total number of inmates was 62%
Total	98	

Saffron Walden workhouse had the highest percentage of children in 1841 compared with the other 16 Union workhouses although the total number of inmates was rather low. The workhouse master and his wife and those employed to teach the children are usually fairly mature people. In the case of Saffron Walden though in 1841 the master was a single man of 30 with the schoolmaster and the schoolmistress being married and also both 30 years of age. They had their 10 year old daughter living with them in the workhouse.

Enlargement in the 1840s

The workhouse was built for 300+ inmates in 1836 but by the time that an infirmary had been built and also four fever wards which were completed by 1848 the workhouse could accommodate 400 inmates. Whilst the majority of Essex workhouses increased the potential number of inmates over the first twenty years or more of building mainly by increasing the medical facilities, the actual number of inmates at Saffron Walden did not increase accordingly as the following figures demonstrate.

Number of inmates at	1841 census	94
	1871	193
	1891	173
	1901	105

The number of inmates peaked in about the 1870s and fell consistently after that. Consequently the workhouse was nowhere near full compared with its potential of 400 inmates. Saffron Walden had the smallest inmate population of all the Essex workhouses in 1901.

1890s
The Guardians' minutes
I have looked at the Guardians' minutes for the 1890s which now begin to demonstrate a more caring attitude towards paupers with treats and outings being seen. We also see more examples of boys being taken into apprenticeships and also extra staff being employed to look after the young

The census of 1891
The census data for 1891 saw the population of the workhouse at 180 including a staff of six and the matron's daughter. Unlike the 1841 figures the workhouse master and his wife were more of an age that one saw at the other workhouse being 47 and 39 respectively. The age break for teenagers was different for this census at either up to or over 15 years old. The figures are as follows:

Staff	Workhouse master	
	Matron (wife)	
	their daughter (aged 5)	
	Caretaker (boys)	
	Cook	
	Porter	
	Nurse	
Total		7
Inmates	Adult single males	51
	Adult single females	29
	Widowers	34
	Widows	14
	Three families	7
	Children up 15 - males	22
	Children up 15 - females	16
Total		180

July 1892
Treat for children
The Board of Guardians wrote a letter of thanks to Mr Henry Stear for his kindness in organising a trip to Clacton on Sea for the Union children.

September 1892

A criminal offence by Charles Johns

Mr Johns was one of the relieving officers for the Saffron Walden Union. A report in the local paper said that he had on trial but had been "acquitted of a criminal offence". Although the details were known to the Guardians the clerk did not record them in the minutes but he was asked to check with the court in case there had been any mistakes in the newspaper. This was done and the Guardians decided to advise the Local Government Board of the circumstances and asked for their advice. The Local Government Board said that Mr Johns should resign and so his resignation was obtained by the Guardians. I do not think that someone would resign so easily today especially as Mr Johns was not found to be guilty. Subsequent minutes record that Mr Johns received an ex-gratia payment of £20 a year for the next four years presumably out of workhouse funds as the Local Government Board was not obliged to pay a pension. This bequest by the Guardians seems to indicate that they were not in agreement with the decision by the Local Government Board.

February 1893

Boys' caretaker and tailor

This was a fairly new appointment and a recent advertisement for a new boys' caretaker and tailor attracted sixteen applications. Two were selected for interview and Mr Whiffen was offered the position at a salary of £25 a year together with board and lodging.

June 1893

Royal marriage

The Local Government Board authorised the various Unions that "rules were to be relaxed on the occasion of the Duke of York's marriage". The Guardians were also authorised to spend an extra £7 towards a dinner for the inmates. The Guardians added a further £3 towards tea and cakes. Queen Victoria's second son George was married to HRH Princess Victoria May of Teck on the 6th July 1893.

July 1893

Stone breaking

The Guardians resolved that the daily amount of stone to be broken shall be 7cwt or less if the master so decides. Although no previous amount is quoted in the minutes it was possibly 8cwt as a later case in 1898 surprisingly quotes this higher amount.

Local Government Act 1894

This act saw the dissolving of the parish vestry which was the body which ran a parish. The parish vestry was an informal body which was to be replaced by an elected Parish or Town Council. This new status for the Saffron Walden Town Council prompted them to ask the Union if their number of representatives could be increased from four to eight. The minutes record that Saffron Walden was "fully represented" and their request was declined. Subsequently in December of the same year the number of representatives for Saffron Walden was increased to six.

August 1894

Recruits for the navy

The Guardians received a letter from the Recruiting Officer for the Navy at Cambridge looking for suitable young men for naval service. The Boys Committee reported that none of the Union boys were up to the standard required for apprenticeship for the Navy.

September 1894

Tailor apprenticeship

A letter was received from a Mr Spencer a tailor of Abergavenny requiring boy apprentices. The clerk was asked to obtain references on Mr Spencer and if satisfactory the Union would pay a premium of £5 to Mr Spencer with the employer to provide board and lodging. The employer was to pay the apprentice one shilling a week in the first year with rises of one shilling for the next three years.

October 1894

Criticism of the nurse

The Local Government Board inspector reported to the Guardians that he did not consider the nurse to be efficient and lacked nursing experience. He suggested that the Guardians employ an experienced nurse to help the present nurse. It is clear from the comments made in the minutes of many of the Union Workhouses that the position of nurse was not one that we recognise today. The person seems to have had no nursing training and was probably someone who was just prepared to be a carer for the sick and infirm. The Guardians advertised for a nurse aged between 30 and 45 with some knowledge of nursing to assist the present nurse. The salary was to be £15 per annum "with rations and beer". The successful applicant was Miss Eliza Abbott who was appointed Assistant Nurse to someone with less experience than herself. In March 1896

Eliza's salary was increased to £18 a year and obviously the Guardians recognised the contribution she was making.

February 1895

Drainage and sewage

It is clear that inspectors from the Local Government Board made regular inspections and in February 1895 they commented, not for the first time, on the lack of proper sewage facilities at the Union Workhouse. The workhouse used cesspits and was not linked to the town's sewage system. The Guardians wrote to the Urban Sanitary Authority but they said that there was no sewer closes enough to the workhouse to which it could be connected. It would also cost too much to lay a link to the town system.

Girls' caretaker

One of the Guardians felt that in addition to there being a caretaker for the boys that there should also be one for the girls. A further recommendation was that both the boys and the girls should have a female caretaker. A female caretaker, the Guardian said, could also teach the boys tailoring and the mending of clothes and also instruct those of below school age with 'elementary knowledge'. The Guardians took up this suggestion and the job went to Miss K Newland at a salary of £20 a year 'with rations except beer'. Presumably, Mr Whiffen, who was the caretaker for the boys, retained his job and Miss Newland looked after the girls and also assisted Mr Whiffen as suggested above.

Saffron Walden Union Workhouse Goal.

August 1895
Punishment
All Union Workhouses had a punishment book and there was no need to record these misdemeanours in the Guardian's minutes. For some reason though the minutes record that William Cornell, aged 17, was ordered for the crime committed to serve 24 hours of solitary confinement with only bread and water for this period.

Report of the Asylum Committee
The Asylum Committee reported to the Guardians that they had visited the Essex County Lunatic Asylum at Brentwood to check on inmates from Saffron Walden who were now resident at that institution. The report said that five patients were at other locations and were not seen. All the others were seen and the recommendation of the doctors was that they remain at Brentwood with the exception of John Inman. The doctors said that his condition continued to improve and he could shortly be returned to the Saffron Walden Union. The report said that the committee found the conditions at Brentwood satisfactory. The three committee members were granted total expenses of £3 for the visit.

September 1895
Sanitation report
The February 1895 report by the inspector commented on the inadequate drainage and sewage arrangements at the workhouse. The Guardians had obviously commissioned a report on the situation and Dr W Armisted submitted his report. He said that dry and solid waste was collected daily by staff in small wagons and used as manure. He is probably referring to kitchen waste. Liquid sewage is transported by underground pipes and allowed to soak into the chalk soil through cesspits. The Union had a large oval shaped hole which was 40 feet wide and divided in the centre. The sewage drains from the first chamber discharged into the second chamber. Both were covered with wood and topped with a foot of soil. The soil covering was to keep the smell down and the inspector's report said that he could not report any 'nuisance' (smell). He felt that the system would need improving in the near future and he had already passed a copy of his report to the Local Government Board. The inspector also reported the situation to the Saffron Walden District Council who did have plans to continue the town sewer along Sewards End Road (now Radwinter Road) which would be capable of accepting sewage from the workhouse. The surveyor of the Urban District Council felt though that the cost of the sewer extension would be prohibitive as the sewer would have to be very deep to accept a gradient from the

workhouse. Compensation would also have to paid to owners of land through which the workhouse pipes would pass. In the interim Dr Armisted recommended some in-house improvements to the present cesspit system whereby some sewage is directed into a new separate container.

October 1895
A month after the above report was submitted the Guardians reported that the Saffron Walden District Council had decided to extend the sewer along Sewards End Road to a point opposite the workhouse. It was then for the workhouse at its own expense to make a connection to the town's sewage system. The Guardians were obviously pleased about this but wished to check that the extension along the road to the workhouse would be deep enough to accept their sewage by gravity.

November 1895
Children's caretaker
Miss Kate Newland had been appointed as caretaker to both the girls and partly to the boys in February. The master now reported that this lady 'had neglected to do her duty'. The Guardians adjourned the meeting for the House Committee (a number of the Guardians) to conduct an investigation and reconvene in half an hour. They reported back that the charge against Miss Newland was sustainable but that there was no charge against her character. The Guardians recommended that she be asked to resign. No action was taken immediately and a further report by the House Committee the following week reversed their recommendation and she was not asked to resign. The minutes record that Miss Newland resigned of her own free will three months later in February 1896.

April 1896
Buns for inmates
Mr H Stear provided hot cross buns for the inmates on Good Friday. The Guardians sent their thanks for his generosity. It was Mr Stear who organised the trip to Clacton in July 1892. The minutes also recorded that gifts had been provided for the inmates the previous Christmas but the donor was not mentioned.

November 1898
Murder at the workhouse
I have jumped a couple of years to record this very serious offence that happened at the workhouse. A tramp, Thomas King, aged about 30, had been admitted to the workhouse on Sunday 31 October 1898. On the

Monday morning he was required to break up 8cwt of granite which he initially refused to do. He was threatened with an appearance at the Magistrates Court and so he set to work. The tramp master, William Woolard, was working in an adjoining yard and suddenly Thomas King left his work and proceeded to the yard where Mr Woolard was sweeping up. Mr King had taken with him the six pound hammer he was using and beat Mr Woolard about the head with the tool until he fell to the ground. Two men attempted to pull him away but he managed two more blows before he was overpowered. The doctor arrived and pronounced Mr Woolard death at the scene. Thomas King was arrested and charged with murder. He later appeared at Chelmsford assizes. The minutes unfortunately do not record the eventual outcome but if found guilty his punishment would have been very serious.

The twentieth century
The census of 1901

Males	70	The total includes 7 staff and no children.
Females	42	
Total	112	

By 1901 there were no children at all in the workhouse. The reason why the numbers at Saffron Walden were so low and why there were no children in the workhouse in 1901 is more of a reflection of the population growths of the other Union workhouse areas rather than any special employment features in this part of north Essex. Saffron Walden's catchment area of parishes was about 18.000 people in 1831 and most of the other sixteen Union areas also had catchments of below 20,000 with Chelmsford having the largest at 24.000. Over the next 70 years to 1901 the population of all the other 16 areas grew at a much faster rate than the rural Saffron Walden parishes.

When Saffron Walden workhouse was taken over by Essex County Council in 1930 the old workhouse buildings and infirmary first became known as the Public Assistance Institution before being renamed St James' Hospital which later changed its name to the Saffron Walden Community Hospital. The main workhouse buildings have now been converted into apartments.

The entrance block of Tendring Union workhouse built 1837/38
in course of modern conversion (see page 299)

Chapter 16

TENDRING AND ITS ENVIRONS

PARISH WORKHOUSES

The following 30 parishes in the large rural area east of Colchester were grouped together in 1834 following the Poor Law Amendment Act to form the Tendring Union. Before 1834 each parish may have had its own poorhouse or workhouse.

Alresford, Ardleigh, Beaumont with Moze, Bradfield, Frating, Great Bentley, Elmstead, Frinton, Great Bromley, Great Clacton, Great Holland, Great Oakley, Kirby, Lawford, Little Bentley, Little Bromley, Little Clacton, Little Holland, Little Oakley, Manningtree, Mistley, Ramsey, St Osyth, Tendring, Thorpe-le-Soken, Thorrington, Walton-on-the-Naze, Weeley, Wix and Wrabness.

Subsequently **Harwich and Dover court** joined the Union very shortly after inception although these two parishes were not mentioned in the original list of 30. Later **Brightlingsea** was transferred from the Lexden & Winstree Union. The Tendring area was very largely rural in the eighteenth and nineteenth centuries and it took in all the parishes east of Colchester to Walton-on-the Naze in the east, Manningtree in the north and St Osyth in the south. The parish of Tendring itself only had a population of a few hundred in earlier centuries but the name was taken for the Union workhouse from its historic connection with the area which was called the Tendring Hundred from back in Saxon times. The modern local authority is called the Tendring District Council. Although Clacton-on-Sea is the largest area of population area today the situation in the 1830s was very different. Clacton then had less than 1000 people with St Osyth being the largest parish with 1583 falling to Frinton with only 35. The Essex seaside resorts had not been discovered in the 1830s when leisure time was at a premium.

The government undertook a survey of parish workhouses in 1777 and the following parishes in the Tendring area had a workhouse open in that year.

Ardleigh	Beaumont/Moze	Lt.Bentley
Bradfield	Gt. Bromley	Gt.Clacton
Dovercourt	Harwich/St.Nich	Lawford
Manningtree	Gt.Oakley	Ramsey
St. Osyth	Tendring	Thorpe-le-Soken
Weeley	Wix	

Subsequent to 1777 the following parishes had a workhouse for at least a portion of the time between 1777 and the 1830s:

Elmstead	Kirby	Little Clacton
Mistley	Thorrington	

Taking the original 30 parishes that formed the Tendring Union and including Harwich and Dovercourt, which were included very quickly after inception, twenty two out of thirty two parishes had a parish workhouse at some time. Compared with the other sixteen Unions in Essex the Tendring Union had the highest number of parish workhouses and also the highest percentage of workhouses to parishes - 68%. For the Tendring area I have not on this occasion included jottings on some of the parish workhouses but conducted an exercise dividing the parishes into total population groups to see what population supported a parish workhouse. As can be seen from the chart below all the parishes with a population of over 750 in 1801 had a workhouse which fell only slightly for those parishes in the next two groups with populations above 250 with 14 parishes having a workhouse out of 16. For the eight small parishes with a population of under 250 there was only one workhouse.

Great Bentley was the only parish in the 500 - 750 population group without a workhouse but the smaller Little Bentley did have a workhouse. The Little Bentley workhouse probably served both parishes. The break point for having the need for a parish workhouse seems to have been about a population of 250/300. Most parishes owned one or two cottages in which they placed homeless families and it seems that when the total number in a parish needing accommodation was less than ten then the parish poor houses would probably suffice. Beyond this number a parish vestry might consider building or renting its own workhouse if it could not persuade an adjacent parish to look after its homeless poor for a fee. If an individual or family had a roof over their head, but there was a financial need, then the parish would place the individuals on out-relief which would be a weekly allowance from the parish overseer.

The first parish in the 'Over 1000' category is Ardleigh with a population in 1801 of 1145. The parish workhouse could accommodate up to 40 inmates which was 3.5% of the population. The average percentage of all the workhouse populations in the Tendring area to the parish populations, that were open in 1777, was 3.7% and although the years are different the figures are a good guide. If the breakpoint for the need for a parish workhouse is a population of about 250/300 then 3.7% of this total is between nine and eleven persons. This number appears to bear out the previous assumption that if a parish has a need for accommodation for more than 10 persons then this could be the case for having a parish workhouse. This little exercise relates to the rural Tendring parishes and may not apply across the rest of Essex.

As one would expect the larger the parish the larger the size of the workhouse. It seems that if there was a need for a parish workhouse it would usually be built to accommodate up to 15/20 inmates although as the chart shows a few were smaller.

Population and workhouses compared for the year 1801

Parish	Population	Workhouse	Max.no.in 1777 if open in that year
Over 1000 population			
Ardleigh	1145	yes	40
Harwich	2371	yes	60
Manningtree	1016	yes	20
St Osyth	1168	yes	20
750 - 1000 population			
Thorpe le Soken	974	yes	50
Gt Clacton	904	yes	30
Gt Oakley	769	yes	20
500 - 750 population			
Gt Bentley	617	No	
Bradfield	582	yes	12
Elmstead	550	yes	-
Kirby-le Soken	664	yes	-
Mistley	554	yes	-
Ramsey	595	yes	14
Tendring	522	yes	20
Wix	573	yes	25
250 - 500 population			
Lt Bentley	331	yes	26
Gt Bromley	492	yes	30
Lt Bromley	295	no	
Lt Clacton	475	yes	-

Gt Holland	300	no	
Lawford	467	yes	22
Thorrington	271	yes	-
Dovercourt	390	yes	8
Weeley	387	yes	16
Under 250 population			
Alresford	210	no	
Beaumont	240	yes	14
Frating	176	no	
Frinton	31	no	
Lt Holland	59	no	
Lt Oakley	153	no	
Walton le Soken	221	no	
Wrabness	162	no	

THE TENDRING UNION WORKHOUSE

Of the original 30 parishes the Board of Guardians record in their minutes at their first meeting that 25 parishes would have one representative each as a Guardian and five would have two representatives. The parishes with two Guardians were Ardleigh, Manningtree, Mistley, St Osyth and Thorpe-le-Soken making a total 35 Guardians. The parishes of Harwich, St Nicholas and Dovercourt were added shortly after the first meeting.

The first meeting of the Guardians was at the Maids Head Inn at Thorpe on the 18 November 1835. At the first meeting the Guardians divided the area up into districts and listed all the parishes with their populations in 1835. The five parishes with an extra representative are all the largest parishes with the exception of Mistley which only had a population of 876 although there were five other parishes with larger populations. There must have been some reason why Mistly was given an extra representative despite not being one of the top five although the minutes are silent on this point. The Guardians appointed various officers at their first meeting and also set up a committee to inspect the existing parish workhouses in their area. They reported back that four parish workhouses were suitable for conversion and use by the Union pending the building of the new Union workhouse as soon as minor alteration had been made. There was no mention of the names of any rejected workhouses. The four parish workhouses were at Mistley, St Osyth, Great Bromley and Thorpe. It was decided that the Mistley workhouse should be used for the aged and infirm paupers, the one at Thorpe for the able-bodied males, the one at St Osyth for the able-bodied females and finally the workhouse at Great Bromley for the children under 16 years old. It later transpired that the Great Bromley workhouse was not owned by Great Bromley parish but by trustees in respect of a charitable trust and consequently the Guardians had to agree a reasonable rent for the premises.

December 1835
Relieving officer's report
The appointed relieving officers informed the Guardians the number of poor that were not in a parish workhouse but currently receiving out-relief in each parish. The numbers are as follows:

St Osyth	101	Mistley	79
Bradfield	56	Kirby	52
Wix	43	Gt Oakley	43
Manningtree	35	Lt Clacton	34
Weeley	33	Gt Bromley	24
Lt Bentley	24	Wrabness	12
Walton	11	Lt Holland	5
Lt Oakley	4	Frinton	2
Total number on out-relief			558

Harwich, Dovercourt and Brighlingsea do not feature in the above list as they had not been brought into the Tendring Union at this stage. During the month of December the Guardians reviewed the above paupers in each parish and agreed their weekly allowance or increased or reduced their allowances as necessary.

Many parish workhouses had a hand operated corn mill and as there was not one in the four selected workhouses the Guardians agreed to purchase one for installing in the Thorpe workhouse for use by the able-bodied males. The Guardians had also reviewed the furniture and decided to order 30 new beds and blankets for distribution around the four workhouses.

January 1836
New appointments
The next job for the Guardians was to appoint new masters and matron for the four workhouses and also to appoint a schoolmaster and schoolmistress for the Great Bromley workhouse to look after the children. Advertisements were placed in the Colchester and Ipswich newspapers and there were three or four application for each job. The master and matron had to be a husband and wife and the Guardians interviewed all the applicants. The successful couples were told that they would take up their appointments when the paupers had all been

transferred to their appointed workhouse and any alterations had been completed.

Food and provisions
When the parish workhouses were working independently the parish ordered all the food supplies together with any other necessities the workhouse or the paupers required. The job was now taken over by the Union Guardians and much of every meeting was taken up by arranging contracts for bread, meat, vegetable, coal and all types of groceries for the four workhouses. Once the new workhouse was built then there would be only one contract for each item instead of four at present.

May 1836
Architect to be appointed
The Guardians now got down to the business of selecting a site for the new Union workhouse and appointing architects. Messrs Scott and Moffatt were eventually awarded the contract after an initial list of about a dozen architects was whittled down to three. Their brief was to design a workhouse to accommodate up to 350 paupers. The new Union workhouse was built in 1837/38 on Tendring Heath which was roughly in the centre of the large rural area.

The census of 1841
The first national census after the workhouse opened was in 1841 and the census figures are as follows:

Males	103	The total included 6 staff and 82 children under 14.
Females	99	The percentage of children to the total number of inmates was 42%
Total	202	

The total number of inmates, 196, was high compared with the other Essex workhouses in 1841. Only Romford and West Ham had more inmates at this time with the Chelmsford workhouse also having 196 paupers . This high number of inmates in 1841 is probably a reflection of the economic climate in this rural area. Even back in 1777 there were seventeen parish workhouses which are listed at the start of this chapter which could accommodate over 400 inmates.

One of the original blocks of Tendring Union workhouse

I have looked at the Guardians' minutes for the turn of the nineteenth century to see what was cropping up at the meetings which by this time had moved from a weekly meeting to one every two weeks.

April 1899

Workhouse Committees

By the end of the nineteenth century the administration of the workhouse was getting more sophisticated with many more committees being appointed. At the annual election of officers in April there was a Finance Committee, a Visiting Committee, a School Attendance Committee and a Ladies Committee. These committees are all made up of elected Guardians and are in addition to the external officers like the medical officers or the relieving officers.

The case of William Page

William Page was in the workhouse and was chargeable out to St Osyth parish which appeared from the records to be his place of settlement. This would be normally the place of his birth or his father's birth. The clerk had drawn the Guardians' attention to the fact that William had been born in Harkstead, Suffolk which was the place of birth of his father. The father had lived all his life in Suffolk apart from one year in Brighlingsea. The clerk would now communicate this information to the local Union workhouse in Suffolk and that workhouse would now be charged for William's keep at Tendring.

Tendring Union workhouse infirmary built in 1901 showing modern front wings

Housing the ambulance van

The Guardians discussed where they should keep their ambulance van which appears to be a new acquisition. Agreement was reached that the Guardians would hire the barn of an adjacent resident. The internal combustion engine was just becoming commonplace and maybe the workhouse had invested in a motorised ambulance. At the same meeting the Guardians looked into the state of the (horse drawn) hearse which appeared to need repairs and painting at a cost of £7.

May 1899
Emily Lee

Lewisham Union workhouse had taken in Emily Lee a widow aged 48 who they described as a lunatic. They produced evidence that her place of settlement was Walton and consequently they were seeking approval of the Tendring Union that she could be charged out for her board and lodging. The clerk confirmed that Emil's place of settlement was Walton and advised Lewisham that Tendring would accept her charges. A month later the Lewisham workhouse arranged for Emily to be transferred from the London County Asylum at Banstead to the Essex Asylum at Brentwood. The bill for Emily's keep would now come from Brentwood.

Appointment of new schoolmistress

The schoolmistress had resigned and the Guardians had selected a replacement. The Local Government Board, which replaced the Poor law

Commissioners, was requested to approve her new salary. Whilst approval was obtained the Local Government Board expressed surprise that none of the children in the workhouse were attending the Public Elementary Schools which were set up in 1870 when the Education Act of that year made education compulsory up to the age of thirteen. It was usual from this date onwards for workhouses to send some of their children out to a village school. By the latter part of the nineteenth century some of the Essex workhouses did not educate any of their children in-house. It was agreed that all the older children would be sent to school in Tendring. There would be an extra expense for the Union as pauper children were all dressed the same and arrangements would have to be made to purchase jackets and waistcoats for the boys. Some of the other Essex workhouses did not send their girls out to school. One of the reasons that none of the children were having their schooling outside the Union was probably because Tendring was a very small parish, with a small school, which could probably not cope with the extra workhouse children. Tendring was only chosen for the site of the workhouse as it was the centre of the rural area. Two years later in 1901 there were 34 children under fourteen in the workhouse and the Tendring village school would undoubtedly not be able to cope with this number.

Inability to contribute to father's keep

The Guardians considered two letters regarding William Coe a recent inmate of the workhouse. It was usual for relatives to contribute to the keep of the person taken into the workhouse if they were not able to look after them if they were sick or did not have the finances to keep them at home. One letter was from James Coe, the son, saying that he did not have the finance to look after his father and the other was from the Vicar of St Osyth confirming the son's letter. The clerk was asked to make further enquiries and if the facts were proved to be correct then the son would not have to pay for his father.

A similar case was considered by the Guardians in respect of William Dove's father. William had written to the Guardians saying that although the court had reviewed his case and ordered that three shillings out of his wages of ten shillings be sent to the Union for the keep of his father he could not afford this sum. The Guardians decided, that as the case had already come to court, that proceedings be taken against William Dove for the arrears. There were no further comments in the minutes on both the above cases and one can presume that in the case of William Coe the Guardians did nor pursue the matter and that James Coe did not have to contribute to the cost of his father.

Church Army mission week

The master reported to the Guardians on the Church Army Mission Week and said 'that it was a pleasant and helpful week. The Missioner had been received everywhere with the greatest goodwill by both inmates and staff and I feel great pleasure in stating that the Mission will undoubtedly have done much good'.

August 1899

Mrs Mary Shea and 13 children

The master reported to the Guardians the case of Mrs Shea and 13 children who had been sent into the workhouse by Mr Hurrell the overseer of Clacton. The family came from 71 Ashburnham Grove, Greenwich and were admitted at 3am on the Monday morning. Although the report does not say it looks as if the group had missed the steam boat back to London having taken a day trip to Clacton. The group consisted of Mrs Shea aged 49 and one child of her own, Dorothy aged 14 years, together with 12 other children. Two of the children were her grandchildren aged two and three years. It looks as if Mrs Shea earned her living by looking after children as accompanying her was Mary Rowley aged 13 who was her general help at Greenwich. The remaining nine children were all aged between three months and 10 years old. When the group were taken in the master enquired into Mrs Shea's income to satisfy himself that she could afford to look after such a large number of children. She said that she received sufficient income from the parents of each child to look after them. The master then checked what money Mrs Shea had on her and ascertained that she had eleven shillings and the return tickets on the steamship to London. Mrs Shea and her party of 13 left the workhouse at 12 noon on the Monday to catch the boat back to London but she was required to pay for the transport to the workhouse and back to the boat and also eight shillings towards her board and lodgings. The boat probably left from Clacton pier and consequently it would have been quite expensive for Mrs Shea for the transport to the workhouse at Tendring Heath and back to Clacton. As a follow up the clerk was asked to write to the Greenwich Union to see if Mrs Shea was licensed to 'baby farm'. A letter was subsequently received from the Greenwich Union confirming that Mrs Shea was duly licensed under the Infant Life Protection Act 1897.

Mr F Grant the porter

Mr Grant the porter had obviously left the employment of the workhouse under a cloud as he had just completed a prison sentence in Pentonville

Prison. On his release he wrote asking for any salary that was due to him and also were there any letters for him. He also asked for a reference. The clerk replied that that there were no letters for him, no salary was due and the Guardians declined to give a reference.

September 1899

The workhouse horse

The Visiting Committee reported that they considered that the workhouse horse was no longer fit for work. It was recommended that the horse be sold and another obtained as the horse was in daily use with a cart probably for collecting provisions for the workhouse.

November 1899

The case of Samuel Gibson

Samuel was six years old and the son of Elizabeth Gibson and lived with her in Colchester. Mrs Gibson was housekeeper to a Mr Blather. Samuel had been taken into the Colchester Infectious Hospital suffering from scarlet fever. This hospital which must have been under the control of the Colchester Union were asking the Tendring Union to pay for his hospitalisation. The Gibson family came from Great Clacton and as this was his place of settlement the Tendring Union would have to pay for his treatment and care.

Arthur Francis apprenticed

Arthur Francis was a 14 years old inmate and George Bowell of Little Bentley had agreed to take him as an apprenticed shoemaker. An agreement was signed by the Guardians and Mr Bowell with the following arrangements:

A premium of £5 was to be paid to Mr Bowell now.
A further £5 to be paid after one year.
The term of apprenticeship to be three years.
Arthur was given £1 to buy clothes.
Wages of one shilling per week to be paid for the first year and two shillings for the second year and three shillings for the third year.
Mr Bowell to provide board, clothing, lodging and medicines.

A lucky lad to get out of the workhouse and have this opportunity to learn a trade.

The case of John Saddler

A youngster who was not as lucky as Arthur Francis above was John Saddler who was sent to the Buxton, Norfolk Industrial School. John was only nine and he had been previously brought before the court for continually failing to attend school. The instruction was that he was to be 'detained' at the Norfolk school until he was sixteen. It sounds as if this was more like the present day remand centre for young offenders.

December 1899
Christmas fare
The Guardians agreed that 'the usual Christmas fare be provided for the inmates'. A roast dinner and plum pudding is what other Essex workhouses provided on this occasion. It was suggested by the Guardians that instead of beer (weak beer) inmates be provided with tea, cocoa or another non-alcoholic drink. It was eventually decided that inmates could have the choice of beer or the other suggested drinks.

March 1900
Vagrancy return
The Tendring Union were asked to submit figures for the number of vagrants that passed through the workhouse for the year 1899 compared with five years earlier.

1894	847 vagrants
1899	635 vagrants

For Essex as a whole the number of vagrants that passed through the workhouses was down from 42,276 to 22,812 over the five year period. Essex was down by nearly 50% but Tendring only dropped by 25%. The 30 or so parishes that made up the Tendring area were all rural, apart from Harwich, whereas the other Union areas all had larger centres of population which were all expanding at the turn of the century. Whereas jobs were easier to find in larger communities, the make up of Tendring possibly meant that the vagrant's numbers had not reduced as much as in other parts of Essex. The figures for Essex and Tendring are not those for individual vagrants but cumulative as some may have visited the workhouse on more than one occasion in a year.

The case of Edith Sparrow a lunatic
Edith was the daughter of Mr and Mrs Robert Sparrow of Great Bromley and was most probably in the workhouse because she had been classed as a 'lunatic'. The Guardians were chasing Mr Sparrow for financial support for his daughter. Mr Sparrow wrote to the Guardians to say that he had now given up his small farm at Great Bromley and was now only a farm labourer and consequently could make no provision for his daughter's keep.

June 1900

Inspection of school and workhouse

Two separate inspections took place in June by different inspectors. The summary of the school inspection said that 'the children are well taught and have passed a good examination except that those in the third standard do not spell very well'. The initial report of the workhouse inspector was that the workhouse 'was clean and in good order'. A more detailed report would be submitted to the Guardians in due course.

September 1900

Assault on master

The master reported that Thomas Smith and John Woodham and another man applied for permission to enter the Casual Ward. The two named were very drunk and refused to answer the standard questions asked when vagrants are taken into a workhouse Casual Ward. When the master cautioned them as to their behaviour his report said:

...they commenced to use disgusting language and to threaten me. I decided to summon the police and at this time they made an assault on me. I managed to dispose of one man by getting him outside the gate but Smith was still inside and struggling with me for nearly two hours. I was unassisted the whole time as the porter was on leave. Help was eventually rendered by the foreman. The police arrived at 11.50pm. I put Smith in the care of the police who brought charges for the wilful damage of Guardian's property and assaulting me. Mr Smith was brought before the magistrate the next morning and remanded in custody until a later date. Mr Smith was brought before the magistrate again and sentenced to two months imprisonment. There were 32 previous convictions against him.

The census of 1901

Males	111	The total included 14 staff and 34 children under 14.
Females	90	The percentage of children to the total number of inmates was 18%
Total	201	

The breakdown of the total of 201 was as follows:

Staff and families	15	
Able bodied paupers	2	
Aged and infirm	61	
Single pauper inmates	67	
Imbeciles	10	
Children	43	(9 over 14 years old)
Vagrants	3	

At the end of the census document the enumerator summarised the workhouse population of 201 into the above categories. I am not sure why he decided in his summary to separate the two able bodied paupers from the single inmates.

During the period 1899/1900 the Guardians had been discussing the building of a large infirmary and eventually this building was erected in 1901. The infirmary/hospital could accommodate up to 94 patients and you will notice from the 1901 census figures that there were as many sick/infirm or of unsound mind in the workhouse as there were fit paupers. Like all the other Essex workhouses the turn of the century saw workhouses being utilised as much as a hospital as a residence for paupers. The building project also included a self contained nurses' home. Essex County Council took control of the Tendring Union Workhouse at the end of March 1930 and in the post 1930s period the old workhouse became the Heath Hospital for the Chronic Sick and later the Tendring Meadows Nursing and Residential Home. The original workhouse buildings still stands, although the front is much changed, and it is presently in the course of redevelopment.

Chapter 17

WEST HAM AND ITS ENVIRONS

PARISH WORKHOUSES

The following seven parishes in the above area were grouped together in 1834 following the Poor Law Amendment Act to form the West Ham Union. Before 1834 each parish may have had its own poorhouse or workhouse.

West Ham, East Ham, Walthamstow, Leyton
Wanstead, Woodford, St Mary, Little Ilford

The government undertook a survey of parish workhouses in 1777 and the following parishes in the West Ham area had a workhouse open in that year.

West Ham   Leyton   Walthamstow

The survey return recorded that the West Ham parish workhouse could accommodate up to 155 inmates with Leyton and Walthamstow capable of housing up to 30 and 50 respectively. Subsequent to 1777 other parishes opened workhouses and of the seven parishes six had workhouses during the period up to the 1830s. The six were:

West Ham   East Ham   Leyton
Walthamstow   Wanstead   Woodford

Only Little Ilford did not have a workhouse and of the above six only Wanstead was not open when the new West Ham Guardians took over the parish workhouses in 1836.

West Ham

The vestry minutes for the West Ham parish mention that the poor were housed in 1663 in 'two rooms in the churchyard'. This was probably a cottage owned by the church at that time and the church and the parish arranged jointly for this property to be accommodated by the poor. Later in 1686 the minutes make mention of a badge for paupers which would have been worn probably on their sleeve to show that they were in the poorhouse or on parish relief.

The West Ham parish vestry first talked about a workhouse for the parish in 1725 and it was built the same year. Rules were drawn up for the diet of inmates and also there were rules covering the discipline of inmates. John Woodward and his wife were appointed governor and matron in November 1725 at a joint salary of £30 a year. The minutes of the 27 December record that the new parish workhouse was ready to receive the poor.

In 1754 the parish arranged for the all the doctors in the West Ham area to administer to any sick paupers in the workhouse on a rotation basis. A few years later in 1760 the parish vestry had to increase the size of the workhouse by building an extra two rooms. By 1777 the workhouse could accommodate up to 155 inmates according to a government survey of that year. There was a fire at the workhouse in 1786 and in the following year the vestry were discussing building a new workhouse although thereafter it seems their discussions had changed to only a further enlargement. A new workhouse was not built for in 1815 the discussion was about 'another enlargement to the workhouse'.

It does seem that a new parish workhouse was built as records show that sometime between 1815/20 a new workhouse was built in Abbey Road, West Ham. In 1818 the number of poor in the area was increasing at a 'rapid and alarming rate' and consequently the vestry appointed a committee to look into ways of bringing down the Poor Rate which of course increased as the number of poor increased. The report mentioned a number of reasons why the Poor Rate had risen but one interesting reason related to itinerant Irish agricultural labourers. The labourers had during the time of the August harvests been employed in the rural areas surrounding West Ham but thereafter had come into West Ham parish for the autumn potato harvest. The Irish would have been accompanied by their wives and families and when they could find no more work they would get accommodation in West Ham and then apply to the parish for out-relief. The families would stay until the following Spring before moving out of the area to the many market gardens in the suburbs.

Whilst the itinerant labourers were a drain on the parish in respect of out-relief the number in the workhouse was also increasing as the following table shows:

Number of inmates

1812	101
1818	189
1819	227 including 58 children under 12 years

One of the outcomes of the 1818 committee report was that the vestry formed three committees, the Workhouse Subcommittee, a Pensions List Subcommittee and a Casual Poor Committee. These three committees turned the financial affairs of the parish around by enforcing a policy of strict economy and putting the affairs of the workhouse in good order. They also economised on the vestry's purchases of food and items needed for the workhouse and they examined in more detail the casual poor and in particular the information that was taken from them when they entered the workhouse. Presumably the information taken regarding the finances of the prospective inmate was sketchy and the committee felt that this aspect needed to be improved. The committees also examined the profits being made from workhouse industries and scrutinised all the workhouse accounts. The three committees worked hard over a three month period in 1819 and by the end had reduced the Poor Rate from four shillings in the pound to two shillings in the pound. In 1823 the parish installed a unit for making sacks in the workhouse.

West Ham parish workhouse closed in 1841 when the new Union workhouse opened at Leyton although the building survived until it was demolished in the early 1960s.

Walthamstow

The first mention of a parish workhouse in Walthamstow was in 1726 when rented premises in Hoe Street were used for this purpose. In 1730 the Walthamstow parish vestry decided to build a purpose built workhouse which would also serve as the offices for the vestry. The site chosen was on Church Common which in 1730 covered 27 acres and the parish vestry acquired a one acre piece of the Common for £6 near to the St Mary the Virgin church. The small green outside the workhouse is all that remains of the village green for this historic section of Walthamstow which is only a quarter of the mile from the main shopping centre in Hoe Street. The building, which still remains, is two storeys and built with brown stock bricks and originally had eight rooms and could accommodate up to 40 inmates. This attractive building is called Vestry House and now owned by the London Borough of Waltham Forest and houses the local history museum. The cost of building was £343 and originally it was symmetrical in shape. Above the front door the plaque read as follows with the capital letters as in the inscription:

THIS HOUSE ERECTED
An. Dom. MDCCXXX
If any would not work
neither should he eat

Walthamstow parish workhouse built in 1730

The ground floor room to the left of the front door was used by the parish vestry for their meetings and in 1756 there were enlargements to the rear of the property to provide a workroom downstairs and more sleeping accommodation above. In 1779 the vestry room at the front was extended into the front yard. This front extension also provided more workrooms upstairs. The workhouse master had his accommodation at the rear of the property with his wife where they had their own fireplace and kitchen area. To the side of the property is the garden where there were fruit trees and the paupers grew vegetables to supplement their meagre diet. Leading off the rear of the house was an exercise yard which had twelve foot high wall surrounding it. The enlargements of 1756 and 1779 saw the workhouse capable of taking up to 50 inmates. By the 1820s the number of inmates numbered up to 80 and there were still 73 being accommodated when the workhouses closed in 1841.

The pauper inmates were given plain clothes and a plain diet. The plain pauper uniform had a badge put on the shoulder which read 'W P' standing for 'Walthamstow Poor'. The inmates received three meals a day which was usually porridge, soup, bread and weak beer. The adults and the children all had to work in the workroom during the day to earn their board and lodgings.

The property was used until 1841 when the inmates were transferred to the new Union Workhouse at Leyton. After the inmates had been transferred the administration side of the Walthamstow parish vestry occupied some of the empty rooms with the remainder being used as a local police station complete with cells.

THE WEST HAM UNION WORKHOUSE

The Poor Law Commissioners had decided that only seven parishes would make up the West Ham Union. Although the total population of the seven parishes in 1834 was the standard of about 25,000 the individual parishes were more densely populated than elsewhere in Essex with the largest, West Ham parish, having a population of about 11,500 in the 1830s. The number of representatives from each parish to serve on the Board of Guardians was as follows:

West Ham	10	East Ham	2
Walthamstow	4	Leyton	3
Wanstead	2	Woodford, St Mary	2
Little Ilford	1		
Number of Guardians	24		

West Ham's ten representatives is a reflection of its 11,500 population at that time compared with the next highest in Essex which was Chelmsford who had four people on their Board for its population which was just under 5500. Colchester was divided up into a number of parishes and although cumulatively they exceeded Chelmsford no one parish exceeded a population of 5500.

1836
First meetings of Guardians
The first meeting of the new Board of Guardians was held on the 7 June 1836 at the Swan at Stratford. The first couple of meetings dealt with the appointment of officers and the usual relieving officers and medical officers were allocated to the various areas.

A letter from the West Ham Union to the clerk at the Woodford parish workhouse dated the 24 June 1836 chased that workhouse for names of their elected Guardians which should have been submitted to the West Ham workhouse board meeting at their first meeting on the 7 June 1836. A postscript to the letter was addressed to the wife of the clerk at the Woodford workhouse from the wife of the writer (the Union clerk) trusting that 'she will soon have plenty of juvenile inmates to amuse her'!!! As the census data below shows the majority of the children in the West Ham Union area were sent to the Woodford workhouse.

Before, of course, the children could be transferred to the Woodford workhouse the adult inmates had to be moved out and these were transferred to the Walthamstow workhouse in August 1836. The clerk at Woodford drew up a comprehensive list of the paupers in the Woodford workhouse on the 1st August 1836 with comments as to their state of health and a list of their possessions of those that were being transferred. There were 11 men, 11 women and 5 children - total 27 inmates. All the 11 men were over 61 years old ranging up to 85 with the women of a similar age range including three under 60. The five children were three aged five, one aged eight and one aged thirteen. The clerk added at the bottom of his report a list those that had left the workhouse in the preceding month.

The details are as follows:

July 8	Sarah Wheller left the House with her infant child
July 17	Sarah Watson absconded with Clara her youngest child - she left behind Emma aged 5 (one of three mentioned above)
July 26	Alfred Watson, aged 9, absconded, presumably Emma's brother.

Of the 11 men six were transferred to the Walthamstow parish workhouse. Of the 11 women eight were also transferred to Walthamstow. The five children stayed at Woodford to be joined by other children in due course. One can only presume that the men and women that were not transferred were too ill to be moved. The list of possessions of those being transferred was very similar and they consisted entirely of clothes. A typical list for one of the men was:

> 2 shirts, 2 suits, 1 flannel waist coat, 2 pair stockings, 2 neckchiefs, 2 hats, 1 pair shoes

The women's clothes included petticoats and aprons.

July 1836
West Ham's paupers

The Guardians investigated the circumstances of those West Ham paupers who were on out-relief to see if the weekly allowance paid to them was justified or whether their circumstances had changed. The Guardians reviewed 86 cases at a July meeting and decided that 21 cases should be transferred to the West Ham parish workhouse. Five more had their weekly allowance discontinued and further enquiries were to be made on four others. The remainder continued to be on out-relief at the same rate as before.

At a subsequent meeting the Guardians looked at 34 more cases and these seemed to be ones that needed further research. This time the clerk explained in a few lines the outcome of each case.

Elizabeth Baker - Widow for four years with eight children. The eldest son was 27 and married and five more children were also in work. Elizabeth had one daughter aged 11 who "has clothes found for her" and one further daughter aged seven. The out door relief was five shillings a week. The Guardians decided to discontinue the relief. Mary Rowett - Mary's husband was a gardener and milkman. They had one child of their own. Mary is also looking after three children by her father's second wife aged nine, five and three years. The father had now died. Mary had been getting five shillings a week to look after the children whom the Guardians decided to continue. Sophia Holbrook - Widow for seven years with three children aged 12, 10 and seven. The allowance was previously three shillings per week. All four have been ordered into the workhouse.

The Buildings Committee

One of the sub committees appointed the previous month was the Buildings Committee whose brief was to inspect the existing parish workhouses and recommend what changes should be made, if any. Their report in July 1836 said that there were presently five parish workhouses at:

West Ham	East Ham	Leyton
Walthamstow	Woodford	

The West Ham workhouse was by far the largest and could accommodate all the able bodied men and women and also all the children under the age of seven presently housed in all five workhouses. Of the remaining four the recommendation was that Walthamstow should house the aged or infirm men and women and that Woodford would take all the boys and girls from the age of 7 to 16. Consequently there would be no further use for the East Ham and Leyton parish workhouses. Although the official report by the Building Committee was not presented to the Guardians until July 1836 it appears that everyone seemed to know in advance who was going where as the correspondence to the wife of the Woodford clerk in June mentioned above informs her that she is to receive the children in due course.

The seven parishes that made up the new Union were continually having to make returns to the main Board of Guardians at the West Ham Union Workhouse not just on the situation at their particular workhouse but also on the paupers in their area who were on out-relief. One that survives at the Essex Record Office was from Wanstead parish in 1837 when they submitted their list of paupers on out-relief for the quarter and also how many of their residents were inmates of the workhouse although they do not specify in which workhouse they refer as they had now bee segregation and spread around the various parish workhouses. Forty nine residents of Wanstead were on out-relief and sixteen were inmates of one of the workhouses. All of those on out-relief were adults with the exception of two five year olds who were both described as 'bastards' and would have been placed with a family at the expense of the Union. Of the sixteen in the workhouse they included the Hawkins family of father, mother and children aged five and one year old with the comment that they were all in the workhouse because the mother was ill and the father did not have any employment. The family would of course now have been split up although the two children would still be with their mother if she was well enough to look after them. The list of names also includes how long the inmates were in the workhouse for that quarter. Most were there for the 91 days of the quarter but it was pleasing to see that the Hawkins family left after 24 days.

November 1838
Building Committee
This committee seemed to have changed its name from the 'Buildings' to 'Building' committee. Previously the committee was charged with looking into the situation regarding the existing parish workhouse but their brief had now changed to all aspects of the building of the new Union workhouse. At their November meeting they discussed the appointment of a surveyor and also discussed how many inmates the new workhouse should accommodate. The Guardians conducted research to ascertain what the greatest number of inmates was at one time in the three parish workhouses. The maximum was 423 and consequently the Guardians decided that the brief to the architect, when appointed, would be to design a workhouse to accommodate up to 500 inmates. Little did the Guardian know at this time that the number of inmates at the West Ham Union workhouse would be over 1000 forty years later.

March 1839
Purchase of land
The Guardians approved the recommendation of the Building Committee to purchase four acres of land in Leyton at £200 per acre for the purpose of building the new Union workhouse.

February 1840
Acceptance of tender
The Guardians had advertised for tenders to be submitted for the building of the new workhouse. Seven tenders were received and these ranged from £10,484 to £12,780. The lowest tender submitted by Messrs Curtis and Sons was accepted with the work to commence forthwith.

April 1841
The new workhouse
The month of April saw the completion of the building of the workhouse and during this month all the new furniture for the schoolrooms, kitchens, and bedrooms was being ordered. At this time the Guardians were also advertising and interviewing for all the appointments in the new workhouse. It was during this month that the Guardians started having their meetings in the new Guardians Board Room.

The census of 1841
At the date of the national census in April 1841 the new Union workhouse at Leyton was partially functioning but the old parish workhouses at Walthamstow and Woodford still accommodated pauper inmates. The temporary arrangement in 1836 was that the children and young adults would be transferred to the Woodford parish workhouse and these were still there in 1841. The old parish workhouses at Walthamstow and Woodford were now referred to as the Union Workhouses but they would both be closed within a few months when the new Union Workhouse at Leyton was fully operational.

West Ham Union Workhouse, Union Road, Leyton

Males	104	The total includes 4 staff and 39 children under
Females	115	14. The percentage of children to the total number of inmates was 18%
Total	219	

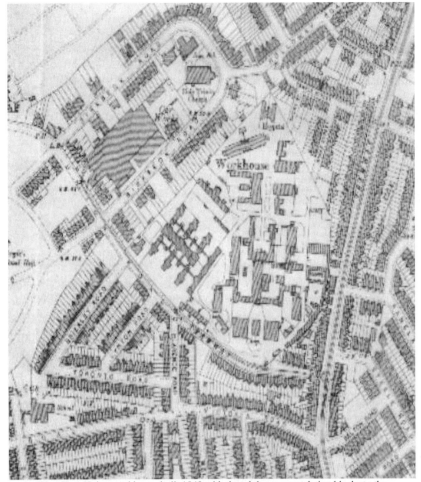

West Ham Union workhouse built 1842 with the adult accommodation blocks to the right and the childrens' "barrack" blocks to the left

Walthamstow Union Workhouse

Males	34	The total includes 2 staff and one child aged 10 -
Females	42	daughter of an inmate
Total	76	

Woodford Union Workhouse

Males	39	The total includes 4 staff and 62 children under 14
Females	35	with the other 8 being young persons up to the age of 18.
Total	74	

During the summer of 1841 the two existing parish workhouses at Walthamstow and Woodford closed and all the inmates were housed in the new Union workhouse at Leyton. At their first Christmas together in December 1841 the Guardians agreed that all categories of inmate could have plum pudding for Christmas dinner. In addition beer was ordered at the price of twenty six shillings per 36 gallons. All adults were allowed one pint each and the children half a pint. The cost of the plum puddings and the beer came from donations and not out of the workhouse funds.

1867

Commissioners in Lunacy Report

The Commissioner visited a sample of workhouses throughout the country and the figures for the West Ham Union showed that there were 24 male and 21 female inmates who were described as being either 'insane, idiotic and imbecile inmates'.

One of the accommodation blocks at the West Ham Union Workhouse
at Leyton

1878

Deputation by parishes

The Local Government Board was the successor to the Poor Law Union and a deputation was made to the Board by four of the parishes that made up the Union, namely, Walthamstow, Leyton, Woodford and Wanstead. Their argument was that in 1836 when the Union was founded the total population of the seven parishes was under 20,000 (actually it was just under 25,000). Forty years later the total population had risen to 150,000 and despite enlargements to the Leyton Union workhouse the deputation said that 'the present accommodation is wholly inadequate'. The total number of paupers accommodated in the workhouses was 869. In addition the report to the Local government Board said that the amount of out-relief was increasing at a high rate due to the Guardians not undertaking sufficient checks on prospective cases for out-relief due to the high population of the area which was too large for them to cover. Consequently the report by the four parishes recommended that the Union area be split into two with West Ham, East Ham and Little Ilford forming one Union and a new Union area be created comprising Walthamstow, Leyton, Woodford and Wanstead.

This rise in population from about 20,000 to 150,000 was tremendous reflecting the spread of London outwards in the middle of the nineteenth century with its row upon row of terraced houses. Whilst all the seven parishes grew at a fast rate the parish of West Ham was the fastest with its 11,500 population in 1836 rising to 100,000 by 1878. Nothing came of the deputation.

The West Ham Union workhouse Guardian's board room at Leyton

By 1891 the Guardians had built separate accommodation and a school for the children in the grounds of the workhouse where the children lived and went to school. Even if they had parents in the main workhouse buildings they were kept separate apart from those under school age.

The census data for 1871, 1881, 1891 and 1901

Union Road, Leyton workhouse.

1871	Staff	13	
	Inmates	771	including 228 children
	Total	**784**	

1881	Staff + fam	32	
	Servants	10	
	Messengers	9	
	Inmates	1129	including 352 children
	Total	**1180**	

1891	Staff + fam	41	
	Domestics	20	
	Inmates	1074	including 21 very young children with mothers
	Total	**1135**	

Union School in workhouse grounds

Staff	16	
Servants	11	
Children-boys	101	aged 7 and over
Children-girls	62	aged 7 and over
Boys and girls	39	under 7
Total	**229**	

Grand total	**1364**	**(1891)**

The census of 1901

By 1901 the population of the area making up the West Ham Union was 580,000 and this very large number compared with the other Essex Unions is reflected in the number of inmates which was just under 2500 in 1901.

The West Ham Union workhouse chapel at Leyton

Census 1901
West Ham Union Workhouse, Union Road, Leyton (today it is Langthorne Road)

Males	919	The total includes 85 staff and no children
Females	924	up to the age of 14
Total	1843	

West Ham Union Workhouse School (adjacent to main workhouse)

Males	199	The total includes 17 staff and 333 children
Females	151	up to the age of 14
Total	350	

The number of children in the workhouse school also grew at a fast rate with 202 children in 1891 rising to 333 in 1901 and by 1906 this number had increased to 500. The separate area for the children was known as the Barrack Schools as they lived in three story blocks adjacent to the schoolrooms. The twentieth century saw the end of this type of institution for children and by 1913 there were 235 children housed in the Aldersbrook Homes and 660 were scattered in small homes throughout the Union's area. Training workshops were established at Aldersbrook for the boys and the Union encouraged the boys to take apprenticeships. Many joined merchant navy training ships and others emigrated to Canada.

In 1901, in addition to the main workhouse and the workhouse school at Leyton, the Union also had 285 inmates at Forest House, Leytonstone.

Forest House, Leytonstone branch of the West Ham Union (now Whipps Cross Hospital)

Males	290	The total includes 5 staff. The inmates were
Females	nil	basically all males over 60 years old.
Total	**2483**	**(including staff of all three premises)**

The Forest House estate at Upper Walthamstow comprising 44 acres was purchased by the West Ham Union in 1889 and by 1895 planning permission was granted for a purpose built infirmary. The building work started in 1900 and as the census figures above for 1901 show there were 290 inmates and staff accommodated on the estate in 1901. Whilst the building work was going on the West Ham Union were using the old Forest House as a home for able bodied old men. Forest House was not being used for the sick as these were at the time catered for at the larger Union Workhouse at Leyton. It looks as if initially the first patients at the new infirmary were the sick and aged transferred from the West Ham Union Workhouse at Leyton and when the infirmary proper opened in 1903 under the control of the West Ham Union there were 672 beds in 24 wards covering four large blocks. As we have said before with the other Essex workhouse infirmaries, the inmates in the twentieth century were not just the pauper class but the infirmaries were now catering for the general sick and infirm of the area. Consequently the workhouse infirmary gradually turned into a hospital and the site of the original Forest House, Walthamstow is now the impressive building now known as Whipps Cross Hospital. One of the distinctive features of the 1903 building, which has changed little today, were the fire escape bridges in tiers which linked the four large blocks. There were 91 nursing staff when the infirmary opened of which 28 were qualified and 63 unqualified. The old Forest House continued to be occupied by old men until well into the 1920s when there were over 300 in occupation with 200 sleeping in one large room side by side said to be the largest bedroom in the country. Forest House Cottages, also in the grounds of Whipps Cross Hospital, were originally built for aged married couples but subsequently used solely by aged women. Ninety women were accommodated in the cottages.

The 1901 census data also listed a Bethnal Green Union school that had 373 children within the West Ham residential area but this belonged to the Bethnal Green Union. The Forest Gate Workhouse School with 634 children was also sited within the West Ham area but this school belonged to the Whitechapel Union.

The West Ham Union workhouses in 1841 had a total of 360 inmates whereas by 1901 the total number of inmates was nearly 2376 and the number totalled nearly 2500 when staff are included. Four years later in 1905 the number of inmates had increased by a further 1000+ and a ten year comparison is shown below.

1895 to 1905 Compared

	Number in workhouse	Population of area
1895	1814	451,000
1905	3597	667,000
	Inmates increased by 98%	Population increased by 48%

	Number on out-relief
1895	7644
1905	16320

an increase of 113% compared with population increase of 48% for same period

As the above figures show that whereas the population of the West Ham Union area increased by 48% over a ten year period the number of in-house inmates increased by 98% and those on out-relief by 113%. Economists put the reason for the disproportionate increase in the number of poor compared with the increase in population to the house building boom in the West Ham area at the turn of the century. Demand for property was great in 1897 and many builders moved into the area. A lot of the house-building was by small building firms where large numbers of semi-skilled building workers were attracted to the area. In times of boom there is always bust and many of the casual labourers were out of work by 1901 when the supply of labour exceeded demand. There was also a high incidence of bankruptcy with the small builders with the ultimate consequence that both labourers and employers became reliant on the parish as paupers. Over the next couple of years from 1905 to 1907 the number of people on out-relief fell from the peak of 16320 to under 13000 whereas those in the workhouse continued to grow from 3597 to 4000.

The unemployment situation in the period 1895 to 1905 was getting so bad that the workhouse was full and the Guardians opened a 'labour yard'. The unemployed could come to one of the workhouse yards, undertake work and be fed and then return to their lodgings. The yard could take about 200 people and even with this number the yard was crowded and supervision was impossible. A report of the time said that men were drafted to the infirmary grounds to dig but it always seemed to rain when this work was scheduled and little got done. Painting was another job given to the men and the report said that 'men were swarming about the place with paint pots, painting'. It was probable a case of too many cooks. On other occasions when unemployment was running at a very high rate up to 1000 men over a period came to the yard for work and relief. The 'yard' system was not a success and so this form of relief was discontinued and it was changed to the standard form of out-relief under the control of the relieving officer for the district in which with applicant resided. The yard did open again in 1905 but this time the Guardians had got their act together with allocated work better supervised and the payment of relief also better organised. The statistics of the time show that the recipients of the yard relief were mainly from the dock area and also from Stratford with their occupation being almost exclusively that of a casual labourer.

1905

The South Ockendon Colony

West Ham County Borough formed a Distress Committee in 1905 as a result of the acute unemployment situation in the West Ham area. The County Borough purchased the same year farmland at South Ockendon, Essex and established a market gardening concern called the South Ockendon Colony. The Committee consisted of 12 persons from the Borough and 12 from the West Ham Union Guardians and a further six persons 'experienced in the relief of distress'. The Guardians regularly sent the jobless, who would otherwise have ended up in the workhouse, to the Colony. By 1927 the Colony was no longer being used as a centre for the jobless but now utilised for the mentally defective to which the Union's Guardians sent many of their cases. The name changed to the Hospital Farm but for many years after it was still known as the 'Colony'.

1906

Complaint against coal contractor

The auditors noticed that there had been a large increase in the consumption of coal notwithstanding that the price of coal had decreased and the cost of that used by the workhouse had increased. At the same time complaints were being made that there were large amounts of smoke being generated by the boiler house at the infirmary and investigations concluded that the reason was the inferior quality of coal being supplied to the workhouse. It was taking much more of the inferior coal to generate the heat required which resulted in the high costs. An action was brought against the coal contractor for obtaining money by false pretences. He was found guilty and sentenced to six months imprisonment.

Cheating by Guardians, master and officials

In the same year the auditors noticed that the cost per head of inmate for food, necessaries and clothing was rising. The auditors decided to get some comparable figures from other local Unions to see if this trend was the norm. The outcome following an internal investigation was that the West Ham Union was not necessarily accepting the lowest tender for goods. On November 26th 1906, three Guardians, the workhouse master and two other officials were arrested and charged that 'on divers dates between 1903 and 1906 they did unlawfully conspire, combine and confederate together with Elijah Bond, a contractor, to unlawfully obtain by divers false pretences.........large sums of money from the Guardians of the West Ham Union'. The court case showed that by collusion the contractor Bond had delivered short weight coal, that the quality was inferior and that the books of the Union had been altered and readjusted in an attempt to hoodwink the auditors. In addition the prosecution showed that there were elaborate systems of corruption within the Guardians in that sums of money passed to secure votes (presumably so that Bond got the contract). The contractor appeared as a witness for the prosecution and confirmed what had been going on including that he paid some of the Guardians to get the coal contract. Subsequently one Guardian committed suicide and another attempted suicide. Two more Guardians were arrested and also one more official. In total five Guardians and four officials were found guilty and sentenced to terms of imprisonment ranging from six months to two years.

The source of the above two frauds does not actually give the name of the coal contractor who supplied the inferior coal in the first jotting. Presumably he was the Mr Bond of the second jotting and he was brought from prison as a prosecution witness.

1906 to 1930
Pauper children

In 1906 the workhouse Guardians removed all the children from the workhouse and lodged them in houses within the area of which there were up to 50 properties at any one time. From the age of fourteen children went out to work or in some cases arrangements were made for them to emigrate. A report made by an Inspector on behalf of the Canadian government in 1915 was investigating the conditions of children in British workhouses prior to accepting them as immigrants into Canada. The Canadian Inspector was taken round a number of children's homes controlled by the West Ham Union and in his report he mentioned the English government's changing policy to pauper children which was 'the determination to afford children under the poor law with surroundings as nearly as possible like the normal home life of children in their natural homes'. As far as the West Ham Union was concerned their policy, which complied with government guidelines, was to accommodate poor law children in one of the following five types of establishment:

> Boarded out with working or middle class families.
> Barrack schools where all children live together.
> Village homes where children and staff are a community
> Cottage homes which are the same as village home but with limited access to the outside world.
> Houses containing a few children who fully integrate with the community.

In 1909 the English government decided that no child under the age of 14 would be allowed to emigrate to Canada 'owing to the inadequate educational facilities in the farming districts of the Dominion'.

1918
Whipps Cross Infirmary

By 1918, like the other Essex Unions, there were no longer any children in the workhouses and only sick children in the infirmaries. The Whipps Cross Infirmary had now become the Whipps Cross Hospital although still under the control of the West Ham Union. The problem that was being experienced at this time was that the hospital was accepting a high proportion of fee paying patients to the detriment of the pauper sick. There was of course no National Health Service in 1918. The hospital history records that the paupers were separated from the fee paying patients to the extent that the paupers were crowded into wards not intended for that many patients. The hospital could accommodate 744 at this time but hospital records show that the total number of patients peaked at 1051.

1929

Guardian's Final Report

The West Ham Guardians published a final report for the public in July 1929 a year before control passed to the West Ham local authority. The bulk of the report was about financial matters but there were some interesting data when the Guardians were comparing the number of people on outdoor relief in 1926 to 1929. The reason the Guardian picked 1926 was because of the General Strike that year when they had on their outdoor relief books 27,853 cases covering 66,001 people which was costing the Union £28,000 a week. By 1929 though, the number of cases had dropped to 6,759 covering 14.541 people which was costing a more sensible figure of £3860 a week. The Guardians also stated that the number of people resident in their institutions was 4160. Although the 1901 census data gave the number of inmates as just fewer than 2500 I believe that the figure of 4160 includes the many children's home that the Union was running in various locations throughout the West Ham area. No children were now in the workhouse but boarded out with families or in cottage homes.

Post 1930

After 1930 the West Ham Union workhouse at Leyton became the Langhorne Hospital. Part of the workhouse has now been demolished but part has been converted into flats. The separate board-room block remains as does the chapel and the stores block. The Union school barrack blocks have all gone but the school remains and is now a medical centre.

Whipps Cross Hospital was originally part of the West Ham Union and built during the period 1900/03

Chapter 18

WITHAM AND ITS ENVIRONS

PARISH WORKHOUSES

The following seventeen parishes in the above area were grouped together in 1834 following the Poor Law Amendment Act to form the Witham Union. Before 1834 each parish may have had its own poorhouse or workhouse.

Great Coggeshall, Fairstead, Faulkbourne, Feering, Great Braxted, Hatfield Peverel, Inworth, Kelvedon, Little Braxted, Little Coggeshall, Marks Hall, Messing, Rivenhall, Terling, Ulting, Wickham Bishops and Witham.

The government undertook a survey of parish workhouses in 1777 and the following ten parishes in the Witham area had a workhouse open in that year.

Gt Braxted	Gt Coggeshall	Lt Coggeshall
Faulkbourne	Kelvedon	Hatfield Peverel
Messing	Rivenhall	Terling
Witham		

Witham

Some time between 1620 and 1639 Dame Katherine Barnardiston left £100 for the poor of Witham to purchase a parcel of land. With this £100 and a further £20 the trustees purchased a piece of land on the east side of Church Street and the income from this land enabled twelve poor persons to be provided with two penny loaves every Sabbath.

In 1714 part of this land was used to build the parish workhouse and the initials 'IW, SN and FR, WS' together with the date 1714 can still be seen on a plaque on the front of the block. The formal government act giving parishes permission to erect a parish workhouse was not until 1723 and consequently Witham's workhouse was one of the first built in Essex. The parish raised the sum of £300 to build the workhouse by way of a loan from Miss Alice Bird a spinster of Great Coggeshall. The repayment was to be by the 4th May 1718 with interest to be paid at 5%. An itemed account of the £300 expended included beds, bedding and clothing for the inmates.

Witham parish workhouse built 1714 from the churchyard across the road

The plaque over the Witham parish workhouse

In 1715 the Justices made the workhouse a House of Correction for the receipt of 'vagrants and vagabonds ....and disorderly persons .....and to punish the said persons by whipping as ordered by the Justices'.

An inventory of 1757 itemised the rooms as follows:

Hall	Cellar	Kitchen	Pantry
Brewhouse	Workhouse	Master's room	
Five bedchambers			

The government survey of 1777 indicated that up to 60 inmates could be accommodated in the workhouse. This number seems high when one looks at the building as it is now but as a comparison the Great Dunmow parish workhouse could take up to 50 inmates and it is also still possible to identify this building. The Witham and Gt Dunmow properties are of a similar size and maybe therefore 60 inmates could have been housed in the Witham parish workhouse.

The old workhouse is now seven cottages numbered 28 - 40 Church Street opposite the parish church of St Nicolas. The rest of the workhouse site is now occupied by 22 -26 Church Street and also by Chipping Hill Infants School.

Witham's poor, prior to the opening of the workhouse, would have been funded by the Poor Rate. The poor would have either stayed in their own rented accommodation with financial assistance provided by the parish or if for some reason they did not have anywhere to live they would have been housed in a property owned by the parish. The parish workhouse had the effect of reducing the cost of financing the poor of the parish and records show that initially the poor rates reduced by half to £230 in the early 1700s. In 1817 the parish drew up a new agreement with the governor of the workhouse, Thomas Bolingbroke. Besides the usual instruction that the inmates were to be fed and clothed to a certain standard, Mr Bolingbroke was to ensure that all the inmates attended church twice every Sunday 'in decent clothes'. An instruction not often seen in a master's workhouse agreements was that all the men in the workhouse were to be shaved once a week at the expense of the parish. Inflation was high at the beginning of the nineteenth century and the parish arranged with Mr Bolingbroke that if the price of flour rose above one hundred and ten shillings per sack then the weekly allowance per inmate would increase from four shillings a week to four shillings and six pence per week. Conversely the allowance would decrease if the price of flour fell below eighty shillings a sack.

By 1834 the number in the workhouse had reduced to only 14 - eight old men, four old women and two boys - together with the governor and his family. Consequently there would have been plenty of room in the workhouse to take the paupers of the other parishes when their workhouses closed when the new Union Guardians took control of the parish workhouses.

Great Braxted

The Great Braxted workhouse gets a mention in the overseers account's from at least 1749 and continuously until at least 1774 although the workhouse does not get a mention in the government survey of 1777. Possibly the parish failed to make its return or the workhouse had closed by 1777.

The location, as described in the sale particulars of 1838, was a brick built cottage on the road from Great Braxted to Kelvedon. An area on this road is still called 'Workhouse Plantation'. Even if the workhouse was closed in 1777 it must have reopened again as the building appears to have been used as a workhouse by the parish right up to the time that the Witham Poor law Guardians came into existence in 1835. The property was sold for £250 by way of conveyance on the 2nd January 1837.

Great Coggeshall

Great Coggeshall parish forms the northern side of the river Blackwater which divides the parish from Little Coggeshall which is in the southern side of the river. Great Coggeshall has roughly always had twice the area of Little Coggeshall. The Great Coggeshall parish workhouse was built at some time prior to the 1740s.

A new overseer, Edward Powell, was appointed for the parish in February 1758 and it appears that he was unhappy that that no account was held of the contents of the workhouse and so he drew up an inventory. His listing of the rooms is as follows:

Kitchen	Parlour	Buttery
Beer store room	Brewhouse	Great workroom
Officer's store room	Great chamber	Small chamber
Nursery	Chamber over parlour	Chamber over brew house
First garret room	Second garret room	Woodhouse
Old House		

The workhouse, from the above description, was a large building over three floors with five bedrooms on the first floor and two garret rooms above these. The 'Old House' probably refers to part of the property which even in 1758 was an older part of the property. In 1777 the government return stated that up to 50 inmates could be accommodated which seems rather high although the inventory quotes that there were 33 drinking pots and at least 20 beds. Other inmates would probably have slept on the floor. In the Great Workroom there were 17 spinning wheels and 11 carding stocks in 1758. In the brew house there were 18 wooden dishes and 18 wooden spoons. An undated return of the 1750/60s quotes the number of persons residing in the parish workhouse as 40 and consequently the figure of 50 quoted as the maximum the workhouse could take some years later in 1777 could well be accurate.

One of the surviving records for the workhouse is the register of the work done in the workhouse on daily basis - Monday to Saturday. The record for 1759 for spinning and carding lists 30 inmates and the amount of work that they achieved each day. At the end of the list was Ann Boosey and against her name was 'learning to spin'. Her output was, as to be expected, only a fraction of what the adults achieved. Among the 30 names was that of Elizabeth Boosey who was probably her mother. There were five more names after that of Ann Boosey who did no work at all and one must assume that they were infirm or sick. The total number of inmates appears therefore to be 36 in 1759 although a full list of names for 1760 mentions 50 inmates. The Boosey mother and daughter do not appear in the 1760 list and hopefully they were able to leave the workhouse at some time earlier.

The only other record book that includes the names of inmates and their work done on a daily basis is for the period 1812 to 1819. For the year 1812 there were 39 persons listed as inmates which included again an Elizabeth Boosey. So, assuming that it was the same Elizabeth Boosey that was in the workhouse in 1759, she had left the workhouse in 1760 she was back in again some 50 years or so later in 1812 at the age of 86. She died in the workhouse the following year. There was no mention of her daughter Ann who would have been about 60 years old when her mother died and probably married. The names of the inmates in the latter period (1819) indicated that their stay in the workhouse was only for a few weeks or months whereas in the previous century inmates stayed for much longer.

Little Coggeshall

The parish of Little Coggeshall had its own workhouse which was built at some time before 1777 as the workhouse is included in the government survey of that year when the parish said that it could accommodate up to 15 inmates. The location, when sold in 1838, is described as being by the bridge at Little Coggeshall and abutting on one side Grange Farm and on the other side the High Road. The auction on

January 18 1838 described the property as a timber built and thatched cottage. The sale price was £34.

Hatfield Peverel

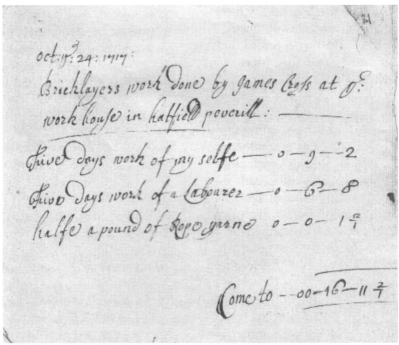

Work done at Hatfield Peverel pariah workhouse in 1717

Hatfield Peverel workhouse was situated on the B1019 Maldon Road near to the junction with the The Street the B1137. It would appear that the workhouse was built in 1717 as there exists a parcel of bills for that year from various tradesmen for work done at the workhouse. The amount of time spent by the tradesmen and the materials used seemed to be more than just remedial work and it would appear that the money spent by the parish was for the building of the workhouse. Carpenters were supplying lengths of elm board, 700 laths and various other planks and boards. The carpenters charged for 26 days work over a two month period. The bricklayers were also on site for many days during the same period. On one of the bricklayer's bills the parish was charged for two quarts of beer for unloading lime.

The cost of running the workhouse to the parish was a never ender expense. This was one of the main reasons that parish workhouses all closed in the 1830s in favour of the Union Workhouse. The overseer's accounts for the 1700s are full of bills for such items as repairing the workhouse pump, having coffins made for deceased paupers together with the replacement of the items that were installed when the workhouse was built. All this type of expense was in addition to the general running costs of the workhouse for the supply of food, drink and clothes for the inmates.

Residents of any village did not like ending up in the parish workhouse but there was one resident in 1822 that refused to leave. The minutes of the parish record the case of Elizabeth Norris who had been in the workhouse for sixteen months. The overseer had sanctioned an out-relief allowance of three shillings per week and would also find her accommodation. Elizabeth refused to leave and the parish vestry ordered that she appear before the local magistrate who would deal with her case.

At the same meeting in June 1822 the vestry passed a resolution concerning paupers generally in the parish which would effect those on out-relief as well as those in the workhouse. The workhouse master ensured that those in his care worked but the vestry resolved that those paupers living in the village would only receive their allowance if they were in employment. A list of unemployed paupers would be posted in the village and those named would have to report to the overseer at 6am every morning with a reason why they could not work or for those that were fit for work the overseer would advise them where they could find work.

At the time of the government survey of parish workhouses in 1777 the Hatfield Peverel workhouse could accommodate up to 30 inmates which indicates somewhat the size of the workhouse which was about the equivalent of three or four Victorian cottages. The workhouse existed into the nineteenth century but closed when the Witham Union was established in 1835.

Kelvedon

Few records remain concerning the parish workhouse but it was in existence in 1777 as the number of inmates it could accommodate in that year was 30. The workhouse was probably much like that of Hatfield Peverel, which had a similar population, and was probably built much earlier than 1777. The workhouse was probably equivalent in size to three or four Victorian cottages. The records do state that a resolution was passed in July 1836 for the workhouse to be sold and consequently, like Hatfield Peverel, it was used up to the time that the Witham Union was formed.

Terling

The overseer's accounts for the parish go back to 1751 and there is expense for the workhouse for this year and probably the workhouse was built in the 1730/40s. The parish minute book shows that in 1776 there were only nine people in the workhouse although the return to the government a year later records that the workhouse could accommodate up to 20 inmates. By the 1780s the number of inmates in the workhouse had increased to 15. An inventory of the workhouse in 1781 shows that there were four rooms downstairs and four bedrooms upstairs. The size of the workhouse therefore was the equivalent of two Victorian cottages of the two up two down style.

Inflation was rising at the turn of the century and in 1799 the parish agreed to supply flour to the poor of the parish at the price of two shillings and six pence per peck (a quarter of a bushel) with an allowance of half a peck per person to those who qualified. By the end of the century the number in the workhouse was still 15 inmates.

In December 1801 the parish vestry passed a resolution 'that there be a new workhouse built'. It is surprising that this was the feeling of the day as by this year there were only six persons in the present workhouse. There was no other property in the village at this time suitable for a workhouse and the suggestion was that a purpose built workhouse be constructed on land to be given by Colonel Strutt. The minutes are silent as to whether a new workhouse was eventually built but in the Essex Record Office is a Deed of Exchange dated 1826 between Joseph Holden Strutt and the parish exchanging the deeds of the old workhouse land for the new workhouse land. It looks, therefore, as if a new workhouse was built.

The parish did not know that within a few years of the new workhouse being built it would be made redundant by virtue of the formation of the Witham Union in 1835. The workhouse did though continue in operation until the mid 1830s.

Farmstead - Faulkbourne - Messing - Rivenhall

Fairstead had a workhouse which was not in existence in 1777 as it does not appear in the government survey of that year. It was probably built at some time later in the eighteenth century. It would have accommodated about 15 inmates as it was converted into three cottages when sold in 1837.

Faulkborne had a workhouse which could accommodate up to 25 inmates in 1777. Unfortunately no other records exist of its further life although it would have closed by at least 1835.

Messing's workhouse was brought into use in 1799 by the conversion of two almshouses. The almshouses were two cottages either side of the old schoolhouse. When the Witham Union was formed in 1835 these was no further use for these two buildings and they were converted back into cottages in 1836.

Rivenhall had a workhouse and this building could accommodate up to 25 inmates according to the government survey of 1777. The governor of the workhouse in 1783 was Edward Ellis who agreed to look after the inmates of the workhouse for four shillings per week per inmate. There was no arrangement for the parish to supply anything which meant that Mr Ellis would have to provide all the food, clothing and firewood. The parish though was responsible for the structure of the building. During the late 1700s the number in the workhouse was about 15. No records exist for the workhouse in the early 1800s but it probably functioned until the Witham Union was formed in 1835.

THE WITHAM UNION WORKHOUSE

Of the 17 parishes that made up the Union area, fourteen in the list at the start of this chapter had one representative as a Guardian with four others having two or three relative to their population. Witham and Great Coggeshall had three representatives each with Hatfield Peverel and Kelvedon having two each. These extra six representatives made the total number on the Board of Guardians up to 23. Witham has the largest population today but in the 1840s Great Coggeshall was the largest with a population of over 3000 even without the number living at Little Coggeshall. At that time Witham only had a population of just less than 3000. The smallest parish was Marks Hall with a population of only 52.

The first meeting of Guardians was on the 17 December 1835 and one of their first tasks after the appointment of officers was to appoint a new master and matron for the Witham parish workhouse. The Guardians took over all the parish workhouses in their new area pending the building of the new Union workhouse. Thomas James Bollingbroke and his wife Elizabeth were appointed to the positions at a combined salary of £50 a year.

RETURN of GUARDIANS.

WITHAM UNION.

I do hereby certify that the Election of Guardians of the Poor for the several Parishes in the Witham Union, was conducted in conformity to the Order of the Poor Law Commissioners, and that the Entries contained in the Schedule hereunder printed are true.

Names of Persons Nominated as Guardians.	Residence.	Quality or Calling.	No. of Votes given for each Candidate.	Names of the Guardians Elected
William Brown	Great Braxted	Farmer	no contest	William Brown
Thomas King Thedam	Little Braxted	Farmer	....	Thomas King Thedam
Richard Meredith White	Great Coggeshall	Gentleman	198	Richard Meredith White
John Hall	Great Coggeshall	Silk Throwster	129	John Hall
William Swinborne	Great Coggeshall	Currier	195	William Swinborne
Stephen Unwin, Jun.	Great Coggeshall	Wool Stapler	70	
Jacob Unwin	Little Coggeshall	Farmer	no contest	Jacob Unwin
Arthur R. Goodday	Faulkbourne	Farmer	....	Arthur Goodday
Joseph Everitt	Feering	Farmer	....	Joseph Everitt
George Ellis	Hatfield	Farmer	....	George Ellis
James Grimwood	Hatfield	Farmer	....	James Grimwood
Joseph Green	Inworth	Farmer	....	Joseph Green
John Hutley	Rivenhall	Farmer	....	John Hutley
William Docwra	Kelvedon	Farmer	....	William Docwra
William Sadler	Messing	Farmer	....	William Sadler
Rev. P. J. Honywood	Markshall, Rectory	Clerk	....	Rev. P. J. Honywood
Joseph Lake	Rivenhall	Farmer	....	Joseph Lake
The Rt. Hon. John James Lord Rayleigh	Langford Grove	Peer of the Realm	....	The Rt. Hon. John James Lord Rayleigh
William Aldham	Ulting	Farmer	....	William Aldham
Josiah Bright	Wickham Bishops	Farmer	....	Josiah Bright
John Crump	Witham	Farmer	....	John Crump
William Hutley	Witham	Farmer	....	William Hutley
Thomas Butler	Witham	Gentleman	....	Thomas Butler

Given under my Hand, this 26th day of March, 1842,

JOSEPH HOWELL BLOOD,

Clerk to the Guardians of the Poor of the

WITHAM UNION.

KNIGHT & KING, PRINTERS, WITHAM.

Witham Union Election of Guardians for 1842

The Guardians set up a sub committee to look at the existing parish workhouses in the group to decide which would continue to be used pending the building of the new Union workhouse. Even at the first meeting the Guardians felt that the parish workhouses at Witham and Great Coggeshall would be sufficient for their purposes but the committee were asked to inspect the workhouses and report back. The subsequent report recommended that two cottages adjoining the Witham parish workhouse be demolished and a brick building erected in its place to accommodate the women with sleeping accommodation above. The recommendation for the Great Coggeshall parish workhouse was that the floor of the long room downstairs be bricked. Presumably the floor was originally only a dirt floor. The Guardians appointed Joseph Knight and his wife Tamar as workhouse master and mistress of the Great Coggeshall workhouse. The Guardians make no mention of any of the other parish workhouses in the Witham area and one must presume that even if they had been open when the new Union Guardians took over then they were closed and did not feature in the future plans for accommodating the area's paupers.

The next major task for the Guardians was to find a piece of land on which to build the new workhouse and to appoint architects. The architects who got the contract were George Scott and William Bonython who also designed the workhouses at Billericay, Dunmow and Tendering. The workhouse was built to accommodate 300 inmates over the period 1837-39 and the site chosen was in the Hatfield Road to the west of the town.

Witham Union workhouse main entrance with the central hub in the background

All those paupers on out-relief throughout the seventeen parishes were personally examined as to their personal and financial situations and the Guardians took over the payment of out-relief from the respective parishes. Some changes were made even to the extent that some of the paupers from Wickham Bishops on out-relief were taken into the Witham parish workhouse. The Guardians also decreed that if any paupers was dissatisfied with their new out-relief allowance then they were to be admitted to the Witham parish workhouse.

The first national census after the workhouse opened was in 1841 and by this time the situation had settled down with the parish workhouses having been closed and all paupers that were not on out-relief were accommodated in the new Union workhouse. The number of inmates and staff in 1841 was as follows:

Males	76	The total included 6 staff and 62 children under
Females	62	14. The percentage of children to the total number of inmates was 47%
Total	138	

Guardians were elected or re-elected on a regular basis and the Return of Guardians for the election of 1842 shows that there were four nominations for the three positions of Guardian for the parish of Great Coggeshall. An election took place with Stephen Unwin being the one that was not elected as he only received 70 votes. Kelvedon was eligible to have two Guardians but there was only one nomination. Willam Docwra was therefore elected with the Union having to go back to the parish for a further nomination.

Witham workhouse did not last until 1930 like other Union Workhouses in Essex but closed in 1880 when the inmates were transferred elsewhere. The Guardians carried on with their duties though until the property was sold with their last meeting being in 1883. Although the inmates had all gone to other workhouses the Guardians still had responsibilities to those residents of their parishes who were on out-relief until arrangements were made for them also to be transferred to the control of other relieving officers.

I have looked at the Guardians' minutes for those years prior to closure to see what was being discussed in the leading up to the decision to close. The last national census before closure was in 1871 and the figures are as follows:

The census of 1871

Males	119	The total included 5 staff and 71 children under
Females	97	14. The percentage of children to the total number
		of inmates was 34%
Total	216	

The percentage growth in the number of inmates was similar to the other Essex workhouses but the institution was working well within its capacity of 300 inmates a few years before closure.

November 1876
Inferior quality produce
Even from day one the management of the Essex workhouses complained as to the quality of food supplied and presumably suppliers thought that as they were supplying to an institution of this type they could get away with inferior quality goods. It had been reported to the Guardians in November 1876 that inferior quality beef and mutton had been supplied to the workhouse and the clerk was instructed to write to Mr Wendon, the supplier, saying that the quality was not in agreement with his contract and that in future sub standard food would be refused and his contract cancelled.

December 1876
Christmas dinner
The Guardians resolved to provide £7 towards the cost of a Christmas dinner for all inmates except the able bodied. Presumably this was just another example of the strict regime in a workhouse to try and get able bodied inmates to get a job and leave the workhouse by not giving them a Christmas dinner.

May 1877
Closure of Union
The first mention that it was proposed to close the Witham Union and distribute the inmates around the surrounding Unions was accompanied by a resolution of the Guardians that they were against the proposition which was carried by 13 votes to 7. It was felt that any closure 'would not be for the benefit of the ratepayers, the Guardians or the poor'. It appears that the Chelmsford Union Guardians had first proposed the closure of the Witham Union and the Witham Guardians had written to the Guardians of the surrounding Unions seeking their support for non closure.

School charges
Compulsory education had been introduced in 1870 by the Education Act which meant that all children had to go to school up to the age of thirteen. School Boards were formed and each major centre of population had its Board School by the 1870s. Prior to Board Schools the government granted funds in 1833 for the Church of England and the Non-Conformist churches to establish their own schools. The Church of England schools were known as the National School and the schools for the other denominations were called the British School.

Whilst it was quite likely that there was a Board School in Witham in 1877, which was free, some of the workhouse children were educated at the British School where a small charge was payable. The clerk to the Guardians was ordered in June 1877 to write to the managers of the British School complaining that workhouse children were being charged three pence a week whereas ordinary village children were charged two pence a week. The reply from the British School said that all children are now charged three pence a week which means that the Guardians were out of date with their information. Nevertheless the Guardians wrote back to say that they would not pay more than two pence a week. In the October of 1877 the Guardians agreed to pay the full charge of three pence per week.

November 1877
Outbreak of measles and scarlet fever
The Guardians were concerned about the recent outbreak of measles and scarlet fever in Witham and the clerk was ordered to obtain a detailed report from the Witham Urban Sanitary Authority asking for the number of people infected and their opinion on how the outbreak started and what the authority was doing to contain the outbreak. The sanitary authority refused to supply the information requested but said that the epidemic was now at an end. Union Guardians throughout Essex were always historically concerned with health matters in their area and did valuable work in controlling the spread of infectious diseases. From 1872, when the Public Health Act was passed, Union Guardians were the official body that looked after health matters in their area unless there was a local Urban Sanitary Authority. In the case of Witham it was not the Guardians' brief to oversee health matters as there was the Witham Urban Sanitary Authority to do this job. Consequently one can understand why the health authority was not cooperative.

February 1878
Consumption of brandy
The clerk was asked to write to Mr Proctor, the medical officer responsible for the workhouse inmates, asking why there had been a great increase in the consumption of brandy. Brandy was only to be consumed 'in extreme cases' said the Guardians. Mr Proctor's name crops up from time to time often in connection with a complaint against him and probably either he or someone on the staff, or even possibly the inmates, was getting access to the brandy bottle which was only to be used for medicinal purposes.

Mr Proctor resigned his position in the September. Following the appointment of the new medical officer he was asked to look into 'the excessive use of stimulants (brandy) in the workhouse'.

Funeral horse at full trot
It had been reported to the Guardians that at the funeral of Elijah Clarke at Coggeshall (presumably a pauper) the funeral hearse was seen to be 'at full trot' through the village. The Guardians instructed that in future when passing through the parish of Coggeshall the cortege should proceed at a walk from the bridge to the church.

April 1878
Salaried staff
The minutes listed the fourteen salaried staff members:

Chaplain	Clerk	Relieving Officers (2)
Master	Matron	Schoolmaster
Schoolmistress	Porter	Nurse
Medical Officer	Poor Rate Collectors (2)	
School Attendance Officer		

January 1879
Staff problems
The nurse reported to the Guardians that the workhouse was being conducted in a disorderly manner and that the matron was frequently under the influence of drink. The master and matron, Mr and Mrs Crockett, were interviewed and denied the charge and declined to resign. Witnesses were interviewed and a report was sent to the Local Government Board. Meanwhile it was proposed that the master and matron be suspended from duty. An amendment that they not be suspended was carried by seven votes to four pending a reply from the Local Government Board. Subsequently the nurse was charged with 'great neglect' and that she should be reprimanded. It seems that the

master and matron and the nurse did not see eye to eye and probably the nurse was the guilty party.

The meeting the following week records a problem between, this time, the master and the porter and it is clear that all was not well with the staff at the workhouse. Apparently the master had reported to the Guardians regarding the porter's absence from duty but it appears he was telling them a 'falsehood'. Notwithstanding the master not telling the truth the porter was eventually dismissed. There obviously must have been some truth in the accusation that the porter was going absent without leave from his duties.

Nothing seemed to come of the nurse/matron complaint but two months later in March the nurse wrote again saying that this time the master had been abusive and threatening to her. The master was interviewed again and said that he felt that she 'was incompetent to perform her duties' and that the doctor had been called twice and that buckets of water had been thrown over her (presumably to calm her down). The Guardians resolved to investigate the matter.

The report the next week supported the nurse's charges notwithstanding the water incident and the Guardians considered the master's conduct to be improper and offensive and he once again told a falsehood. The Guardians this time wrote to the Local Government Board reciting all the various incidents where the master was at fault and recommended that he be dismissed. The Guardians also passed on to the local magistrate the case of assault brought by the nurse. The nurse had obviously decided that there was too much aggravation working in the workhouse and she now resigned.

The Local Government Board wrote directly to the master for his response to the accusations made by the Guardians but the Guardians felt that his explanation was unsatisfactory. Before a final decision could be made on the master and matron a further incident occurred regarding their drunken habits which resulted in them being suspended and the schoolmaster and the new nurse were temporarily appointed in their place. The master and matron finally resigned on the 28 July 1879.

During the year, therefore, the master, the matron, the porter and the nurse all resigned or were dismissed. Although this was obviously a traumatic year for the Guardians, in view of the resignations and dismissals, it is noted from reading all the Essex workhouse minutes that workhouse staff generally did not stay very long. The working environment was obviously difficult compared to being a schoolmaster in a Board School or a nurse in an infirmary and it was not unusual for schoolmasters/mistresses/nurses, for example, to resign after only a year or so.

June 1879

Funeral complaint

The Visiting Committee reported that they were disgusted at the way the arrangements for Charles Cheek's funeral was conducted at the workhouse. They said that the coffin was three inches too shallow and six inches too narrow resulting in the body not being properly laid out in the coffin. No shroud or winding sheet had been provided. Three parties would have been involved in the burial namely an officer of the Union, the funeral contractor and the undertaker and none of these at the time was concerned at the irregularity of the burial arrangements. Consequently the Guardians drew up new rules for burials within the workhouse grounds involving all the parties previously named together with the nurse who should ensure that the body was properly prepared.

August 1879

Workhouse as Lunatic Asylum

It was reported to the Guardians that should the Witham Workhouse close then it may be used as a lunatic asylum.

December 1879

Dissolution of Witham Union

It seems that the Guardians at Witham had finally accepted that their workhouse was to close as a sub committee was formed for this purpose. A meeting was set up with Braintree Union to sort out the allocation of parishes to adjacent Unions.

Christmas 1879

The Guardians agreed to spend £8 in total on the inmates Christmas dinner compared with £7 in the three years earlier.

March 1880

It was decided by the Local Government Board that the Union would be dissolved in March 1880 but whereas a few months earlier it seemed that the Guardians had accepted the situation, they now wished to delay closure as they sent a petition to the House of Commons saying that closure would not be to the public good.

This petition did not seem to do any good as we see in April 1880 that the Guardians are discussing selling off the furniture and effects belonging to the workhouse.

Colonel's Lucas's proposition

It rather looks as if Colonel Lucas, one of the Guardians, had strong views on education and it seems as if he wanted to get his thoughts off his chest before the workhouse finally closed. He made a proposition to the Board regarding the compulsory education of workhouse children which surprisingly was passed by 16 votes to 5. His views were extreme as he only wished to see the children educated up to the age of ten because he was against the upper classes paying for the cost of educating pauper children above their station in life. It was a long resolution and I have extracted the salient points to give the gist of what he, and the Guardians, was saying. The petition was sent to Parliament and said:

That this Board views with alarm the greatly increasing cost to the country of the compulsory education enforced in the Elementary Schools. That admitting that it may be the duty of the country to educate the masses.................they consider (the Guardians) that they should not be called upon to assist by grants of public money in elevating them (the pauper children) beyond their station. That it is unjust to compel the higher classes to supply the means by which the children of the lower classes shall be enabled to compete with their own children for employment for which they shall seek. ....That the advanced education now enforced in Elementary Schools tends to dissatisfy the children in after years with their sphere in life whilst the prohibition of employment till the age of 14 engenders habits of idleness which in after life cannot be overcome. ....Your petitioners therefore pray that the children may not under any circumstances be compulsorily detained at school beyond the age of 10 years and that no public money be expended in teaching in Elementary Schools more than reading, writing and arithmetic sufficient to enable them to pass the Third Standard as it is present framed, with needlework for girls.

In this late Victorian period the class structure was still very evident in the country and this is another example of the Guardians moving outside their brief (see also November 1877) and trying to influence others on matters unconnected with looking after the poor.

May 1880
Sale of workhouse contents

There is no record in the minutes as to when the inmates were transferred elsewhere but it appears that it happened during March and April 1880 as the master and matron were told in May that their services were no longer required. Discussion also took place again regarding selling the contents of the workhouse by auction.

December 1880
Sale of the workhouse

Since the summer of 1880 the Guardians were no longer holding their regular weekly meeting but were meeting on an irregular basis probably when the need arose. Talk now was concerning the sale of the workhouse but there had also been discussion regarding the use of the workhouse for 'an asylum for the chronic and harmless class of pauper lunatics'.

May 1881
Sale offer accepted
Various offers for the workhouse buildings had been made over the last year or so and although the price offered was right the Local Government Board wished the building to be sold for a public purpose rather than be purchased by a private developer. In May 1881 the Managers of the South Metropolitan School District made an offer of £3,000 for the workhouse which was accepted by the Local Government Board.

April 1882
Sale completed
The Guardians met for the first time since June 1881 when the only important item was the receipt of the sale proceeds of £3,000 and the payment of sale expenses.

14 September 1883
Final meeting
The Guardians met twice more in 1883 to tie up the loose ends before conducting their final meeting on the 14 September 1883. The balance standing in the account on the last day was £3021 and the Guardians were instructed by the Local Government Board to pay this amount to the following Unions probably proportionate to the inmates they had received from the Witham Union.

Braintree Union	£2437
Lexden & Winstree Union	£269
Maldon Union	£315

The South Metropolitan School District took over the old workhouse buildings but later the buildings became to be known as Bridge Hospital under the National Health Service. The old workhouse is now closed and in course of redevelopment.

APPENDIX 1

ESSEX PARISHES IN OTHER POOR LAW COUNTIES

Bishop's Stortford Poor Law Union, Hertfordshire
Berden, Birchanger, Elsenham, Farnham, Gt Hallingbury, Lt Hallingbury, Henham, Manuden, Stansted Mountfitchet, Ugley

Edmonton Poor Law Union, Middlesex
Waltham Holy Cross

Linton Poor Law Union, Cambridgeshire
Bartlow End, Hadstock

Risbridge Poor Law Union, Suffolk
Ashen, Birdbrook, Helions Bumpstead, Steeple Bumpstead, Haverhill, Kedington, Ovington, Sturmer

Royston Poor Law Union, Hertfordshire
Gt Chishill, Lt Chishill, Heydon

Sudbury Poor Law Union, Suffolk
Alphamstone, Belchamp Otten, Belchamp St Paul, Belchamp Walter, Borley, Bulmer, Bures, Foxearth, Gestingthorpe, Gt Henny, Lt Henny, Lamarsh, Liston, Middleton, Pentlow, Twinstead, Wickham St Paul, North Wood

BIBLIOGRAPHY

The source of nearly all the information in this book has been from the original documents in the Essex Record Office in Chelmsford and their branch offices at Colchester and Southend together with the Newham Local Studies Library.

The majority of the information on parish workhouses has been gleaned from the respective parish vestry minute books and the overseer's accounts. These records do not exist for every parish that had a workhouse and consequently any omissions relate mainly to those parishes where records are missing or are stored elsewhere. The library at the Chelmsford Record Office of local history books has provided much back up information on parish poorhouses and parish workhouses.

For the information on Union Workhouses the Essex Record Office at Chelmsford has the Guardians' minute books for twelve out of the seventeen Union Workhouses in Essex. In addition there are many other record books for these twelve workhouses. The records for the Union workhouses at Colchester, Lexden & Winstree and Tendring are maintained at the branch office at Colchester. The branch office at Southend houses the records for the Rochford Union workhouse and for the West Ham Union workhouse the records can be found at the Newham Local Studies Library within the Stratford Reference Library.

Whilst the Essex Record Office has been the primary source of information the internet has provided back up data on various aspects of Essex workhouses. Many books have been written on workhouses generally but the source for some of the information in the first chapter on the history of workhouses was Norman Longmate's *The Workhouse*.

Index of Parishes

Index of Parishes

Index of Parishes

Index of Parishes

General Index